Foreword

Foreword by the Rt. Hon David Blunkett MP, Secretary of State for Education and Employment

Creative and cultural education can help raise educational standards by boosting a child's self-confidence and self-esteem. The Government wants to give young people every chance to develop their full potential, to build on their strengths and to believe in themselves. Our cultural heritage, together with creativity through self-expression, offers a way of developing the talent of the individual and their understanding of a diverse and complex world around them. I welcome the recommendations of this report which identify a variety of ways in which we can enable young people to explore their creativity at school and more widely for their future leisure and work opportunities. I am grateful for the committee's efforts and the imaginative proposals they have contributed to this vital part of a balanced and rounded education. I look forward to the results of further constructive debate on the challenge we face in the social and economic climate of a new century.

DAVID BLUNKETT

Foreword by the Rt. Hon Chris Smith MP, Secretary of State for Culture, Media and Sport

The opportunities to explore the best of contemporary culture and to express individual creativity are two vital components of any education system committed to developing the full potential of all its pupils. They also play an essential role in nurturing a lively society and a dynamic economy. I welcome the vigorous way in which this report addresses these issues and, in particular, the emphasis it places on developing effective partnerships between schools and the wider community. My Department will be looking at ways of building on its recommendations.

CHRIS SMITH

Contents

Terms of Reference

The National Advisory Committee on Creative and Cultural Education was established in February 1998 by the Secretary of State for Education and Employment, the Rt. Hon David Blunkett MP and the Secretary of State for Culture, Media and Sport, the Rt. Hon Chris Smith MP. Our terms of reference were:

To make recommendations to the Secretaries of State on the creative and cultural development of young people through formal and informal education: to take stock of current provision and to make proposals for principles, policies and practice.

This report makes recommendations for provision in formal and informal education for young people to the age of 16: that is, to the end of compulsory education. Our inquiry coincides with the Government's review of the National Curriculum. This report includes specific recommendations on the National Curriculum. It also includes recommendations for a wider national strategy for creative and cultural education.

Membership of the Committee

Professor Ken Robinson (Chairman), *University of Warwick*
Professor Lewis Minkin (Vice-chair), *Sheffield Hallam University*
Professor Eric Bolton CB, *Formerly Senior Chief Inspector*
Dawn French, *Actor/Comedian*
Lindsey Fryer, *Vice-chair, Engage The National Association of Gallery Education*
Professor Susan Greenfield, *University of Oxford; Director, Royal Institution*
Valerie Hannon, *Chief Education Officer, Derbyshire*
Lenny Henry CBE, *Actor/Comedian*
Dawn Holgate, *Director of Education, Phoenix Dance Company*
Dame Tamsyn Imison, *Head, Hampstead School, London*
Clive Jones, *Chief Executive, Carlton Television*
Judith Kelly OBE, *Artistic Director, West Yorkshire Playhouse*
Professor Sir Harold Kroto Kt., FRS, *University of Sussex*
Sir Claus Moser KCB, CBE, FBA, *Chairman, Basic Skills Agency*
Sir Simon Rattle Kt., CBE, *Conductor*
Lord Stone of Blackheath, *Managing Director, Marks & Spencer plc*
Professor Helen Storey, *Fashion Designer*
Carol Traynor, *Head, St Boniface RC Primary School, Salford*

Research Officer
Mathilda Joubert

Administrative Officer
Lynn Green

Observers
Department for Education and Employment
John Connolly (from August 1998)
Julian Critchley
Janet Dawson
Teresa Downing (to August 1998)

Department for Culture Media and Sport
Tony Dyer (from December 1998)
Patrick Fallon (to November 1998)
David Fawcett (to November 1998)
Allan Ferries (from December 1998)

Office for Standards in Education
Peter Jones HMI

Qualifications and Curriculum Authority
Tony Knight

Teacher Training Agency
Angela Walsh

Introduction and Summary

The Purpose of this Report

 In 1997, the Government published its White Paper, *Excellence in Schools*. It described education as a vital investment in 'human capital' for the twenty-first century. It argued that one of the problems in education is the low expectations of young people's abilities and that it is essential to raise morale, motivation and self esteem in schools. The main focus of the White Paper was on raising standards in literacy and numeracy. But this will not be enough to meet the challenges that face education, and the White Paper recognised this. It also said:

> *If we are to prepare successfully for the twenty-first century we will have to do more than just improve literacy and numeracy skills. We need a broad, flexible and motivating education that recognises the different talents of all children and delivers excellence for everyone.*

It emphasised the urgent need to unlock the potential of every young person and argued that Britain's economic prosperity and social cohesion depend on this.

 This report argues that a national strategy for creative and cultural education is essential to that process. We put the case for developing creative and cultural education; we consider what is involved; we look at current provision and assess the opportunities and obstacles; and we set out a national strategy. By creative education we mean forms of education that develop young people's capacities for original ideas and action: by cultural education we mean forms of education that enable them to engage positively with the growing complexity and diversity of social values and ways of life. We argue that there are important relationships between creative and cultural education, and significant implications for methods of teaching and assessment, the balance of the school curriculum and for partnerships between schools and the wider world.

What is this Report About?

Our report develops five main themes:

The Challenge for Education
Education faces challenges that are without precedent. Meeting these challenges calls for new priorities in education, including a much stronger emphasis on creative and cultural education and a new balance in teaching and in the curriculum.

Creative Potential
Creativity is possible in all areas of human activity, including the arts, sciences, at work at play and in all other areas of daily life. All people have creative abilities and we all have them differently. When individuals find

---

<blockquote>
"
Our aim must be to create a nation where the creative talents of all the people are used to build a true enterprise economy for the twenty-first century — where we compete on brains, not brawn. "

The Prime Minister, the Rt. Hon Tony Blair MP
</blockquote>

<blockquote>
"
...we cannot rely on a small élite, no matter how highly educated or highly paid. Instead we need the creativity, enterprise and scholarship of all our people. "

Rt. Hon David Blunkett MP, Secretary of State for Education and Employment
</blockquote>

<blockquote>
"
We must change the concept of creativity from being something that is 'added on' to education, skills, training and management and make sure it becomes intrinsic to all of these. "

Rt. Hon Chris Smith MP, Secretary of State for Culture, Media and Sport
</blockquote>

their creative strengths, it can have an enormous impact on self-esteem and on overall achievement.

Freedom and Control

Creativity is not simply a matter of letting go. Serious creative achievement relies on knowledge, control of materials and command of ideas. Creative education involves a balance between teaching knowledge and skills, and encouraging innovation. In these ways, creative development is directly related to cultural education.

Cultural Understanding

Young people are living in times of rapid cultural change and of increasing cultural diversity. Education must enable them to understand and respect different cultural values and traditions and the processes of cultural change and development. The engine of cultural change is the human capacity for creative thought and action.

A Systemic Approach

Creative and cultural education are not subjects in the curriculum, they are general functions of education. Promoting them effectively calls for a systemic strategy: one that addresses the balance of the school curriculum, teaching methods and assessment, how schools connect with other people and resources, and the training and development of teachers and others.

Who is this Report for?

iv

Formally, our report is addressed to the Secretaries of State, and many of our recommendations do call for Government action at various levels. But education concerns everybody: children and young people, parents, employers, those in work, out of work or in retirement. Consequently, our report is also written for a wider audience:

- for parents, who want education to offer the best opportunities for their children;
- for teachers and headteachers who see the potential range and vitality of young people's abilities;
- for school governors, who want their schools to be alive with energy and achievement;
- for other organisations who see themselves as partners in the education of young people and who want to find better ways of engaging with them;
- for business and union leaders who recognise the need for new approaches to preparing young people for the changing nature of work.

Above all, our aim is to urge the need for a national strategy which engages the energies of all of these to provide the kind of education, in substance and in style, that all young people need now, and to enable them to face an uncertain and demanding future.

Why Now?

 There are great opportunities now to promote young people's creative and cultural education:

- The Government is committed to promoting the creative abilities and cultural understanding of all young people through education. At the same time, it is introducing new patterns of funding to support extended curricula, specialist facilities and innovation.

- The business community wants education to give a much higher priority to promoting young people's creative abilities; to developing teamwork, social skills and powers of communication.

- Many professional and other organisations are keen to develop innovative partnerships with education, through visits, residencies and liaison schemes.

- New technologies are providing unprecedented access to ideas, information, people and organisations throughout the world, as well as to new modes of creativity, personal expression, cultural exchange and understanding.

The opportunities are considerable: and so are the difficulties.

 Issues of creativity and of cultural development concern the whole of education. They are influenced by much more than the shape and content of the formal school curriculum. These influences include methods of teaching; the ethos of schools, including the relationships between teachers and learners; and the national priorities that underpin the education service. Our consultations suggest some tensions in current provision.

- Many of those who have contributed to our inquiry believe that current priorities and pressures in education inhibit the creative abilities of young people and of those who teach them. There is a particular concern about the place and status of the arts and humanities. There is also concern that science education is losing its vitality under current pressures.

- Many schools are doing exciting and demanding work but often they see themselves doing this in spite, not because, of the existing climate. This may be more a problem of perception than of fact. There is no comprehensive evidence available either way to us nor to the Government. Nevertheless, the fact of this perception, and how widespread it is, is evidence of a problem in itself.

- Outside organisations - museums, theatres, galleries, orchestras and others - have a great deal to offer the formal education sector. Many already have education and outreach programmes. There is a compelling argument for closer working partnerships and we have found considerable enthusiasm for them. Many say they are poorly funded for educational programmes and that such work still has low priority.

- There are deep concerns about the supply of teachers and the extent to which current training takes account of the importance of creative and cultural education.

vii The key message of this report is the need for a new balance in education: in setting national priorities; in the structure and organisation of the school curriculum; in methods of teaching and assessment; in relationships between schools and other agencies. Over a number of years, the balance of education has been lost. There has been a tendency for the national debate on education to be expressed as a series of exclusive alternatives, even dichotomies: for example, as a choice between the arts or the sciences; the core curriculum or the broad curriculum; between academic standards or creativity; freedom or authority in teaching methods. We argue that these dichotomies are misleading and unhelpful. Realising the potential of young people, and raising standards of achievement and motivation includes all of these elements. Creating the right synergy and achieving the right balance in education is an urgent task, from national policy making to classroom teaching.

Structure of the Report

viii The report is in four parts. In Part One we set out our definitions and framework for creative and cultural education. In Part Two we look at the implications for the school curriculum, for teaching and for assessment. In Part Three, we argue for a broad base of partnerships between schools and other agencies and consider issues of resources and training. In Part Four we present a series of detailed recommendations as a framework for a national strategy. The main arguments of the report are as follows:

Part One: **Facing the Future**

1 The Challenge for Education

Education throughout the world faces unprecedented challenges: economic, technological, social, and personal. Policy-makers everywhere emphasise the urgent need to develop 'human resources', and in particular to promote creativity, adaptability and better powers of communication. We argue that this means reviewing some of the basic assumptions of our education system. New approaches are needed based on broader conceptions of young people's abilities, of how to promote their motivation and self-esteem, and of the skills and aptitudes they need. Creative and cultural education are fundamental to meeting these objectives.

2 Creative Development

There are many misconceptions about creativity. Some people associate creative teaching with a lack of discipline in education. Others see creative ability as the preserve of a gifted few, rather than of the many; others associate it only with the arts. In our view, creativity is possible in all areas of human activity and all young people and adults have creative capacities. Developing these capacities involves a balance between teaching skills and understanding, and promoting the freedom to innovate, and take risks.

3 Cultural Development

Culture too is often associated with the arts. However, we relate the arts to a broader definition of social culture which includes the impact of science and technology on ways of life and the increasing interaction between cultures. Young people need to be helped to engage positively with cultural change and diversity. The dangers of cultural intolerance make this task a particular priority. We argue that creative and cultural education are dynamically related and that there are practical implications for the curriculum and for the classroom.

4 Meeting the Challenge

In this section we draw together our arguments for creative and cultural education and show how, in principle, they contribute to meeting the challenges for education that we have identified. In Part Two we move from principles to practice.

Part Two: A New Balance

5 Developing the School Curriculum

There have been many benefits in the introduction of the National Curriculum. There are also difficulties for creative and cultural education in the existing rationale, structure and levels of prescription. These issues need to be tackled to allow more initiative to schools within a clear framework of public accountability. All schools should review their provision for creative and cultural education within and beyond the National Curriculum.

6 Teaching and Learning

Creativity can be 'taught'. Teachers can be creative in their own teaching; they can also promote the creative abilities of their pupils. The roles of teachers are to recognise young people's creative capacities; and to provide the particular conditions in which they can be realised. Developing creativity involves, amongst other things, deepening young people's cultural knowledge and understanding. This is essential both in itself and to promote forms of education that are inclusive and sensitive to cultural diversity and change.

7 Raising Standards

Assessment and inspection have vital roles in raising standards of achievement in schools. But they must support and not inhibit creative and cultural education. There is a need for a new balance between different types of attainment target in the National Curriculum, and between the different forms and criteria of assessment and inspection. Raising standards should not mean standardisation, or the objectives of creative and cultural education will be frustrated.

Part Three: **Beyond the School**

8 Developing Partnerships

Schools are now able to work in partnership with a wide range of individuals and organisations to enrich provision for creative and cultural education. The benefits of successful partnerships, and the roles of various partners in creative and cultural education, are different but complementary. There is a great deal of good practice, but there is an urgent need to establish better systems of funding, training and quality assurance.

9 Funding and Resources

Local management of schools has reduced many services and facilities that were once provided by local education authorities to support creative and cultural education. Co-ordinated action is needed to provide these services in new and imaginative ways in the short and longer term. There are also many new sources of funding available to schools and organisations through a wide range of schemes and initiatives. New patterns of partnership are needed between government departments and funding agencies to make more effective use of resources.

10 Training People

The new provisions in initial teacher training present serious difficulties to the future of creative and cultural education. Urgent action is needed to ensure a continuing supply of appropriately trained teachers. We also see new roles for continuing professional development and the need to review the priorities for funding. New training strategies are needed for specialists other than teachers. Action is needed to improve the quality of training for youth workers to promote the creative and cultural development of young people.

Part Four: **A National Strategy**

We welcome the Government's commitment to developing the creative capacities and cultural understanding of young people. We recommend that it should now co-ordinate a national strategy to promote higher standards of provision and achievement. This strategy should include action by the Government itself and by the national agencies for the school curriculum, inspection and teacher training. It should also include action by local education authorities and schools and by other national and regional organisations. Throughout this report we make a wide range of specific recommendations that provide a framework for this strategy. In Part Four, we draw these recommendations together, indicate how they are related and the time scale over which some of them should be implemented and by whom. All of these recommendations are addressed to three principal objectives.

a. *To ensure that the importance of creative and cultural education is explicitly recognised and provided for in schools' policies for the whole curriculum, and in Government policy for the National Curriculum.*

b. *To ensure that teachers and other professionals are encouraged and trained to use methods and materials that facilitate the development of young people's creative abilities and cultural understanding.*

c. *To promote the development of partnerships between schools and outside agencies which are now essential to provide the kinds of creative and cultural education that young people need and deserve.*

If these objectives were achieved, the benefits would be felt by all young people, the education sector and by society as a whole.

How Important is This?

ix

There is intense concern with raising standards in education, and schools and the education sector in general are already deluged with reports. How important is this one? For some people, the very theme of this report may seem a distraction from the main business of raising standards. We do not think so. Our concerns are the same as everyone else's. How can education enable our children to make the most of themselves and take the best advantage of the opportunities and uncertainties that they face in a fast changing world? Let us anticipate some of the legitimate questions that might be asked of this report.

1. Isn't an emphasis on creativity and culture a distraction from the core concerns with literacy and numeracy?

We are not advocating creative and cultural education as alternatives to literacy and numeracy, but as equally relevant to the needs of this and of future generations. We support the need for high standards of literacy and numeracy. These are important in themselves. They can also enhance creative abilities: equally creative teaching and learning can enhance literacy and numeracy. These are complementary abilities, not opposing objectives. The Government and the vast majority of people in education recognise this.

2. How are creative and cultural education relevant to raising academic standards?

Ability comes in many forms and should not be defined only by traditional academic criteria. Academic ability alone will no longer guarantee success or personal achievement. Every child has capabilities beyond the traditionally academic. Children with high academic ability may have other strengths that are often neglected. Children who struggle with academic work can have outstanding abilities in other areas. Equally, creative and cultural education of the sort we propose can also help to raise academic standards. The key is to find what children are good at. Self confidence and self esteem then tend to rise and overall performance to improve. High standards in creative achievement require just as much rigour as traditional academic work.

3. What has this got to do with helping young people get jobs?

We live in a fast moving world. While employers continue to demand high academic standards, they also now want more. They want people who can adapt, see connections, innovate, communicate and work with others. This is true in many areas of work. The new knowledge-based economies in particular will increasingly depend on these abilities. Many businesses are paying for courses to promote creative abilities, to teach the skills and attitudes that are now essential for economic success but which our education system is not designed to promote.

4. Is this committee a lobby group for the arts?

This report does not represent a particular lobby. It expresses concerns across a wide range of public and professional interests about the balance and priorities of education as we move into the twenty-first century. Our members come from different professions and backgrounds: including science, the arts, education and business. Creative achievement is obvious in the arts but it is essential to achievement in all other fields including the sciences and business.

5. Is this a return to the progressive teaching ideas of the 1960s?

No. We are advocating a new balance between learning knowledge and skills and having the freedom to innovate and experiment — a system of education that fosters and channels the diverse abilities of young people and which gives everyone the opportunity to achieve on their own merits. This is why we link creative education with cultural education.

6. Teachers are already under enormous pressures. Are these recommendations going to add to the burden?

Good teachers and many high performing schools are already doing what we are recommending. We want to emphasise the importance of their work and to establish national priorities for creative and cultural education in all schools. The curriculum is already over-full and we think it should be thinned out. We want teachers to have more freedom to use their own creative and professional skills. Greater freedom for teachers in the classroom will help to promote creative teaching and this is essential to promote creative learning.

Looking Forward

x The issues we are dealing with in this report are essential to the overall quality and standards of education. They are also difficult in terms of definition, policy and practice. We have found our own debates as a group exciting and enlightening. We have had an opportunity which is all too rare to meet across specialisms and to talk from a wide range of different backgrounds. We continually found that ideas and values that we thought particular to our own fields are common to us all. Too often, our own education had taught us otherwise. In what follows, we have tried to say as directly and clearly as we can what we are concerned with and what we are concerned about. We have tried to balance a discussion of definitions and principles with recommendations that are practical and feasible. We have not dealt in detail with all of the issues we raise: we have not done justice to every subtlety of argument on the way. Our task has been to balance depth with breadth, theory with practice and detail with brevity. In publishing this report we believe with even more strength than we did at the outset, that the tasks we identify are urgent and the arguments compelling; that the benefits of success are enormous and the costs of inaction profound.

xi In his introduction to *Excellence in Schools* (DfEE 1997), the Secretary of State for Education and Employment relates the Government's aims for education to five priorities:

- the need to overcome economic and social disadvantages;
- the creation of greater fairness within the education system;
- the encouragement of aspiration;
- economic competitiveness;
- unlocking the potential of each individual.

We believe that these are the right priorities for education; and that they are all related. Our aims are to show how these priorities can be realised through a systematic approach to creative and cultural education; to promote higher standards in creative and cultural education in all disciplines; to promote parity of provision between the arts, humanities, sciences and other major areas of education; and to stimulate a broad base of partnerships between schools and outside agencies. We see all of these as essential to realising the potential of young people; and to promoting the quality of national life and of individual achievement that are the ultimate purposes of education.

The foundations of the present education system were laid at the end of the nineteenth century. They were designed to meet the needs of a world that was being transformed by industrialisation. We are publishing this report at the dawn of a new century. The challenges we face now are of the same magnitude, but they are of a different character. The task is not to do better now what we set out to do then: it is to rethink the purposes, methods and scale of education in our new circumstances. This report argues that no education system can be world-class without valuing and integrating creativity in teaching and learning, in the curriculum, in management and leadership and without linking this to promoting knowledge and understanding of cultural change and diversity. The arguments and proposals that follow are to help set a course for the next century while addressing the urgent demands of the present.

Professor Ken Robinson; Chairman

Part One:
Facing the Future

1 The Challenge for Education

Educating for the Future

1 Countries throughout the world are re-organising their education systems. Like us, they are engulfed in rapid economic and social change. Everywhere, education is seen as the main way of enabling individuals and nations alike to meet these changes. Schools have a complex task. We expect education to prepare young people for the world of work and for economic independence; to enable them to live constructively in responsible communities; and to enable them to live in a tolerant, culturally diverse and rapidly changing society. Perhaps above all, we expect education to help young people to build lives that have meaning and purpose in a future we can scarcely predict. The burning question, for everyone involved, and increasingly that is everyone, is how is this to be done? What kind of education is needed? In our view the answers involve much more than increasing the amount of education that goes on: and more than doing better what we have always done. They involve reviewing some of the basic assumptions on which education so far has been based. We need new approaches, because the challenges we all face are unprecedented. What are these challenges?

The Economic Challenge

2 *To develop in young people the skills, knowledge and personal qualities they need for a world where work is undergoing rapid and long-term change.*

One of the most basic expectations of general education is that it will enable young people to get a job when they leave school. The modern system of education in England was introduced by the 1944 Education Act. The Act was planned, in part, to provide a workforce for the post-war industrial economy. It was estimated that this would consist of roughly 80 per cent manual workers and 20 per cent clerical and professional staff. More than fifty years on, the economic context has changed completely: in some fields of employment this ratio is being reversed. This is because of the radical transformations world-wide in both the nature and the patterns of work.

The Nature of Work

3 For a number of years, the balance has been changing between traditional forms of industrial and manual work and jobs that are based on information technology and providing services of various kinds. As a result, the growing demand in businesses world-wide is for forms of education and training that develop 'human resources' and in particular the powers of communication, innovation and creativity. This is because of the incessant need for businesses to develop new products and services and to adapt management styles and systems of operation to keep pace with rapidly changing market conditions. Creative abilities are needed in all forms of business and in all types of work including traditional manufacturing and trades. They are also at the centre of some of the most dynamic and rapidly expanding areas of the world economies.

New Work for Old

4 Whereas the dominant global companies used to be concerned with industry and manufacturing, the key corporations today are increasingly in the fields of communications, information, entertainment, science and technology. In the United States, the 'intellectual property' sectors, those whose value depends on their ability to generate new ideas rather than to manufacture commodities, are now the most powerful element in the US economy. The Intellectual Property Association in Washington has estimated these sectors to be worth $360 billion a year, making them more valuable than automobiles, agriculture or aerospace. They are growing at twice the rate of the economy as a whole and generating jobs at three times the underlying rate. The intellectual property sector is more significant when patents from science and technology are included: in pharmaceuticals, electronics, biotechnology, and information systems among others. These are all based on fundamental advances in the sciences and in engineering and are creative fields of huge significance.

5 A subset of the intellectual property sector are what have been called the 'creative industries'. These include: advertising, architecture, arts and antiques, crafts, design, designer fashion, film, leisure software, music, performing arts, publishing, software and computer services, television and radio. The Department of Culture, Media and Sport has recently estimated that these now generate annual revenues for the UK of over £57 billion and employ more than 1.7 million people (DCMS 1998). Unlike many other industry sectors, the creative industries continue to benefit from high growth rates, in part because they build on, and interact with, innovations in science and technology. The communications revolution, increasing bandwidth and the advent of digital networks are creating new global markets, multiplying outlets and increasing consumer demand. In Britain, employment in the creative industries has grown by 34 per cent in a decade against a background of almost no growth in employment in the economy as a whole. These are fields of significant opportunity for the creative abilities of young people.

> *The arts, business and society all interact, all derive support and enlightenment and life from each other. Creativity in its widest sense is at the heart of much of what we in this country are good at. It is the foundation of a new generation of high-tech, high-skills industries. Ideas are the building blocks of innovation and innovation builds industries.*
>
> *Chris Smith MP, Secretary of State for Culture, Media and Sport*

> *The business world is in a turbulent process of change from the old world of steady-state mass production to one of constant innovation and the pursuit of creativity in all forms and on a global scale.*
>
> *John Wybrew, Executive Director, Corporate Affairs, British Gas plc*

The Patterns of Work

The Need to Adapt

6 Most young people starting out can expect to change not just jobs but occupations, several times in their working lives. There is a growing emphasis on freelance work, short contracts, self-employment and entrepreneurial ability. Trans-national companies now use workers from anywhere in the world on the basis of available skills: including facilities with information technologies and languages. These economic shifts are operating independently of national boundaries. Young people need to have high level skills for this complex new world of global markets and competition. They also need to be able to adapt to change and to new opportunities. Raising standards of literacy and numeracy is essential: but it is not enough. Nor is raising standards of academic qualifications. All of these are important, but the assumptions about human resources that education made in 1944 will not meet the challenges of 2004. Employers are now looking for much more than academic ability.

Academic Inflation

7 In a world where many traditional forms of work are ever changing, good academic qualifications alone will no longer guarantee work. This is partly because of the transience of many contemporary forms of work. It is also because there are many more people with academic qualifications. As the nature of work changes, education itself is becoming one of the world's biggest industries. In Europe and America, the communications, entertainment and education sectors are growing faster than any other area of the economy and are now outstripping many conventional areas of employment[1]. It has been estimated that education and training now account for six per cent of world gross domestic product (GDP). The United Nations predicts that in the next thirty years more people will be looking for qualifications in education than since the beginning of civilisation (Puttnam 1998). This has profound implications for the sorts of education people need, and for the value of the qualifications they receive. One emergent issue is academic inflation.

8 Qualifications are a form of currency. Their value is related to the prevailing exchange rate for employment or higher education. Like all currencies, they can inflate when there are too many in relation to the opportunities available. Two or three A-levels once secured a university place: the baseline for many courses is now much higher. A first degree once guaranteed a job: the baseline can now be masters degree or even a PhD. This is a structural problem for all education systems, and it may compound as the number of people in formal education continues to increase. Whatever other issues it raises, one consequence is already clear. Academic qualifications alone are no longer enough. Increasingly, employers and others emphasise the need for the qualities and aptitudes which academic qualifications are not designed to produce — powers of creativity, of communication, of empathy and adaptability, and social skills.

> Every single person in business needs the ability to change, the self confidence to learn new things and the capacity for overview. The idea that we can win with brilliant scientists and technologists alone is nonsense. It's breadth of vision, the ability to understand all the influences at work, to flex between them and not to be frightened of totally different experiences and viewpoints that holds the key. The specialist that cannot take a holistic view in business is no use at all.
>
> *Sir John Harvey-Jones*

The Technological Challenge

9

To enable young people to make their way with confidence in a world that is being shaped by technologies which are evolving more quickly than at any time in history.

The real long-term effects of the revolution in information technology have still to be felt. The rate of technological change is quickening every day. Information technologies are transforming how we think, how we communicate, how we work and how we play. The new frontiers created by nano-technology and extreme miniaturisation promise a wholly new era of information systems. In the near future, there will be a convergence of information and communication technologies as personal computers and television systems combine. The next generation of computers may be small enough to wear on the body and be powered by the surface electricity of the skin. The rapid growth of understanding of the brain, in particular, and of genetic systems in general, is matched by the speed of development of information systems. In the foreseeable future, these different fields of innovation may converge to produce 'intelligent' computers which can interact with human consciousness.

10

New technologies in all their variety are having profound consequences in all areas of our lives. Young people are often more alert to the possibilities of new technologies than their teachers. Schools have been seen traditionally as points of entry to a wider world of information and knowledge. Young people now have direct access to more information than previous generations could guess at, and are often more expert than adults in finding their way to it. Schools will need to think through the implications of this for their own future roles. New technologies offer unprecedented opportunities for young people to broaden their horizons; to find new modes of creativity and to deepen their understanding of the world around them. Schools also have resources available through these technologies to transform methods of teaching and learning. There are benefits and there are risks.

11

In future, new technologies may create divisions between those who can use them and those who cannot. This argues for systematic and comprehensive programmes of IT education in schools. On the other hand, there are concerns that the use of these technologies in schools

> We need an education system that gives our children an edge, the ability the Industrial Society has identified to survive and prosper. We need to equip our young people with powers of innovation and creativity they need for the rapidly-changing economies of the future. The education system has to develop a new emphasis on creativity and discovery to give pupils the tools they will need to cope with the fast and continuing changes in the nature of work, employment and growth in the world economy that lie ahead.

Clive Jones

> Like it or not, we are living in a time of immense technological change; the world of education is being asked to grapple with challenges and opportunities which almost boggle the imagination.

Lord Puttnam of Queensgate

could become too pervasive. There are fears that long exposure to screens, and the processes they involve, may have harmful effects. One fear is that young people are not having enough direct contact with others and that this may affect their social development. Second, there are emergent concerns about the possible effects on young people's emotional and imaginative development. These and other possible effects have not been evaluated fully from an educational perspective. The best that can be said is that they are simply not understood. Whatever strategies schools do develop, the need will remain to promote other modes of learning and human contact so that the full capacities of young people are developed through and alongside the use of new technologies.

The Social Challenge

12 *To provide forms of education that enable young people to engage positively and confidently with far-reaching processes of social and cultural change.*

The combined effects of economic and technological change are transforming the social landscape. In some areas, the breakdown of traditional patterns of work, particularly in heavy industry and manufacturing, has had cataclysmic effects on social and community life. The effects have been more than economic. In areas worst affected by long-term unemployment, there are mounting problems of social exclusion. The Government's Social Exclusion Unit is involved in a wide range of measures to generate new work opportunities for communities and to promote the confidence and employability of those out of work. In some areas, there has been a particular emphasis on regeneration through the creative and cultural industries — a strategy which can have both economic and community benefits. Advances in science and technology are affecting many other areas of social life. Developments in genetics and fertility in particular are changing perceptions of gender roles and identity. The prospects of longer lives and better healthcare have profound demographic implications for the balance of relations and responsibilities between the generations. At the same time there is a breakdown in traditional family structures and in patterns of parenting and childcare.

13 Over the last three decades, the cultural profile of Britain has widened enormously. There have been profound changes in the food we eat, in how we speak and dress, and in how we see ourselves in relation to other countries and cultural communities. Many British families have links across several continents. Many young people now live in a complex web of interacting cultures and sub-cultures: of families, gender, peer groups, ideological convictions, political communities and of ethnic and local traditions. They also live in a global culture which is driven by the interplay of commercial interests, the creative energies of young people themselves, and the enveloping influence of information technologies. Information and communication technologies and the mass media — films, television, newspapers and magazines — form a torrent of ideas, images and lifestyles which compete for young people's attention and sense of identity.

14 There is a growing awareness of the need for education to respond practically to the increasing diversity of British society, and to the growing interaction between world cultures. The Macpherson report on the Stephen Lawrence inquiry (Macpherson 1999) documents the catastrophic consequences of the breakdown of intercultural relations. It points to the need for schools and others to go beyond a general policy of multicultural education: to combat extreme forms of cultural intolerance and racism. Racist attitudes, though always pernicious, are in the minority. Nonetheless, the education sector as a whole must now look at a range of strategies to address racism wherever and however it occurs.

The Personal Challenge

15 *To develop the unique capacities of all young people, and to provide a basis on which they can each build lives that are purposeful and fulfilling.*

All young people have different capacities, aptitudes and biographies. They have different pasts and different futures. One of the roles of education is to help them find their future and understand their pasts. This begins by helping them to discover their own strengths, passions and sensibilities. Young people spend their most formative and impressionable years at school. There needs are not only academic. They are social, spiritual and emotional. All young people need an education that helps them to find meaning and to make sense of themselves and their lives. For some the need is acute. In a recent report the Mental Health Foundation (1999) found that growing numbers of young people are experiencing emotional problems and disturbances. The report argues that schools must find ways of enabling young people to explore and express their own emotions and feelings in positive and constructive ways. The conventional academic curriculum is not designed nor intended to do this. Yet the need for action is obvious.

16 The rising tide of drug use, of gang culture and street violence is harsh evidence of the pressures and tensions that young people face. A growing number are less and less convinced of the value of education itself. Truancy and disaffection still affect the minority of school pupils: but it is a significant problem. The problems of disaffection are particularly acute among young people who feel a conflict between their own cultural values and identities and those of the schools they attend or the areas where they live. A recent report from OFSTED (1999a) has confirmed the problems of underachievement among children from ethnic minority families. There is an acknowledged and particular problem among African-Caribbean boys, growing numbers of whom are excluded from school.

17 The evidence is that the majority of young people have positive attitudes towards schools and are well behaved in class. There is also evidence of less positive attitudes. For example, research based on the Keele database of schools (Barber, 1994) showed that up to 70 per cent of secondary school pupils 'count the minutes to the end of lessons' and 30 - 40 per cent thought that school was boring and would rather not go to school at

> **"** Life is more than work. If we give children the idea that they need high-level skills only for work, we have got it all wrong. They are going to need even higher-level skills to perform in a democratic society. We have got to get this absolutely right: the issue is not technology, but what it means to be human, what kind of future we want for the human race. **"**
>
> *John Abbott 1998*

all. Clearly there are many factors affecting pupil motivation and interest in education. But one of the most effective solutions is to develop active forms of learning which engage the creative energies of young people. A small proportion of pupils can be classified as disaffected. One estimate puts it at about 10 per cent of Year 6 and 7 pupils (Keys et al 1995). Such pupils may feel that school has nothing to offer them and is a waste of time. Disaffection is often internalised and may be manifested in unhappiness, lack of motivation, truancy and disruptive behaviour. Poor behaviour can lead to exclusion.

18 Although permanent exclusion is relatively uncommon, it has been increasing over the past few years and there is an increase in exclusions from primary schools. Official figures (DfEE 1998b) show that in 1996-97, 12,700 pupils were permanently excluded from mainland schools in England. This was a rise of 15 per cent in the three years from 1994-95. Exclusion is costly in terms of arranging alternative provision for pupils as well as the 'hidden' costs of social service, health, police and criminal justice service involvement. It has been estimated that the total cost of excluding pupils in 1996-7 amounted to £81 million (Parsons & Castle 1998). There is a worryingly consistent picture of excluded pupils. Those excluded are often (Sharp & Cato 1998):

- male;

- black - African and Caribbean;

- from families of low socio-economic status;

- have special educational needs;

- have low levels of academic achievement.

Research evidence highlights the following individual factors associated with exclusion (Sharp & Cato 1998):

- Excluded pupils may have difficulties in establishing positive relationships with teachers and other pupils. They may seek the company of other deviant peers.

- Excluded pupils may experience particular difficulties with literacy.

- Parents of excluded pupils are likely to have experienced difficulties in controlling their child's behaviour.

Equally there is evidence that the experience of excluded pupils from African-Caribbean backgrounds differs from that of white pupils. OFSTED (1996) found that the exclusion of black pupils was less likely to be associated with under-achievement or trauma than was true of white pupils. Many research studies have suggested that structural changes to the educational system may be contributing to the causes of exclusion, including increased competition between schools which has increased the emphasis on conventional academic attainment and fewer resources and less time to support disaffected pupils.

Back To Basics

19 In all of these ways the tasks of education are complex and difficult. They include raising academic standards, but these alone will not answer the questions that education now faces. A motif of educational debate over the last ten years has been the need to get back to basics. The transformational changes we have outlined here are enough to raise questions about what these basics are. Many developed countries are now asking how education can:

- motivate young people and raise their confidence and self esteem;

- increase their employability;

- develop their skills of communication and of social interaction;

- encourage cultural tolerance and understanding;

- promote a sense of social responsibility and political participation;

- promote inclusion and combat exclusion in a world of rapid social and economic change.

20 The Government has in hand a number of initiatives in education to address these challenges. A central strategy is the identification of six key skills:

a. communication;

b. application of number;

c. use of information technology;

d. working with others;

e. problem-solving;

f. improving one's own learning and performance.

We endorse these priorities and we want to add to them. We are living in times of enormous opportunity. Our education system has been largely shaped by the needs of an industrial economy and by particular views of ability and intelligence. In our view, the result has been that many areas of young people's potential — of their real resources — are untapped and neglected. Among them are powers and talents that will be of fundamental importance to them and to society in meeting the challenges we have described. A commitment to developing human resources must involve a fundamental review of what these resources are; of the types of teaching that are needed to develop them; and of who should be involved in education. The strategy we propose for creative and cultural education is intended to contribute to this. The starting point is to say what we mean by creative and cultural education, why they are so important, and how they are related.

2 Creative Education

Introduction

21 The word 'creativity' is used in different ways, in different contexts. It has an 'elusive definition'[1]. The problems of definition lie in its particular associations with the arts, in the complex nature of creative activity itself, and in the variety of theories that have been developed to explain it. Some people doubt that creativity can be taught at all. They see creativity as a natural capacity with limited room for improvement through education. Our proposals are intended to show that creativity can be developed and how this might be done. In this section we offer our definition of creativity and the implications we see for promoting the creative development of young people.

Defining Creativity

22 Creativity is obviously to do with producing something original. But there are different views of what is involved in this process and about how common the capacity for creativity is.

Sectoral Definition

23 Many people associate creativity primarily with the arts[2]. Music, drama, art, dance, literature, and the rest, are often called 'the creative arts'. As we said in Chapter One, the professional arts and associated fields are now known as the 'creative industries'. The 'creative arts' are often contrasted with the sciences, which tend to be thought of as uncreative. One of our aims in this report is to emphasise the importance of the arts and their essential place in creative development. But creativity is not unique to the arts. It is equally fundamental to advances in the sciences, in mathematics, technology, in politics, business and in all areas of everyday life.

> *There are few areas of life where the nation's priorities for education, health, employment and industry are not dependent on the development and application of creative practical skills.*
>
> *Crafts Council 1998*

Élite Definition

24 It is sometimes thought that only very rare people are creative and that creativity involves unusual talents. The literature of creativity often focuses on the great men and women who have produced or made path-breaking compositions, paintings, inventions or theories. Such people, it is sometimes said, make their mark without special help and may even gain strength from educational failure. For both reasons it is assumed that there is limited scope and little point in trying to educate for creativity. Obviously, there are people with exceptional creative gifts. The élite conception of creativity is important because it focuses attention on creative achievements which are of historic originality, which push back the frontiers of human knowledge and understanding. These achievements constitute the highest levels of creativity. Education must certainly nurture young people who are capable of such achievements. But there are other considerations.

Democratic Definition

25 In our view, all people are capable of creative achievement in some area of activity, provided the conditions are right and they have acquired the relevant knowledge and skills. Moreover, a democratic society should provide opportunities for everyone to succeed according to their own strengths and abilities. Meeting the various challenges we have described, economic, technological, social, and personal, involves realising the capacities of all young people, and not only those with obviously exceptional ability. There is no doubt that some highly creative individuals do thrive in adversity — we have such people on this committee. But others do not. There is no way of knowing the current scale of frustration or waste of creative capacities in our schools. In our view:

a. creative possibilities are pervasive in the concerns of everyday life, its purposes and problems;

b. creative activity is also pervasive: many people who are being creative do not recognise that this is what they are doing;

c. creativity can be expressed in collaborative as well as individual activities, in teamwork, in organisations, in communities and in governments.

For all these reasons, we favour a democratic conception of creativity: one which recognises the potential for creative achievement in all fields of human activity; and the capacity for such achievements in the many and not the few. To justify this approach we need to say what we mean by creativity.

Creativity: Our Definition

26 Defining a process that covers such a wide range of activities and personal styles is inherently difficult. Ours is a stipulative definition, but it takes account of what we understand about the nature of creative processes and of the ways in which key words are used in different contexts. It is also in a sense an indicative definition in that it points to features of creative processes that we want to encourage for educational purposes. Our starting point is to recognise four characteristics of creative processes. First, they always involve thinking or behaving *imaginatively*. Second, overall this imaginative activity is *purposeful:* that is, it is directed to achieving an objective. Third, these processes must generate something *original*. Fourth, the outcome must be of *value* in relation to the objective. We therefore define creativity as:

Imaginative activity fashioned so as to produce outcomes that are both original and of value.

We want to comment briefly on these four characteristics. On this basis we will develop our view that creativity is possible in all areas of human activity and that everyone has creative capacities.

Four Features of Creativity

Using Imagination

27 Imaginative activity in our terms is not the same as fantasising or imaging, although it may involve both. It is not simply producing mental representations of things that are not present or have not been experienced. Imaginative activity is the process of generating something original: providing an alternative to the expected, the conventional, or the routine. This activity involves processes of thinking or behaving. The behaviour may include activities where thought is embodied in the movement: such as in performance and other forms where there is not necessarily prefigurative thinking. Imaginative activity is a form of mental play — serious play directed towards some creative purpose. It is a mode of thought which is essentially *generative:* in which we attempt to expand the possibilities of a given situation; to look at it afresh or from a new perspective, envisaging alternatives to the routine or expected in any given task. Creative insights often occur when existing ideas are combined or reinterpreted in unexpected ways or when they are applied in areas with which they are not normally associated. Often this arises by making unusual connections, seeing analogies and relationships between ideas or objects that have not previously been related.

Pursuing Purposes

28 Creativity carries with it the idea of action and purpose. It is, in a sense, applied imagination. To speak of somebody being creative is to suggest that they are actively engaged in making or producing something in a deliberate way. This is not to say that creative insights or breakthroughs may not occur unexpectedly along the way, for example by intuition or non-directed thought, but they occur on the way to something: to meeting the overall objective, or to solving the central problem. This can be a highly dynamic process, whose eventual outcomes can be quite different

"I decided I was only going to do things for the fun of it and only that afternoon as I was taking lunch some kid threw up a plate in the cafeteria. There was a blue medallion on the plate — the Cornell sign. As the plate came down it wobbled. It seemed to me that the blue thing went round faster than the wobble and I wondered what the relationship was between the two — I was just playing; no importance at all. So I played around with the equations of motion of rotating things and I found out that if the wobble is small the blue thing goes round twice as fast as the wobble. I tried to figure out why that was, just for the fun of it, and this led me to the similar problems in the spin of an electron and that led me back into quantum electrodynamics which is the problem I'd been working on. I continued to play with it in this relaxed fashion and it was like letting a cork out of a bottle. Everything just poured out and in very short order I worked the things out for which I later won the Nobel Prize."

Richard Feynmann, Nobel Prize-winning Physicist

than from those anticipated at the outset. Sometimes the objective changes as new ideas and possibilities come into view: sometimes, as with inventions and discoveries, new purposes are found when an initial product or idea has emerged.

Being Original

29 Creativity always involves originality. But there are different categories of originality[3].

- *Individual*
  A person's work may be original in relation to their own previous work and output.

- *Relative*
  It may be original in relation to their peer group: to other young people of the same age, for example.

- *Historic*
  The work may be original in terms of anyone's previous output in a particular field: that is, it may be uniquely original.

There can also be degrees of originality within these categories: of greater or less originality in relation to individual or group output. Originality in creative work will often be judged to be of the first two categories. For reasons we come to, this can be of considerable importance in the general education of each individual. But in our view exceptional individual achievement - that is, of historic originality - is also more likely to emerge from a system of education which encourages the creative capacities of everyone.

Judging Value

30 We described imaginative activity as a generative mode of thought; creativity involves a second and reciprocal mode of thought: an *evaluative* mode. Originality at some level is essential in all creative work, but it is never enough. Original ideas may be irrelevant to the purpose in hand. They may be bizarre, or faulty. The outcome of imaginative activity can only be called creative if it is of value in relation to the task at hand. 'Value' here is a judgement of some property of the outcome related to the purpose. There are many possible judgements according to the area of activity: effective, useful, enjoyable, satisfying, valid, tenable. The criteria of value vary according to the field of activity in question.

31 Creative activity involves playing with ideas and trying out possibilities. In any creative process there are likely to be dead-ends: ideas and designs that do not work. There may be many failures and modifications and much refashioning of imaginative activity before the best outcomes, the best 'fit' is produced. A similar process may then take place in terms of the application of creative outcomes. Evaluating which ideas do work and which do not requires judgement and criticism. In this way creative thinking always involves some critical thinking. Understanding this is an important foundation for creative education. There is a distinction, and there may be differences, between the evaluations made by the creator and those made by others. Equally, the value of something may only be recognised over time. We will come back to this later in discussing the links between creative and cultural development.

32 Critical evaluation involves a shift in the focus of attention and mode of thinking as we attend to what is working or not working. This can happen throughout the process of creativity and not only at the end. It can permeate the process of generating ideas: it can involve standing back in quiet reflection. It can be individual or shared, involve instant judgements or long-term testing. In most creative work there are many shifts between these two modes of thought and focus of attention. The quality of creative achievement is related to both. Helping young people to understand and manage this interaction between generative and evaluative thinking is a pivotal task of creative education.

The Processes of Creativity

33 Creative abilities are developed through practical application: by being engaged in the processes of creative thought production: making music, writing stories, conducting experiments and so on. A key task for teachers is to help young people to understand these processes and to gain control of them. These are particular techniques and skills which are specific to different disciplines and forms of work. But there are also some general features of creative processes which young people need to experience and recognise.

34 Creative processes in all disciplines normally involve an initial phase of drafting: of giving an idea a rough shape or outline. This may be the first notes of a melody; a first image or metaphor; the first sketch of a problem in mathematics. The process of development is commonly one of 'successive approximations' in which the idea is shaped and clarified in the process of exploring it. The final phases are often to do with refining the detail of the expression: with producing the neat copy, so to speak. The classical division of stages in creative thought - preparation-incubation-illumination then verification[4] - is contested in various ways by different

> As I watched my sister, a developmental biologist, from a distance in her own environment, I could tell that her lab processes were not that different to my studio ones. In science at the bench much as the potter at his wheel, or the sculptor at his block of wood there is a process of preparation, some questions posed early on and a distinct feeling of grafting away until a result wins through. There follows a period of stepping back, more questions, what does this result say to me? How can I change the outcome? Is there anything that 'failure' can teach me? And then back again, to retry or reshape the work in hand.

Professor Helen Storey

scholars but it does alert us to the common pattern of focus, withdrawal and then breakthrough and to the key point that creativity is a process, not an event. The form of this withdrawal from thinking about a problem, and the best circumstances for its success, are personal to the individual but often involve waking/sleeping moments, or a 'moving meditation' as we do other things. Creative activity involves a complex combination of controlled and non-controlled elements, unconscious as well as conscious mental processes, non-directed as well as directed thought, intuitive as well as rational calculation.

35 Deferment of judgement is an invaluable element as we produce ideas and then stretch them and connect them imaginatively as far as they can go. Although there is always a stage, maybe many stages, where critical appraisal is necessary, if only to assess coherence and relate ideas to evidence, practicability, utility and audience response, generative thinking has to be given time to flower. At the right time and in the right way, rigorous critical appraisal is essential. At the wrong point, criticism and the cold hand of realism can kill an emerging idea.

36 This dialogue between initial conception and final realisation can be delicate. It can be halted or inhibited by trying to do too much too soon or at the same time. For example, asking children to write a poem right away in their best handwriting can destroy the spontaneity they need in the initial phase of generating ideas. They need to be helped to understand that creativity often develops in phases; and to have some sense of where they are in the process and what to expect of themselves there. We have identified two modes of thought: generative and evaluative. The balance between these must be right. In most situations, trying to produce a finished version in one move is for most people an improbable task. Not understanding this can make young people and adults alike conclude that they are not really creative after all.

37 We said earlier that creativity is possible in all areas of human activity and not only in the arts. This is clearly true. Creative insights and advances have driven forward human culture in the sciences, in technology, in philosophy, the arts and the humanities. The history of science, indeed the essential process, is one of continuous conjectures and of re-evaluations of established ideas: of new insights or information, challenging and building on existing knowledge. This is the source of the intellectual excitement and creative impulse of science: that it is concerned not only with facts, but with what count as facts; not only with observation but with explanation — with interpretation and with meaning. The processes of scientific analysis and investigation can involve the highest levels of creativity and insight. Discovery in science is not always strictly logical. It often results from unexpected leaps of imagination: from sudden moments of illumination in which the scientist grasps the answer to a problem and then sets out to verify it by calculation. This can be as true for children setting out as for experienced scientists.

Leap of the Imagination

Some of the most common science activities can provide opportunities for teachers to witness a creative leap of the imagination where children suddenly make a connection and move their own learning forward. Children were testing different materials to find out which one was waterproof. They used a range of materials, looked at them under a microscope and made the connection that those materials with holes allowed water to flow through and that the bigger the hole the faster the water flowed through the material. Whilst most children accepted that some fabrics were waterproof and some others were not, one child, silent for a while, obviously pondering on the different aspects of the activity, suddenly exclaimed, "We need to fill the holes to make it waterproof. If we crayoned over the fabric the wax would go into the holes". This illustrates creative thinking in science where a child does not take the obvious route and also shows real understanding of the key idea.

Information provided by the Association for Science Education

38 The creative process of the arts involves developing forms of expression which embody the artist's perceptions. This is not a matter of identifying an idea and then finding a form in which to express it. It is through shaping the individual work that the ideas and feelings are given form. Often it is only through developing the dance, image or music that the perception itself is clarified. The meaning is uniquely available in the form in which it is expressed; and it is in these forms that we express our most human perceptions and feelings. The creative processes of the arts centre on the shaping and refining of a work in which its aesthetic qualities are central to its meaning. The look, sound and feel of work in the arts is inseparable not only from what it means, but from how it means.

39 It is essential for education to provide opportunities for young people to express their own ideas, values and feelings. In recent years, there has been a new recognition of the vital importance of what Daniel Goleman (1996) calls emotional intelligence: the ability to understand, express and use our feelings and intuition. Goleman, and many before him, points to the changes and the problems that can follow from difficulties in understanding and expressing our emotions. The recent report by the Mental Health Foundation (see paragraph 15) confirms these concerns. There are many ways in schools of enabling young people to discuss and express their feelings and emotions. Among the most important are the arts. Discussions about the arts in education often emphasise the value of self-expression, and this is an important idea. But there is a difference between giving direct vent to feelings — as in a cry of pain or a jump for joy — and the creative processes of the arts. Composing and playing music, writing poetry, making a dance may all be driven by powerful emotional impulses; but the process is not simply one of discharging feelings — though it may involve that — but of giving them form and meaning.

❚❚ This expression is unique. If you block it, it will never exist through any other medium and will be lost. ❚❚

Martha Graham

❚❚ The arts are quite simply a magic key for some children and within the hands of gifted committed teachers of the arts they are a key to *all* children, not only do they open the mind of the learner, they then reveal a cast cornucopia of endless delight, challenge and opportunity. ❚❚

Professor Tim Brighouse, Chief Education Officer, Birmingham City Council

Problem-Solving

40 Problem-solving is now recognised as a key skill in education. Developing young people's abilities to solve problems is fundamental to preparing them for an independent life. Creative education can contribute directly to problem-solving abilities in all disciplines and fields of work. But creativity and problem-solving are not the same thing. Not all problems call for creative solutions or original thinking. Some can be solved routinely and logically. And not all creative thinking is directed to solving problems, in the conventional sense. Composing poetry, painting pictures or 'playing' with abstract ideas in science or mathematics are not always problem-solving as normally understood. The value of creative thinkers is not only that they solve problems we know we have, but that they find problems we hadn't imagined and lead us on to new horizons. More opportunities should be given to young people to sense and define problems for themselves, as well as identifying solutions to given problems. More opportunities should be given to the generation of ideas; looking at the world in different ways and playing with different possibilities and alternative solutions. Familiarity with a wide range of problem-solving activities can lead to greater competence in seeing underlying patterns and analogies.

Creativity and Intelligence

41 Creativity is a basic capacity of human intelligence. Human intelligence is not only creative, but multifaceted. It is for this reason that we argue that all young people have creative capacities and they all have them differently.

The Variety of Intelligence

42 A key characteristic of human intelligence is our capacity for representing experience in various ways. This capacity is basic to how we think and communicate. Verbal language is the most obvious example. As they learn a language, children are not only learning how to name things: they are acquiring the patterns of ideas and understanding which are inherent in their language. In learning to speak they are also learning ways to think. But we think and communicate in other ways too. Our experiences are of many kinds and we use a wide variety of ways to make sense of them. Words help us to formulate some ideas but not others: equally mathematics makes

possible ideas which are otherwise inconceivable. There are ideas, feelings and perceptions that will not go into either. To understand these we turn to other modes of expression and communication.

43 Our primary perceptions of the world are through the senses: through light, sound, shape, texture, smell and movement. We do not only experience the world in these different ways, we think in them too. A person painting a picture is thinking visually; a musician is thinking in sound. Dancers think in space and movement. These are not substitutes for words; they illustrate the rich diversity of human intelligence and the many different modes in which we think and communicate. A painter is not producing images of ideas that could be expressed equally well in words or numbers. He or she is presenting visual ideas. Musicians are expressing ideas that can only be fully understood through music. Conventional education tends to emphasise verbal and mathematical reasoning. These are vital to the intellectual development of all young people but they are not the whole of intelligence.

44 Most children spend most of their time in school reading, writing and thinking in words or numbers. In higher education, essay writing and note taking are the principal forms of study. Using words and numbers are among the highest achievements of human intelligence, but if it were limited to these, most of personal experience would be incommunicable and most of human culture would not have happened. The worlds we live in are as rich and various as they are because our minds are so complex and diverse. Philosophers, psychologists and educationalists have long recognised this diversity of human intelligence. A recent formulation is Howard Gardner's theory of multiple intelligences (Gardner 1993). Gardner identifies seven forms of intelligence: linguistic, mathematical, spatial, kinaesthetic, musical, interpersonal and intrapersonal. This is not a fixed list. There are other ways of categorising types of intelligence (White 1998). The numbers of intelligences and the exact ways in which they are classified are less important than the fact that intelligence is multifaceted. There are two important implications of this argument, for education in general and for creative education in particular.

45 First, the tendency now is to think of children as 'able' or 'less able', mainly on the basis of academic performance. Academic ability consists primarily of a facility for propositional knowledge and linear forms of reasoning. All children have such abilities to varying degrees and it is essential that they should be developed. But it is neither accurate nor responsible to judge children's intellectual abilities in general on the basis of these abilities alone. It would be more accurate to think of all children having a profile of abilities across a wide range of intelligences. Second, children who perform poorly in conventional academic tests may have strong abilities in other areas. Children with high academic ability may be highly able in other areas too. A child with poor spatial abilities may have high linguistic or aural intelligence. Some children have particular capacities for mathematics, for music, for dance, for languages, or for

> *"The creative artist is an observer whose brain works in new ways making it possible to convey information about matters that were not a subject for communication before. The discoveries of the artist and the scientist are exactly alike in this respect. Artists have discovered new aspects of space with one symbolism just as physicists had with another."*
>
> *J. Z. Young 1987*

> *"There is no such thing as a single general intelligence, which we all possess to a greater or lesser degree. We all have a unique combination of different kinds of abilities, which can and do change throughout our lives."*
>
> *Scottish Consultative Council on the Curriculum 1996*

several of these. When children discover their real strengths, there can be a dramatic change in their overall motivation in education. Judging children against a single standard of ability can misrepresent their own individual strengths. Discovering them can enormously increase self-esteem, confidence and achievement as a whole. A commitment to developing children's human resources must begin from a recognition of how wide, rich and diverse these resources really are.

The Dynamics of Intelligence

> Each of us have a different mosaic of intelligences. Uniform schooling ignores these differences.
>
> *Howard Gardner*

46 Intelligence is multi-dimensional: it is also dynamic. In the 1960s, research in the USA suggested that the two hemispheres of the brain have different functions. The left hemisphere was found to be largely concerned with logical, analytical thought: the right hemisphere with more 'holistic' modes of thinking, with recognition of faces, patterns and with spatial movement. The two halves of the brain are joined by a shaft of nerve fibres, the corpus callosum. This facilitates interaction between the two hemispheres and between different modes of activity. More recent studies confirm that different areas of the brain are strongly associated with different types of activity: with speech, emotions, touch, spatial orientation and so on. They also show that the brain does not work in separate, isolated compartments, but as a whole dynamic system. Different areas of the brain work together during different types of activity. During speech, for example, the patterns of brain activity are different according to whether we are speaking our mother tongue or a second language.

47 Some modes of thinking dominate in different types of activity — the aural in music, the spatial/kinaesthetic in dance, the mathematical in physics. But these, and most other forms of intellectual activity, draw on different areas of intelligence simultaneously — they are multi-modal. Mathematicians, for example, often talk of 'visualising' problems and solutions. Dance is closely related to musical understanding: visual arts draw deeply from spatial intelligence. The composition of music is often informed by an understanding of mathematics. Research in Europe and the United States (Fox & Gardiner 1997) has suggested for example that music education can have a direct effect on improvement in mathematical ability. Equally, drama can be a powerful way of promoting skills in reading, writing and in speech. Creative insights often occur when new connections are made between ideas or experiences that were not previously related. This happens across as well as within different modes of thinking.

Learning through your Body

Susie attends a special school where she has a weekly session with a dance-movement specialist. Susie likes writing and has a lot to say. But her teachers can only read a portion of what she writes, because Susie doesn't notice the edge of the paper. As she writes, she works her way across the paper, then onto the desk, until she comes to the end of her reach. Then she returns to the page and starts all over again. No amount of talking about it made any difference; bigger paper didn't help. Then her teacher asked the dance-movement specialist if she could help. They worked with an aspect of movement called 'flow'. It concerns the way a person allows energy to pass through and out of the body, or, at the other end of the spectrum, the way they hold it in. Susie moved with lots of 'free flow'. Her movement seemed to go on and on; if you clapped your hands and said stop, it took her a long time to come to some sort of stillness, but even then there was movement. Together they played 'flow' games; letting the energy go, then trying to stop it and hold it inside. Gradually the games moved closer to the skill of stopping at the end of the page. They played, move your arm against the floor and now "stop!". They got out paper and played, move your arm across the paper and then "stop!". Susie returned to the classroom and never wrote off the paper again. She needed to learn this through her body, not her intellect.

Information provided by Jabadao

> **"** Intelligence is multifaceted. The arts are also multifaceted. They involve intellectual, emotional, social, cultural, spiritual, moral, political, technological and economic understanding and inquiry, as participants and as viewers. Each of these facets can dominate at any one time, but can combine. Our knowledge and understanding of intellectual abilities are extended through the participation in and study of the arts. Through this participation and study intellectual and other intelligences are extended and nurtured. **"**
>
> *Lindsey Fryer*

Developing Creativity

48

There is considerable debate about, and a growing body of research into the idea of transferable skills: that is, skills of creative thought and production that apply in different domains of activity. The literature and many of the practical programmes on creative thinking certainly suggest that there are general skills that can be used across many different fields. It is also the case that some people are creative in many areas. The following themes are suggested by experience and research and are important in planning policies and strategies for creative education.

- *Creativity is best construed not as a single power, which you either have or do not, but as multidimensional:* Creative processes involve many different mental functions combinations of skills and personality attributes[5]. They involve special purposes for familiar mental operations[6] and the more efficient use of our ordinary abilities, not 'something profoundly different' (Boden 1990:259).

- *Some creative abilities are 'domain specific'.* Some of the specific skills and techniques of mathematics or physics or drawing or playing the piano are specific to those activities and do not necessarily transfer to each other nor to other areas.

> **"** Look and you will find it. What is unsought will go undetected. **"**
>
> *Sophocles*

- The creative strengths of any one person may be specific to particular fields or types of activity: Creativity involves working in a medium. The medium may be conceptual, as in mathematics. It may involve a physical medium: an instrument, clay, fabrics or steel. For many people, creative ability is stimulated by the 'feel' of the materials and the activity in question. If a person does not find their best medium, they may never discover what their creative potential is, and never experience the pleasures, satisfactions and achievements that follow.

Experience suggests that some, perhaps many people feel disaffected by education and suffer a sense of failure precisely because they have never discovered where their own unique abilities lie. For all of those reasons, schools need to promote a broad approach to creativity across the curriculum and a broad and balanced curriculum. In doing so, it is important to recognise two fundamental dynamics of creative processes.

Freedom and Control

49 Creativity is not simply a matter of 'letting go'. It is sometimes assumed that creativity only emerges from 'free expression' and lack of inhibitions or constraints. This is very misleading. Freedom to experiment is essential for creativity. But so too are skills, knowledge and understanding. Being creative in music, or in physics, or dance, or mathematics, involves knowledge and expertise in the skills, materials and forms of understanding that they involve. It is possible to have a limited creative impact in some fields with little knowledge of them. But sustained creative achievement involves knowledge of the field in question and skills in the media concerned. Creativity in music requires increasing control in the production and dynamics of sound: creativity in mathematics or science requires increasing skills in numeracy. It is possible to teach all of these and not promote creative ability at all: indeed, to stifle it. But the alternative is not to disregard the teaching of skills and understanding, but to recognise the mutual dependence of freedom and control at the heart of the creative process.

Creativity and Culture

50 There is a further point which has important implications for teaching methods and for the curriculum. Creativity is sometimes seen as an entirely individual process. The popular image of creative genius is of the lone individual producing unique insights out of the air. Some individuals do work alone, and the course of history has been changed by the extraordinary creative insights of particularly gifted people. But for everyone, creative achievement always draws from the ideas and achievements of other people: from the books, theories, poems, music, architecture, design and the rest that mark the trails of other people's creative journeys. Just as different modes of thinking interact in a single mind, individual creativity is affected by dialogue with others. In these ways, creative development is intimately related to cultural development.

> People assume that as an innovator, I break rules. I don't. I relish rules. I just like rewriting them.
>
> *Lord Stone of Blackheath*

Conclusion

51 In this section we have defined what we mean by creativity and what we see as its main features. Creativity is possible in all fields of human intelligence; and this is diverse and multifaceted. Genuine creative achievement involves knowledge, control and discipline combined with the freedom and confidence to experiment. In the next chapter we relate these arguments to our conception of cultural education.

3 Cultural Education

Introduction

52
In this section we set out our definition of culture and of the roles of cultural education. We argue that creative education and cultural education are closely related and that there are important implications for the balance of the school curriculum and for teaching and learning.

Defining Culture

> **"**
> Human life depends upon language, art and all the complications of culture as much as on food — it would ultimately collapse without them.
> **"**
>
> *J. Z. Young 1987*

53
Like creativity, culture is a term that is used in many ways in different contexts. It is a term with a complicated history and with a range of different, sometimes conflicting meanings. Like creativity, culture is strongly associated with the arts and letters. While accepting the importance of this particular sense of culture, we want to adopt a more general definition which includes, but goes beyond, it. The exclusive association of culture with the arts overlook many other aspects of human culture, including, not least, science and technology.

Sectoral Definition

54
Since the late eighteenth century, culture in one sense, has meant a general process of intellectual or social refinement. This is the sense in which a person might be described as 'cultured'. This process has been linked particularly with an appreciation of the arts. By extension, culture has also come to mean the general field of artistic and intellectual activity through which this process of refinement was promoted. It is this meaning of culture that is implied in describing the arts and related fields as the 'cultural industries'. Ministries of culture throughout the world, and national cultural policies often focus specifically on the development of the arts, including music, cinema, literature, dance, visual art and also traditional and folk culture, especially traditional music and dance.

Élite Definition

55
Within this particular conception of culture, a further distinction is often made between high art and popular culture. In Western European terms, high art normally means opera, classical music, ballet, contemporary dance, fine art, serious literature and some forms of cinema. Culture, in the sense of high art fits well with Matthew Arnold's famous formulation, "the best that has been known and said". Popular culture, on the other hand, is taken to mean those forms of creative practice that have mass appeal, including commercial music, popular cinema, television, fashion, design and popular fiction.

56
On this basis, two assumptions are sometimes made which are relevant to our argument and both of which we want to challenge. The first is that

cultural education should consist principally, if not wholly, of teaching young people to understand and appreciate high art, particularly works in the classical European tradition. We think that all cultural education should certainly include this, but in relation to particular roles which we set out later. We also think that cultural education must go much further. The second assumption is that there is an unbridgeable gap between high art and popular culture. We think that this assumption is wrong for two reasons. The first is that there is in practice an interaction and overlap between different cultural processes, including high art and popular culture. The second is that many people enjoy and contribute to both, as informed and dynamic audiences and makers. The interaction between different types of cultural practice, including high art and popular culture, is significant for the conception of cultural education that we want to promote.

57 There is, then, in the sense set out above, a strong association between the arts and culture. Practising and understanding the arts in all their forms are essential elements of creative and cultural education. But the definition of culture must, in our view, go beyond an exclusive association with the arts in general and high art in particular. The importance of these can only be fully recognised in educational terms within a more general social definition of culture: a definition which embraces the importance of other significant fields of creative activity.

Social Definition

58 'Culture' as we have said has a long association with the arts. But in this century particularly, the term 'culture' has also been used in a more general sense to mean a community's overall way of life. This definition of culture has been developed particularly in anthropology and sociology. It recognises that different social groupings are held together by shared values, beliefs and ways of relating which are characteristic of them, and which distinguish them from others. Most people now belong to many different cultural groups — national, local, ethnic, religious, ideological and professional. Each has its own values and ways of doing things, its own distinctive culture. The culture of a group includes its sense of identity — its sense of what makes it a group; and the various ways in which its identity is expressed and maintained — its patterns of behaviour and organisation.

> **"** Culture is where we live our shared mental lives. We need a way of understanding this habitat, of treating it with the respect and care it deserves. **"**
>
> *Brian Eno*

59 At the heart of the social definition of culture is the concept of values: those things — the ideas, beliefs, attitudes — which the group considers worthy and important, and which it holds in common as a group. These values are shaped by many factors: by human nature itself, which may be taken more or less as a constant; by the physical environment, including climate and geography; by relations with, or isolation from, other communities; by religious beliefs or lack of them; by science and technology, by economics and by 'events'. These values underpin and shape social institutions such as the law, education and the family, and personal behaviour. In turn they are influenced by changes in knowledge, understanding and experience.

60 Cultural identity is expressed and maintained in many ways. Traditionally, one defining factor of cultural groups has been a shared language and, at more specific levels, shared dialects, accents and vocabularies. This continues to be so for cultural groupings of all sorts, even within the increasingly pervasive use of English as an international language. Customised vocabularies, styles and rhythms of speech are among the most common ways that cultural groups and sub-groups define themselves in relationship to others. In the fast-changing world of youth culture, new slang, styles and rhythms of speech are among the most important ways in which cultural identities are created and recreated. Cultural identity is also expressed in many other ways, from styles of dress, to patterns and structures of social relationships.

61 Our concern in this report is with ways of enabling young people, through education, to understand and make their way in the increasingly challenging social and personal circumstances of the contemporary world. For these reasons, and because of its inherent importance for education, we will also use the term 'culture' here in this broader social sense. Accordingly, we define culture as:

The shared values and patterns of behaviour that characterise different social groups and communities.

Most national communities, including our own, are a complex mix of ethnic, generational, religious, ideological and political cultural groupings which overlap with and affect each other. Many young people live in, and move among many different cultural communities, each of which might contribute more or less to their individual sense of cultural identity, or lack of it.

62 The ways of life — the 'cultures' — of groups are often intricate in themselves and in how they relate with others that surround and intersect them. A key example is the sense of multiple identity felt by young British people whose parents or grandparents were born in other countries and traditions, and who now live in and between several different cultural communities. Understanding the complexities of cultural experience and identity is essential in many fields of study: in social history, sociology, cultural anthropology and in the emergent disciplines of cultural studies. For our purposes, we want to point to three features of the social cultures of the late twentieth century which are significant for our proposals for creative and cultural education: they are *dynamic, diverse* and they are *evolving*.

The Dynamics of Culture

63 Social cultures can be described and analysed in terms of their different systems and elements: legal systems, religious beliefs, technologies, economic activities and patterns of social relations. But they can only be fully understood in terms of how all of these various elements affect each other. Three important examples of this interaction are particularly relevant to our arguments: first, the cultural impact of science and technology;

> "
> Creative practical engagement provides opportunities to share different cultural influences, challenge received thinking, develop means for expression, critical thought and problem-solving skills. "
>
> *Crafts Council*

second, the dynamic relations between the arts, technology and design; third, the interaction between different cultural forms and traditions.

The Impact of Science

64 Science and technology interact with the social culture in many ways and at many levels. From time immemorial, technology - the design and use of tools - has changed the conditions and possibilities of human culture. In the last three hundred years particularly, and with increasing speed in our own time, science and technology have transformed human perceptions of how the world works and of our roles within it. Galileo, Darwin, Newton, Einstein and the rest are towering historical figures and not only in science. Their ideas, and the shifts of perception they provoked are woven into the fabric of global culture and have profoundly influenced the nature and course of it.

Exploring Science through the Arts

Get SET is a science-theatrical showcase consisting of ten pieces by school groups ranging in age from 11 to 18 years. These pieces focus on explaining and exploring scientific themes through drama, dance and music, using a range of styles, and were given two performances at the Everyman Theatre, Liverpool. The pupils devised and performed the pieces themselves as part of a production which was linked by the disembodied voices of a father and daughter from the future, learning about how science was viewed by young people from the 'past'. The pieces all lasted between 5-10 minutes and provided a genuine response by young people to science, engineering and technology, and how these things relate to them. The pieces were imaginative, entertaining, informative and thought-provoking, and the audience was instantly engaged and encouraged to take more interest in areas of science and technology explored. 150 pupils participated and the themes of physics, biology, chemistry, computer science, technology, engineering and the past, present and future of science were all given consideration. Both the schools' matinee and the evening performance played to packed houses, with demand for tickets far outstripping the theatre's capacity.

Information provided by North West Arts Board

65 Through technology, science has also directly changed the practical circumstances of human life and culture. From harnessing electricity to the new frontiers of bio-genetics; from the steam engine and motor cars to nuclear fission; from antibiotics to birth control; from railways to the Internet, science and technology have changed how we think, what we think about, what we do and what we are able to do. For example, developments in contraceptive techniques, notably the Pill, have revolutionised patterns of sexual morality and behaviour and deeply affected roles and relationships between men and women. The current

"Science is the dominant culture of the 20th Century and is set to become even more dominant in the 21st. However, as we become even more dependent on scientific and engineering advances, society appears to become less and less aware of it and how they have freed the human race from the slavery of existing merely to survive. As the next century approaches, the need thus becomes even more urgent that everyone should have some deeper understanding of the way scientific principles underpin their daily life. In fact, the intrinsic cultural nature of these principles, as well as the way they have been applied for the benefit of society, need to be revealed. Judicious use of these advances in the future is necessary and this will only occur if some key scientific principles are understood at every level of society."

Professor Sir Harold Kroto

revolutions in information technology are transforming the world of work for men and women and the economic relationships between them. Science and technology offer profound evidence of the variety of human creativity and they are implicated at every level in the formation and expression of the social culture of the late twentieth century. Any definition of cultural education must take account of this.

The Arts and Technology

66 There is a powerful relationship between science, technology and the arts. Artists make things: new tools and materials generate new forms of creative practice. In 1980, the House of Commons Select Committee defined the arts in this way (House of Commons 1982):

> *The term 'the arts' includes, but is not limited to music, dance, drama, folk arts, creative writing, architecture and allied fields, paintings, sculpture, photography, graphic and craft arts, industrial design, costume and fashion design, motion pictures, television, radio, tape and sound recording, the arts related to the presentation, performance, execution and exhibition of such major art forms and the study and application of the arts to the human environment.*

Many of the art forms listed here in the early 1980s were inconceivable in the 1780s. Film, photography and television are among the dominant art forms of the twentieth century: they did not exist in the eighteenth. It was not only impossible to make films then, it was probably inconceivable. The technology of the moving image not only made film possible, it made the idea of film possible. Shakespeare did not read nor write novels. There were none in the sixteenth century. The evolution of the novel, now one of the most popular art forms of our time, was only possible in the cultural circumstances that followed the invention of the printing press.

67 The relationship between the arts and technology has always been dynamic. Technology makes new forms of expression possible: artists drive technology to new levels of sophistication. This is happening now with digital technologies. At one level, the new technologies are making existing processes of creativity easier. There is software for musical composition, for choreography, theatre design and architecture, and this facilitates many existing forms of work. But new technologies are also generating new

> **"**
> In the future, creativity in industry, founded on the interaction between design and technology, will be the driver of national and international growth. Therefore, very early in education pupils should see these two fields, arts and science, not as two cultures to be separated, but facets to be conjoined for the good of mankind. **"**
>
> *Lord Stone of Blackheath*

forms of creative practice — in computer animation, sound synthesis and digital graphics. Some of the most adventurous developments in the arts are taking place at the boundaries of the new technologies: in multimedia and cyber-technology. The new technologies are providing for new languages and methods and modes of creativity in the arts, now as they have always done. A further example is the interaction of design and technology and their interactions in industry and economics. Throughout industry designers and technologists work together; they create new product systems and services. Britain, because of the diversity of its population and its tradition of freedom of expression, has been, in the past, one of the primary sources for this type of innovation.

High Art and Popular Culture

68 The conventional view of high art is that there are some works in music, painting, literature, dance and so on that are qualitatively superior to others in their depth of understanding of the human condition, and in the power and eloquence of their expression. In contrast, elements of popular culture are thought of as ephemeral and shallow. Both of these statements are true. There are examples of artistic expression, in all cultures, of transcendent beauty and power and which are in the highest reaches of human achievement. Much of commercial or popular culture makes no such claims. But this division is too neat. There is, and has always been, a traffic between different areas of cultural expression. The fact that something is popular does not disqualify it as high art. Some of the greatest classic writers are amongst the most widely-read. In recent years, opera has become hugely popular through television, CDs, the Three Tenors, football, fashion shows and film. The fact that large audiences now enjoy opera does not detract from its expressive power or its high aesthetic claims.

69 Equally, art forms that have their deepest roots in popular culture — contemporary dance, cinema, jazz, rap and rock music — have produced work of intense power and eloquence. Artists of every sort live within, not outside the social culture — and they draw deeply from it in their ideas, themes, and forms of expression. A great deal of classical music is rooted in popular and 'folk' music. Jazz draws from the themes of classical music as much as from the rhythms of popular song. Developments in contemporary dance, through Rudolf Laban and Martha Graham,

> *Young people tend to view listening to or playing classical music as activities which create a poor impression among their peers. These beliefs do not necessarily stem from something that is inherent in the music itself, but rather from the cultural 'positioning' of classical music relative to other forms of music which young people have come to associate with their own sub-cultures.*

Dr Susan O'Neill, Department of Psychology, Keele University were deeply influenced by the patterns and rhythms of ordinary human movement at work and play. These processes of influence and inspiration, borrowing and conversion are at the heart of creativity in the arts in all cultures and also across them. For example, some of the key figures of modern art, including Picasso were inspired and influenced in their work by African art and imagery. Increasingly in contemporary cultures, the use of new technologies and the free access to many different cultural forms they provide, is generating dynamic fusions of forms within and across different cultural genres and traditions - between Asian, European, African and American cultures - and at all levels, from the concert hall to the street.

70 We have defined creativity as a process with outcomes that are both original and of value. But just as values differ between cultures, they also change within cultures over time. There are many examples in the arts as in the sciences of innovations that were not valued or understood at the time they were made: of discoveries whose significance was unrecognised, even condemned or ridiculed by contemporary audiences. The music of Stravinsky, the paintings of Van Gogh, and Picasso, jazz, blues, rock and rap music were all rejected before being absorbed into the mainstream. As social and aesthetic values change, avant garde works of high culture can become icons of popular taste, just as work produced for mass audiences can be assimilated into the canons of high culture. This process of re-evaluation is also true in science. The real significance of scientific discoveries has sometimes become apparent only when social values have changed or when attitudes of other scientists have caught up or when the acceptance of new paradigms changes scientific perceptions.

The Diversity of Culture

71 Britain comprises an extraordinary variety of different cultural communities. Taken as a whole it includes people from many different ethnic traditions and backgrounds, with a wide range of religious beliefs, and of none; of political and ideological convictions and speaking many different languages and dialects. Overlapping all of these there are strong regional traditions and identities; and often stark contrasts between rural and urban communities and the patterns of population and ways of life in our cities. This is not new. It follows from our complex history of economic and political involvement in many different areas of the world and from the patterns of emigration and immigration they have involved.

"
We want a society that has a sense of what distinguishes it from, as well as unites it with, other societies. This will be a society conscious of its own identity or identities, aware of its own past and of the different pasts of its various communities, and respectful without being uncritical of its own customs and traditions.
"

Dr. Nick Tate, Chief Executive, QCA

72 Since the 1950s, there has been a marked change in patterns of population in some cities following the settlement of families from India, Bangladesh, Bengal, Pakistan, Africa the Caribbean and from other former colonies and dependencies. Britain is also home for large numbers of communities whose cultural roots are in many different parts of Europe, in the Middle and Far East: and to many faith communities including Jewish, Hindu, and Muslim as well as Christian. In some of our large city schools there are literally dozens of languages spoken by the pupils: and in some there is a majority for whom English itself is a second language.

73 This diversity is now central to the vitality of our national culture and a distinctive feature of it. There are immense benefits in this and there are deep problems. The patterns of race relations over the past forty years, positive and negative, are well documented: the problems of racism, where they occur, are persistent, and insidious. An approach to cultural education based on the roles we identify later will help to reap the benefits of this diversity and to mitigate the difficulties of intercultural understanding.

The Evolution of Culture

74 Culture in the biological sense implies growth and transformation. This is true of the social culture. One of the consequences of the dynamics and diversity of social cultures is an irresistible process of change. Some years ago a national newspaper campaigned with the slogan, "Times change, values don't". For all the reasons we have suggested, the opposite is true. Many of the values and patterns of behaviour in the closing moments of twentieth century are wholly different from those of the late nineteenth century: as they were from the previous century. Contemporary ways of life are not only different from those of the Victorians, they were largely unpredicted by them and were essentially unpredictable. Cultural change is rarely linear and uniform. It results from a vortex of influences and events which is hard enough to understand with hindsight and impossible to plan in advance. Nonetheless, education has to prepare young people in the best ways possible to engage with these processes of change. What should this involve?

Absolute and Relative Values

75 We have associated the social definition of culture with the idea of values: those things - the ideas, beliefs and attitudes - that groups or communities consider of worth and importance. We have also described contemporary cultures as dynamic and diverse. As a matter of urgency, education must help young people to understand these processes and to engage with and respect cultural perspectives which may differ from their own. In part, this is what we mean by cultural education. We will return to this idea shortly. But first, we want to comment on a view that is commonly taken when discussing cultural change and diversity: this is that there are no longer any core values to be taught in schools and that, instead, young people need to be taught that all values are relative and that there is no basis for choosing between them except personal preference. We do not think that this is the case in our national context. There clearly are some values which are at the core of our national way of life - our national culture. Two in particular underpin many others.

76 The first is a commitment to the unique value and central importance of the individual. On this commitment is built a series of connected attitudes and beliefs. They include a belief in the right of all individuals to fulfilment and self-realisation; to freedom of personal expression and action, providing the freedoms of others are not infringed; and respect for different value systems and ways of life. On these commitments is built a network of legal and political principles including a wide range of democratic rights and responsibilities. These principles permeate our social, legal and educational processes which in turn are meant to express and sustain them. For all its diversity, our national culture is rooted in the core value we attach to the life and rights of the individual. In some national systems this is not so.

77 A second touchstone of our national culture is the idea of contingency: the view that things might be different from how they seem or are currently believed to be. This assumption is the basis of our interests in empirical enquiries and observations in science and of our modes of analysis in the humanities - in history, criticism, politics and philosophy. It is this that encourages us to question current perceptions, knowledge and practices and to believe in the virtues of openness in public and political life rather than closure and censure.

78 These two core values, and the practices and attitudes they give rise to lie at the heart of our national culture. They are not negotiable if individual fulfilment and open enquiry are to continue to characterise our way of life. It is because these are core values that our national culture is so diverse and creative. Benefiting from this diversity and promoting our creative resources is precisely what is at issue on our arguing for a more systematic and sustained approach to creative and cultural education. What does cultural education entail?

Cultural Education

79 Against this background, we see four central roles for education in the cultural development of young people.

a) To enable young people to recognise, explore and understand their own cultural assumptions and values.

b) To enable young people to embrace and understand cultural diversity by bringing them into contact with the attitudes, values and traditions of other cultures.

c) To encourage an historical perspective by relating contemporary values to the processes and events that have shaped them.

d) To enable young people to understand the evolutionary nature of culture and the processes and potential for change.

Taken together these suggest key principles for the balance of teaching and learning in schools and for the balance of the school curriculum. We will come to these shortly but first let us comment briefly on each of these roles.

80 *To enable young people to recognise, explore and understand their own cultural assumptions and values.*

Most young people belong simultaneously to a range of different cultural groups and communities. They do not develop their ideas and values in isolation. They do so in relation to the groups and communities to which they belong and they express them in the clothes they wear, the stories they tell, the jokes they like, and the music they make. All young people, particularly during adolescence, are faced with a complex task of constructing a sense of personal identity from what is now an accelerating traffic of images, ideas, pressures and expectations that surround them, from home, friends, street culture, the media and from commercial interests of every sort.

Recorded music and images, broadcast and printed material, consumer items mainly made mechanically, live entertainment, digital information, games and recreations, educational aids, food and drink, travel and holidays, drugs and cosmetics: these are the languages of commercial culture as spoken to young people An adult view sees them as an ever-increasing mountain of goods and waste which require great effort to manage. For young people, they are important as a means of communication of the identities they are busy creating. Seen in this way and the money used to buy them as a means of independence, the products of commercial culture should be much less frightening to us. Anything can be sold, but how it is used is another matter. Young people select and discard a huge range of available material, ideas, words and images with impressive speed. The past and other contemporary cultures provide them with the material to create an individual style. Strangeness and difference, aspects of the other, are particularly valuable to them in establishing the unique character which will guarantee their presence in the world. Young people require flexibility of the things they take over. Their great skill is in transformation. They can make ordinary and mundane objects special with new uses and combinations. They adapt and they invent. Their language is precise, original and distinctive. They experiment with sensuality, the feel of substances, the pleasure of properties and material goods.

Roger Hill, 1997

81 Commercial culture is sometimes seen as predatory on young people and there is no doubt that the pressures they generate are intense and the markets voracious. But young people are not simply passive consumers of cultural products: they appropriate and adapt them to their own urgent need for a sense of personal and group identity. In doing so, they also shape the commercial environment in which they live. Education has key roles in giving young people the opportunities and the means to reflect on the values and ideas which surround them: to explore them sensitively and critically in a range of different ways.

82 *To enable young people to embrace and understand cultural diversity by bringing them into contact with the attitudes, values and traditions of other cultures.*

Cultural education is a complex field with many dimensions and difficulties. It involves teaching for a diverse society: an education that enables young people to live in a multi-ethnic and multicultural Britain. The need for multicultural education has long been recognised in schools, particularly at the level of policy. It is essential now to go beyond statements of policy to forms of practice and provision which encourage cultural understanding and promote a positive sense of cultural inclusion.

83 There is an important difference between multicultural and anti-racist education. The general aim of multicultural education is to promote understanding of, and respect for, other cultures by deepening young people's knowledge and experience of them. Anti-racist education builds on multicultural education but it includes specific strategies to challenge racist attitudes and behaviour. Both are needed in schools. Increasingly since the 1960s, multicultural education has been a high priority for schools in culturally diverse communities. For them the need to address issues of diversity was immediate and urgent. Schools in more homogeneous or even mono-ethnic areas might have felt less pressure to take up this agenda. But the need for multicultural education in such schools is just as pressing. If young people do not have direct day-to-day experience of other cultures — of having friends from other ethnic traditions and races — they will be less prepared than others for the culturally diverse societies they will eventually encounter.

84 Schools and what goes on inside them cannot guarantee respect for other cultures nor that they will definitely deliver an end to the prejudice and discrimination of racism. But they can and must combat ignorance in what they teach and how they teach it; and confront prejudice and

discrimination in the kinds of institutions they are. All in all, for pupils to emerge from schools as racists, it must be the case that they are flying in the face of all they have been taught and have learnt there, and of their overall experience of the school as a community.

85 *To encourage an historical perspective by relating contemporary values to the processes and events that have shaped them.*

We noted earlier that values and patterns of behaviour are shaped by many factors and that they tend to change over time. Helping young people to understand the processes that have influenced their own and other cultures is an essential role of education. Collectively as well as individually, our sense of our own identity is bound up with memory and knowledge of the past. Discussing the importance of the humanities in education, Sir Alan Bullock (1990) emphasises the necessity of historical understanding to a sense of cultural identity. He notes that any society that turns its back on the past and falls into a 'cultural and historical amnesia', weakens its sense of identity.

86 Multicultural education, as we described it earlier, has to go beyond a familiarity with how other cultures look and sound now, to a deeper understanding of how they evolved and were shaped. Many cultural attitudes and practices can seem strange, even irrational, without some understanding of the contexts in which they emerged and the meanings they have acquired. An historical understanding of cultural development should also enable young people to grasp the many ways in which different cultures have long intersected and shaped each other. Young people need to recognise the distinctiveness of different cultural histories and experience and their roles in shaping global cultures.

87 *To enable young people to understand the evolutionary nature of culture and the processes and potential for change.*

A knowledge of the past is essential to understanding the present. But, as Sir Alan Bullock noted, any culture that is oriented only to the past and 'refuses to identify with the new elements of experience in the future' will stagnate. Education also has to engage young people in the possibilities of change: not only to teach them why things are as they are, but to understand what they might become and how. The task is to avoid the extremes of cultural rigidity - of promoting absolute values with no room for debate; and laissez-faire - the relativity of anything goes. When there is too much rigidity, social institutions, including education, become closed systems in which individuality is discouraged and even penalised. When anything goes and nothing is certain, all that has been learnt and built in the past is lost or abandoned. It is in the balance between closure and openness, between tradition and innovation, that creativity thrives or dies: and with it the diversity and vitality of human culture itself.

Creative and Cultural Education

88 In our view, creative education and cultural education are intimately related. First, creative processes draw directly from the cultural contexts in which they take place. Artists draw from the work and inspiration of other artists, styles and traditions just as scientists build on the insights and achievements of the wider scientific community. Sometimes the relationship between innovation and received knowledge is positive: refining and adding to what is already known or done. Sometimes it is a reaction against them: developing radically new ways of seeing. This is true in all fields of human action.

89 Second, human culture is as rich, complex and diverse as it is because of the richness, complexity and diversity of human creativity. Culture is shaped by, and is the product of, human creativity: it is generated by our different responses to the problems of meaning and practicality with which we are confronted. How we see events is deeply affected by the ideas and values we bring to them. History is marked by the often profound changes in consciousness, in ways of seeing the world, which came about through the constant interaction of ideas and events: between science, religion, morality, politics and the arts, and between tradition and innovation. Education must recognise these intimate relations and promote them throughout the school curriculum. To do so we need to promote three principles of balance in schools.

90 First, *there must be a balance in the curriculum between different fields of creative and cultural education: particularly the sciences, arts, humanities, physical education and technological education.* The school curriculum has tended to emphasise the importance of some of these disciplines over others, largely because some have been thought of as more useful or relevant to employment. This assumed hierarchy is reflected in the division in the National Curriculum between core and foundation subjects; and in the patterns of options in many secondary schools. In our view, and for the reasons we give throughout this report, each of these is essential to the balanced development of the individual, and to the individual's balanced understanding of the social culture: its dynamics, diversity and development.

91 Second, *there must be a balance within the teaching of all disciplines between tradition and innovation.* People are not creative in a vacuum, they are creative at something in a context. Being creative involves a growing understanding of the possibilities, range and methods of a discipline. Consequently, there must be a balance between young people making their own work and the coming to understand the fields in which they are working. Education has a duty to transmit knowledge and culture from one generation to the next: to pass on an understanding of why things are as they are. Education also has to encourage imaginative and critical thinking, the ability to hypothesise, and to question the way things have always been done.

92 Third, *there must be a balance between the teaching of different cultural values and traditions.* The world young people live in and will inherit is multicultural. It is essential that schools reflect and respond to cultural diversity. This means promoting respect for different cultural traditions and practices, and an understanding of different cultural values and perspectives. Schools must take account of this diversity in the forms of cultural practice they include in the curriculum and in the values that are promoted in teaching and learning. We develop these arguments in Part Two.

Conclusion

93 In this chapter we have outlined our understanding of cultural education and its relations to creative education. In Chapter One, we said that creative and cultural education are essential in helping to meet the challenges that education and young people face. In the next chapter we summarise some of the benefits.

4 Meeting the Challenge

Introduction

94 In Chapter One we identified a number of challenges to education. In what ways do creative and cultural education help to meet them?

Meeting the Economic Challenge

95 *To develop in young people the skills, knowledge and personal qualities they need for a world where work is undergoing rapid and long-term change.*

Developing creative abilities is of fundamental importance in meeting the challenges of economic development. New ideas, innovation and ingenuity in the development of products and services are increasingly important to the economic competitiveness of companies, and of countries. These will be needed at all levels, including in primary research, in development, in design, production, marketing and distribution. As the global economies continue to change, the demand for creative resources throughout business and industry will increase. For many of those in work, these creative abilities will be fundamental to the processes of work. So too will be abilities to communicate, to work in teams, and to adapt to new demands and new opportunities. Many companies have now recognised the need to become 'learning organisations' and are investing significantly in programmes of staff development to promote these qualities. The process should begin in school. As the patterns of work change, all young people and adults will need to adapt not only to changes in the work they do, but to the growing likelihood of changing jobs and occupations during their working lives. Promoting creative abilities and the competences and attitudes they require will be central to this process.

Meeting the Technological Challenge

96 *To enable young people to make their way with confidence in a world that is being shaped by technologies which are evolving more quickly than at any time in history.*

New technologies are transforming our lives, and the pace of innovation is accelerating. Creative and cultural education are essential in meeting this challenge in two ways. First, education must enable young people to engage positively with information technologies: to know how to use them, and to explore their potential in creative thinking and action. We have argued that creative processes are purposeful and that they involve growing control over tools and materials. New technologies are providing new means for creative thinking and achievement and new forms of access to ideas, information and people. Young people's command of new

> **"** Creativity is national income. **"**
>
> *Joseph Beuys, The School for Social Research, New York*

> **"** The post-management corporation will be more creative. It used to be assumed that creative individuals should go into the arts, the media, academia, or, if forced into something commercial, then into PR, advertising, merchant banking, consulting or small business rather than into mainstream corporations. This assumption, correct even today, will become outdated. **"**
>
> *Managing without Managers, Koch and Goddin, 1996*

technologies will be enhanced by experiencing them as tools for creative achievement: rather than as ends in themselves. Second, education must enable young people to explore and be sensitive to the impact of new technologies on how we live, think and relate to each other: that is sensitive to their cultural implications. For this reason, we have argued for a central place in the curriculum for the arts and humanities - for those disciplines which not only use new technologies, but which are directly concerned with understanding cultural experience, difference and change.

97 There is a third point to emphasise. It has been estimated that the store of human knowledge is doubling every ten years. However this is estimated, it is clear that we are witnessing an exponential growth in knowledge and information on a scale that is unprecedented, and, for all earlier generations, unimaginable. This expansion is set to accelerate. One result is an increasingly intense form of specialisation in all disciplines: a tendency to know more and more about less and less. This specialisation is necessary. But the risk is that we will lose sight of the larger picture — of how ideas connect, and can inform and contextualise each other. Maintaining a balance between depth and breadth of learning is a major challenge for teaching and curriculum design. In these circumstances, young people need more than access to information and ideas: they need ways of engaging with them, of making connections, of seeing principles and of relating them to their own experiences and emerging sense of identity. These are the essential purposes of creative and cultural education and the need to realise them could hardly be more urgent.

Meeting the Social Challenge

98 *To provide forms of education that enable young people to engage positively and confidently with far-reaching processes of social and cultural change.*

Young people are living through times of immense change. This can be profoundly exhilarating: it can also be disorienting and a source of deep anxiety. Education must help young people to develop the intellectual and emotional resources to deal with change positively and critically. Creative and cultural education provide direct ways of engaging with issues of change: as it affects others and as it affects the life and

> **"**
> Sir Ernest Hall gave a magnificent speech recently, showing how studying to be a concert pianist helped him to be exceedingly successful in business because he realised business entre-preneurialism is essen-tially creative. When he retired at the age of 65 he was able to go back and record piano sonatas, because suc-cess in business gave him the confidence to create art. **"**
>
> *Lord Stone of Blackheath*

> **"**
> In any self-organising system there is an absolute mathematical necessity for creativity. **"**
>
> *Edward de Bono*

feelings of the individual. We noted in Chapter One the profound effects of economic change on communities and ways of life. Creative and cultural education have particular roles in developing the skills and aptitudes which are needed for new and rapidly changing forms of work. They can also be vital elements in developing a sense of community purpose and of social coherence, both in schools and beyond, through a wide network of partnerships and shared enterprise. There are now many examples of initiatives in social regeneration which set out specifically to build on the creative strengths and cultural resources of communities through initiatives in the arts, technology and the sciences. Such initiatives can mitigate the economic problems of changing patterns of work while, and by, restoring confidence and community spirit through shared creative projects.

Regenerating a Whole Town

Huddersfield is midway through its three-year Urban Pilot Project, which aims to demonstrate, on behalf of the European Commission, how creativity might be nurtured, not just in individuals but in a whole town. It is believed that the creativity and prosperity of a town can grow unchecked if a system can be developed for releasing human potential. The Huddersfield Creative Town Initiative (HCTI) is based on the Cycle of Creativity — generating ideas and then turning them into reality, circulating and marketing ideas, setting up platforms for delivery, and promoting and disseminating these ideas. The range of projects which constitute HCTI broadly follow these five stages of the cycle. One of the creative initiatives in this project is that of Artimedia's Enter and Return training courses. Since April 1998 over 100 people have been trained in the creative uses of computing, with courses ranging from 'absolute beginners', for those who have never touched a computer, to 'web weaving', which looks at cutting-edge technology and new developments on the world-wide web. By introducing local people to the creative potential of new technologies, the company is opening up new ways of thinking about and using computers and encouraging people to experiment with computers in their own areas of interest.

Information provided by Huddersfield Creative Town Initiative

"
The Arts Council is already working on how best the arts can play a meaningful role in taking young and long-term unemployed people off benefits as part of the Government's New Deal programme, and how best they can contribute to policies alongside Government departments aimed at tackling social exclusion. **"**

Gerry Robinson,
Chairman, Arts
Council of England

99 Many reports have pointed to the positive opportunities of cultural diversity — and the problems that arise when intercultural understanding breaks down. The Macpherson report (1999) is the most recent, and the most compelling. For all young people, one of the most difficult tasks is to forge a sense of personal identity and belonging. Among the complex effects of economic and social change are those of exclusion: of a sense of being alienated from mainstream society by unemployment, culture or personal loss of motivation. Schools must address these issues with passion and determination.

100
The Government's view, which we endorse, is that there is too often a gap between the community and the schools that exist to serve them. There are 25,000 schools in England, and the majority are doing well. But where there are problems, practical strategies must be found to connect the cultures of schools with the wider community, and to bridge the gap. A starting point is to recognise and validate the cultural experience of minority groups and to engage them in the cultural life of the school. Creative and cultural education can provide powerful and direct ways of achieving this, and of raising the self-esteem and motivation of young people who, for cultural and other reasons, feel marginalised and alienated.

Dance for Expelled Teenagers

Arlette George from Greenwich Dance Agency undertook an intensive four week pilot programme with a small group of 14-year-olds who had been expelled from schools in Camden. The group met four times a week. Although most of these teenagers had been expelled for violent behaviour, their responses were generally inhibited and withdrawn, or full of bravado. Most of their energy was spent in setting up the means to disguise identity and feelings. The prime objective was to use dance, games and discussion to encourage responses that were direct and uncomplicated. A parallel process to the dance work emerged within their everyday interactions before and during session breaks, when the children started to open up about their personal circumstances. Listening became a vital aspect of the work where the realities of racism, sexism, assault, truancy and underage sex were revealed with the 'hype'. The occasions where their depth of confusion was no longer being disguised by tantrums or similarly where laughter broke mounting tensions, acted as encouraging signs of the process they had undertaken. Against all odds the initiative affected their lives and encouraged them to go back to school.

Information obtained from the Spring 1997 edition of animated

Meeting the Personal Challenge

101 *To develop the unique capacities of all young people, and to provide a basis on which they can each build lives that are purposeful and fulfilling.*

Motivation and self-esteem are crucial factors in raising standards of achievement. All young people tend to be considered as able or less-able in education, primarily on the basis of academic performance. But many of these less-able children may have significant abilities in areas which are overlooked by schools. This can be a powerful source of disaffection and under-achievement. This is not a new problem. Many adults have negative feelings about their education. Some think of themselves as educational failures, even when they have had great success since leaving school. This is particularly true of those who failed the 11-plus, by definition a majority of those who took it. Some of the brightest, most accomplished people of our times feel this stigma, no matter what they have achieved since. It may be that they failed because schools were not looking at what they really had to offer. At the same time as raising standards in literacy and numeracy, we must provide opportunities for achievement in other equally important areas of ability. The alternative is that some young people never find out what their real abilities are, and most young people never discover all of them. Research and common sense suggest four key principles:

- all young people have a wide range of abilities;

- these abilities are dynamically related and interactive;

- all children have strengths in different areas of ability;

- success in one area can stimulate self-esteem and encourage success in others.

These principles are important for all children: they are especially important for some.

102 Many children have special needs. For those with disabilities the conventional curriculum can pose particular disadvantages. For those with impairments, in sight, hearing or speech, conventional forms of communication are inherently difficult. It does not follow that they are less able overall, or unintelligent. Many young people with disabilities have profound abilities, but in areas which the conventional curriculum neglects. For others, the opportunity to communicate through other forms of expression, including music, movement or art, can provide essential channels of communication to express ideas which are inhibited by conventional forms of speaking and writing. The point is not that the arts compensate for disability: it is that present conceptions of ability are too narrow. By broadening our understanding of the capabilities of all children, we will reassess the potential of those who, in conventional terms, are thought to be less able.

> **"**
> We must educate the whole child – creatively, culturally, spiritually, morally, physically, technologically as well as intellectually. Good teachers recognise this and develop the child to his/her potential. The greatest gift you can give a child is self-esteem and confidence in their ability. If a child has these, no challenge is too great for him/her. **"**
>
> *Carol Traynor*

"
In all parts of the world, that so-called intangible capital is the most valuable resource of advanced economics, without which the natural endowments of nations — their financial power and fixed capital — will become dwindling resources. No nation can nowadays claim to have achieved a high quality of growth if elements of its human potential remain untapped or under-used. **"**

Ceri Jones

Developing Human Resources

103 We have argued that education must change as we enter the post-industrial world. It is now widely recognised that, during the industrial age, developed nations made very partial use of the earth's natural resources. In the interests of particular industrial processes and products, some of the earth's resources have been over-used and others spoilt or discarded. The force of ecological argument in relation to the environment is now accepted: that there is a delicate balance in the earth's resources and that many resources that were once thought to be useless are now seen to have critical roles in the balance of nature. We see an analogous argument for human resources. Politically and economically much is made of the need to develop human resources. But in practice, education has focused on limited areas of those resources. Many other human resources have been discarded or ignored because there was no obvious use for them. It is now clear that there is a delicate human ecology and that maintaining the balance and developing the breadth of these resources is vital to the individual and to the health and stability of the societies we create. This was always so, but it is becoming ever more important in the new, interdependent and increasingly complex societies of the modern world. If education is to make the most of human resources, we must begin with a fuller and clearer understanding of what those resources actually are.

104   If young people are to make their way in the twenty-first century they will need all their wits about them, literally. The problem in education is not only that standards of achievement have been too low; they have also been too narrow. An education system which focuses only on one mode of intelligence or on a limited range of cultural experiences is underestimating the larger part of children's natural capacities and resources. If education is to develop human resources, we must first recognise how rich and various these resources really are. Outside schools, the fertility of human intelligence is evident in the richness of human culture. A balanced education must provide opportunities for all young people to explore and develop the different aspects of their intelligence, through a balanced curriculum and challenging processes of teaching and learning.

> **"**
> Original thought, and respect for originality of others, must surely lie at the heart not just of creativity, but also individuality — our only chance of twenty-first century escape from zombie-ness.
> **"**
>
> *Professor Susan Greenfield*

Conclusion

105 Our concerns with creative and cultural education point in two directions. First, to making the most of young people's own resources: what they have within them. Second, to helping them to understand the world that surrounds them and of which they are part. We see creative and cultural education as fundamental to meeting the challenges that education now faces. Creative and cultural development are important in themselves: they are also intimately related. In Part Two we consider the implications for the structure of the curriculum, for methods of teaching and learning and for methods of assessment.

Part Two:

A New Balance

5 Developing the Curriculum

Introduction

106 Education consists of three related areas: *curriculum* — what is to be learnt; *pedagogy* — how it is to be taught and *assessment* — how progress and attainment are judged. Our arguments have implications for all three. In Chapter Three we suggested that effective approaches to creative and cultural education need to be based on three principles of balance: a balance in the curriculum between different fields of creative and cultural education, a balance within the teaching of all disciplines between tradition and innovation and a balance between the teaching of different cultural values and traditions. In this chapter we look at the implications of our arguments for the structure and balance of the school curriculum. We make proposals for the development of the National Curriculum for 2000. We also propose a more fundamental review after 2000 to take account of the principles of provision we have identified.

The School Curriculum

107 The 1988 Education Reform Act defined the curriculum at three levels.

    a. *The National Curriculum*

    b. *The Basic Curriculum:*
       the National Curriculum plus Religious Education.

    c. *The Whole Curriculum:*
       the Basic Curriculum and any other provision the school chooses to make.

The National Curriculum

108 The Government is committed to planning an education service that will meet the challenges of the twenty-first century. The centrepiece of the school system is the National Curriculum and this will drive or restrain the developments we are proposing. The National Curriculum has brought many benefits. Teachers have welcomed a national framework for content and attainment targets. There is more consistent provision within and between schools. Ten years on from the 1988 Act, few would argue against the principle of a National Curriculum. Nevertheless, there are significant problems in the current National Curriculum in relation to creative and cultural education.

109 Although the National Curriculum is not the whole curriculum, it is the most significant part of it. It represents the national priorities for learning and assessment. It is the framework for school inspection, accountability and quality assurance; and it is the basis of the National Standards for Initial Teacher Training. The current review of the National Curriculum is not

> **"** A core aim of our education system must be to enable all children to develop their creativity and unlock their creative potential... If the innovative and creative minds of tomorrow are to be nurtured and inspired, teaching has to be developed in a way which appeals to the creative and emotional and which encourages conceptual thinking. The curriculum review is an opportunity to create a new dynamic which will allow this to happen. **"**
>
> *Moira Fraser Steele, Director of Education & Research, The Design Council*

intended to be comprehensive or radical. We understand the reasons for this. A radical change to the current structure will need to be fully evaluated and undertaken over a proper timescale. However, we do believe that such a radical review is necessary over time and the present limited review should be seen as the beginning of a longer-term managed process of change.

110 Our consultations have suggested that the opportunities to promote creative and cultural education in schools are being increasingly restricted by the cumulative effects of successive changes in structure, organisation and assessment since the introduction of the National Curriculum. It is difficult to gather hard evidence of this. The QCA does not have conclusive evidence either way and neither does OFSTED. It would be helpful to the Government and to many others to have a clearer sense of existing provision in this field and also of the impact of specific policy initiatives on other areas of the curriculum; for example, the effects on the broader curriculum of the literacy and numeracy strategies. In the absence of counter-evidence, we think that it is reasonable to listen to the views of the many schools and head teachers who responded to our enquiries. The consistent message was that provision for the arts and humanities in particular and for creative approaches in other areas of the curriculum, including science, have been eroded over recent years.

Undoubted improvements in arts provision have been brought about by the National Curriculum. But they now run the risk of being lost.

Professor Eric Bolton

111 If the school system is to develop young people's creative abilities, steps must be taken to create the conditions in which this can be done. The Government can help to address this situation in two ways. The first is to make explicit provision for creative and cultural education in policy statements and priorities for the future development of the school curriculum. This would send an important signal to schools that the broader curriculum matters. The second would be to reduce existing levels of prescription, to allow schools greater flexibility in devising appropriate programmes of work. This calls for action in five areas of the National Curriculum: rationale, structure, hierarchy, development and prescription.

Rationale

112 The QCA consultation on the aims and priorities of the National Curriculum identified a widespread view that the revised National Curriculum should be based on a clear rationale. We strongly support this view. The 1988 Education Reform Act requires schools to provide a curriculum which:

- is balanced and broadly based;

- promotes the spiritual, moral, cultural, mental and physical development of pupils at school and of society;

- prepares young people for the opportunities, responsibilities and experiences of adult and working life.

The Act did not explain what preparation for adult life meant at the end of the twentieth century, nor how these objectives were met by the ten subject structure which it introduced. The content of the National

Curriculum was developed by ten subject working groups, each of which set out its own aims and objectives. For the last ten years the National Curriculum has been revised and reviewed without any further discussion or agreement on its basic rationale.

113 One of the original requirements of the Act was that schools should provide a curriculum that is broad and balanced. However, it is widely accepted that the National Curriculum has been too congested. Since 1988 there has been a succession of measures to thin it out. For reasons we come to, we welcome attempts to reduce the amount of detailed prescription in the National Curriculum and suggest that these should continue. But the effect of the measures taken so far has been principally to reduce the requirements for the foundation subjects. The result has been to reduce the breadth and to tilt the balance of the National Curriculum. If schools are to meet the challenges they face, and to promote young people's creative and cultural development, both trends must be reversed. The starting point is a clear and agreed rationale.

114 The 1988 Education Reform Act drew from the proposals of *Better Schools* (DfEE 1985). That White Paper set out a list of purposes of education in schools which we commend as a basis for the rationale of the revised National Curriculum. They are to help pupils:

- to develop lively, inquiring minds, the ability to question and argue rationally, and to apply themselves to tasks and physical skills;

- to acquire understanding, knowledge and skills relevant to adult life and employment in a fast-changing world;

- to use language and numbers effectively;

- to develop personal moral values, respect for religious values, and tolerance of other races, religions and ways of life;

- to understand the world in which they live, and the interdependence of individuals, groups and nations;

- to appreciate human achievements and aspirations.

In our view, this list of objectives can only be realised through forms of teaching and learning that promote the creative abilities and cultural understanding of young people in the way we have described. In all events, the new rationale must make explicit reference to the importance

of creative and cultural education and help to create the conditions in which it can be realised in practice.

Structure

115
The National Curriculum in England is divided into three core subjects; English, mathematics, science; and seven foundation subjects — technology (information technology and design and technology), history, geography, art, music, physical education and modern foreign languages. An obvious but important problem in this approach is that there are more than ten subjects in the world. In a ten subject structure, some subjects of the National Curriculum had to be included in others: for example, drama in English and dance within physical education. Beyond education, dance is not normally grouped with sport, games and athletics; drama is not only a verbal art form. In terms of the knowledge and skills they promote, both disciplines have as strong a claim on separate status as other National Curriculum subjects.

116
There are many other ways of conceiving and organising curriculum content. The QCA/NFER INCA archive contains information on curriculum frameworks of different countries. In terms of the primary school curriculum, out of fifteen countries studied, seven countries describe the curriculum in terms of key or essential areas of learning: Australia, Hungary, The Netherlands, New Zealand, Singapore, Spain and the USA. Seven countries group their subjects together: Canada, France, Germany, Japan, Korea, The Netherlands and Sweden. Three countries teach their curricula in multidisciplinary or interdisciplinary ways: Italy, The Netherlands and Singapore. All the other countries studied define their curricula in terms of areas of learning or subject groupings. England is the only country in the archive, which defines its curriculum in terms of ten discrete subjects from Key Stage 1-4. The risk in this approach is in assuming that these subjects are categorically different in all respects. There is considerable overlap between different fields of knowledge. There are continuities in the nature of the creative processes and, often, in subject matter.

The Need for a New Balance

117
In Chapter Three we argued for three principles of balance in education. The first is the need for balance between different areas of education. In providing the education that young people now need, we see equally important roles for English, mathematics, sciences, the arts, the humanities, technological education and for physical education, and fundamental reasons for treating them equally in schools.

118
Literacy and numeracy are the gateways to learning in many other disciplines, and essential skills for social and economic independence. Standards need to be as high as possible, and the national literacy and numeracy strategies have important roles in achieving this. English and mathematics also include more than basic literacy and numeracy. From the beginning of primary school, English should include the teaching of literature, and the expressive and social skills of speaking and listening.

Art is not a diversion or a side issue. It is the most educational of human activities and a place in which the nature of morality can be seen.

Dame Iris Murdoch

It is nonsense to say there are only 10 subjects. By saying this we immediately exclude 90 per cent of the Higher Education experience.

Professor Tim Brighouse, Chief Education Officer, Birmingham City Council

Once the fundamentals of numeracy have been grasped, mathematics evolves into rich fields of abstraction and calculation and the conceptual languages of science and technology. In these ways, both English and mathematics overlap with our concerns for creative and cultural education.

Science comprises three related areas: first, the store of existing scientific knowledge; second, the methods and processes of scientific discovery and inquiry; and third, how this knowledge is applied, and in particular the relations of science and technology. Science education has key roles in the creative and cultural development of young people. First, to provide an essential grounding in gathering and respecting evidence and in intellectual skills of analysis. Second, to provide access to the rich store of existing scientific understanding of the processes of nature and the laws that govern them. Third, to provide essential opportunities for practical and theoretical inquiry by which received knowledge can be verified, challenged or extended. Fourth, in each of these ways, science education can and must promote higher standards of scientific literacy. By this we mean an understanding of how science has shaped the modern world; of the concepts, ideas and achievements that have driven these changes, and of their significance and limitations. A population that is uneducated in science will simply be unable in future to deal intelligently and responsibly with its proposals and consequences.

> We will need to do better than we have done in recent years to convey the excitement of science, to use it to help young people develop a sense of wonder about the world, and encourage them to see its relevance to their lives and how it involves moral issues on which they, as citizens in a democracy, ought to have views.
>
> *Dr. Nick Tate, Chief Executive, QCA*

Unfortunately, traditional methods of education appear to be failing in spite of sterling efforts by our teachers. The sheer complexity of science and technology today, as well as the lure of alternative, often superficially exciting, areas are some of the problems. Chemistry, the discipline central to our socio-economic environment, is suffering as much, if not more, than others, and is a perfect example of the need for urgent measures to develop in collaboration with schools and teachers, better interactive, balanced and personally tailored approaches to education. The wonderful new 'experience' centres and science museums, which are blossoming across Europe, are providing an important component in the solution to these problems. They work closely with schools and science teachers, thereby ensuring that millions of young people are being given a real taste for science and the enthusiasm to learn more is being fostered. The prime purpose of this European project, which has been created by a consortium formed by the museums, the chemical industry and the European Commission, is to help these centres and museums to provide the very best experience of science possible. It must be obvious to any intelligent person from the plethora of serious problems facing the world today that our very survival in the 21st century will depend on a quantum leap in real understanding of science and technology by anyone in a position of any responsibility. Only a crash programme in science education can now help, and I am certain that the exciting 'Chemistry for Life' programme will play a major role in this crucial process.

Professor Sir Harold Kroto, Nobel prize-winning chemist

120 The humanities are those fields of academic study that are concerned with understanding human culture. These include history, the study of languages, religious education and aspects of geography and social studies. The humanities have key roles in creative and cultural education. First, by broadening and deepening young people's understanding of the world around them: its diversity, complexity and traditions. Second, by enlarging their knowledge of what they share with other human beings including those removed in time and culture from themselves. Third, by developing a critical awareness of the society and times in which they live. The humanities overlap in several ways with the sciences and the arts. What they have in common with the arts is a primary concern with understanding the human dimension of experience. They differ in the modes of knowledge they generate and in the forms of study they use.

Dancing the River Thames

During the autumn term, Green Candle Dance Company led a residency in a Newham primary school. With the Year 6 class they started the dance work with creative improvisation about the River Thames. When the children were questioned about their perceptions of the river, they were mostly negative and focused on its pollution and foul smell! Through dance they were enabled to also consider its size, shape, flow and currents. The class teacher was keen to link the dance work to other areas of the curriculum topic 'Rivers', so she asked the children to write poems about the Thames, which could be used in dance. Everyone involved was surprised and impressed by the content and richness of descriptive language used. One of the poems was chosen as the stimulus for creating duets, which were performed simultaneously by the whole class to the accompaniment of their teacher speaking the poem. The children were proud to perform this dance-poem, thus completing a creative cycle of dance, poem, dance and poem in a way that was satisfying to children and adults. This was a clear example of the cross-fertilisation of ideas between artforms and the way both forms, in this case poetry and dance, can be enhanced by the process and, in addition, produce visible learning in other subjects such as English and Geography.

Information provided by Green Candle Dance Company

---

121 The arts are concerned with understanding, and expressing, the qualities of human experiences. Through music, dance, visual arts, drama and the rest, we try to give form to the feelings and perceptions that move us most as human beings: our experiences of love, grief, belonging, and isolation, and all the currents of feeling that constitute our experience of ourselves and of others. It is through the arts in all their forms that young people experiment with and try to articulate their deepest feelings and their own sense of cultural identity and belonging. A balanced arts education has essential roles in the creative and cultural development of young people. First, the arts are essential to intellectual development. We

> The arts are other ways of expressing and communicating experiences, feelings and ideas. Various materials, instruments, tools, techniques and skills are used to express and communicate those feelings and ideas in a creative form. In the creative arts we are training children to look, see and know. To observe fine detail and to develop sensitivity, which remains with them forever, can have a profound effect on the way they view the world and in some cases cause a change in attitude. The creative arts develop thinking and problem-solving strategies in an enjoyable way. This can enhance all other areas of the curriculum.

Carol Traynor

> To communicate through the arts is to convey an experience to others in such a form that the experience is actively recreated actively lived through by those to whom it is offered.

Raymond Williams

argued in Chapter Two that intelligence is multifaceted. The arts illustrate this diversity and provide practical ways of promoting it in all children. Second, the arts provide the most natural processes for exploring and giving form to personal feelings and emotions. The arts engage feelings directly. There is a tendency to think of intellect and emotion as distinct and separate. In many important ways they are closely related. Work in the arts is not about emotions in isolation from the intellect, but about how they connect. Third, the arts are among the most vivid expressions of human culture. To understand other cultures and ways of seeing, we need to engage with their music, visual art, verbal and performing arts where in many ways the pulse of culture beats most strongly.

> There is a hesitancy in many of the primary schools to select areas of work from the Programmes of Study which reflect the pupils' cultural backgrounds — for example, music, famous artists, famous people in history. Indeed, half the primary schools take the view that responding in this way to the ethnic and cultural diversity of their pupil populations is unhelpful and patronising to the groups concerned. Yet National Curriculum Programmes of Study in several subject areas require such a response and a few schools have seized these opportunities to good effect.
>
> *Information from Ofsted 1999a*

122 Physical education is central to the balanced education and development of all young people. First, physical education contributes directly to the physical health of young people. It recognises that we are all embodied beings and that there are intimate relations between mental, emotional and physical processes. Apart from its other benefits, there is now evidence (Steinberg et al 1997) that physical education can also enhance creative processes by quickening concentration and mental agility. Second, physical education and sport, by their very nature, are inextricably bound up in the cultural traditions and practices. For many people games and sport are defining cultural activities and evoke powerful feelings and values both in relation to the games themselves and through the sense of collective activity and belonging they can generate. Thirdly, the diversity and range of physical activity and sport provides young people with many opportunities to experience different forms of physical achievement and

creative expression. In dance and gymnastics there are powerful expressions of creativity and of aesthetic appreciation. In games there are important opportunities to develop individual and team skills and to share success and failure in a controlled and safe environment. In these ways particularly, physical education has essential and equal roles with other key curriculum areas in a balanced approach to creative and cultural education.

123 In Chapter One we emphasised the crucial importance of schools responding to the challenges of rapid technological change, and some of the dangers of an uncritical approach. Young people are growing in a cultural environment which is increasingly shaped by technology in general and by information technology in particular. The Government has in hand a number of far reaching initiatives to increase young people's access to and expertise in information technology; including the National Grid for Learning, actions to install and connect IT equipment in all schools and a massive related programme of continuing professional development for teachers. ICT is at the leading edge of technological change: but it interacts with many other forms of technology, new and old. In 1988 the National Curriculum introduced a new subject, design and technology. This brought together elements of previous subjects and areas of teaching, including craft, art and design, technology and home economics. In the last ten years, a good deal of progress has been made to consolidate this new curriculum area and to explore its relations with the arts, and especially visual art, and science, from both of which it draws ideas and techniques.

124 The heart of design and technology is conceiving and realising practical products and solutions. It involves all the elements of creativity as we have identified them. Design processes are integral to the ways in which the social culture is shaped and expressed: in industrial products, in fashion, in the home, in leisure and in all other areas of daily life. Design and technology as a school discipline is also focused on developing in young people many of the conceptual and practical capabilities that industry and commerce now look to education to develop. For all these reasons we see effective programmes of design technology as essential to creative and cultural education.

125 In setting down our view of these different areas of the curriculum, we are not suggesting a timetable, nor that all subject areas should be taught every day to each child. We are describing an entitlement. We are all too aware of the pressures of time and resources on schools, on local authorities and on national government. Balancing the curriculum equation is complex and difficult . It involves clear national policies and guidelines coupled with expert implementation in schools. The review of the National Curriculum provides a crucial opportunity to look at both the principles and the practicalities of this provision. Our concern is to suggest guidelines and ground rules emerging from our analysis of the importance of creative and cultural education in meeting the national agenda for education, and to counter the imbalance we see occurring incrementally in current provision. In the rest of this chapter we suggest the principles that follow and some of the ways in which they might be implemented.

> *"*
> It has become clear to us how powerful is the contribution of the arts to a whole range of skills and attitudes that are vital to learning right across the curriculum, and indeed to employability. *"*
>
> *Dr. Nicholas Tate,*
> *Chief Executive, QCA*

Making Connections

126 The essence of creativity is in making new connections. These possibilities can be frustrated by rigid divisions in subject teaching which the current pressures tend to encourage. Outside schools, some of the most dynamic developments are the result of the interaction of disciplines. For example, the growth in multimedia technologies is being driven by the relationships between the arts, sciences and technology.

> ### Cross-curricular Teaching
>
> Stoke Newington School (SNS) is a co-educational comprehensive school in the London Borough of Hackney. The school is committed to a broad and balanced curriculum. All students follow an arts subject at Key Stage 4. The examination results are good and the school has developed a reputation for the performing arts as an area of excellence. The arts are an essential part of every student's educational experience, which enhances every aspect of the curriculum, through the development of skills, self-esteem and motivation. Almost all subjects have their own artistic, design, aesthetic and critical aspect. PSHCE can build upon the promotion of physical activity and healthy lifestyle begun in Dance. Drama role-play is also a teaching method relevant to PSHCE as well as many other subjects. The science National Curriculum specifically mentions music in the teaching of sound. Aesthetic and design principles from visual art are intrinsic to the fundamental aspects of technology. Empathy and cultural education in the humanities is greatly informed by the arts. The arts subjects can enhance levels of literacy in the students at SNS in a variety of unique and exciting ways. Discussion skills and the development of oral literacy, often stimulated by visual images, body language, sound, etc. play an important role within the curriculum. Independent research, critical analysis and enquiry play a fundamental role within the arts disciplines. Independent thought and action, alongside the development of team and group work leads to oral negotiation and discussion in the arts. Careers guidance in the performing and visual arts gives weight and credence to a varied range of modes of employment in the expanding arts and leisure industries.
>
> *Information provided by Stoke Newington School*

127 Conventionally, young people have had to choose at the age of 15 or 16 whether to follow arts or science courses in school. The division between the arts and the sciences has its origins in the intellectual revolutions in the seventeenth century and in the industrial and technological revolutions that followed in the eighteenth and nineteenth centuries. The Enlightenment emphasised the pre-eminence of deductive reasoning and propositional knowledge and the need to minimise the influences of feelings and emotions on rational thought. The Romantic movement in art and literature of the eighteenth and nineteenth centuries reacted by emphasising the necessity of feeling, intuition and individuality and the dangers of scientific detachment. These resulting dichotomies between arts and sciences have deeply affected our systems of education and helped to forge popular stereotypes of artists and scientists.

128 Artists and scientists are not necessarily separate beings. Many scientists have deep interests in the arts: a growing number of artists are engaged in science. Any individual may be both artist and scientist according to their interests and activities at a given time. There is a good deal of science in art and in the humanities as there is art in science. The difference between the arts and sciences is not one of subject matter: a work of art can be about anything that interests an artist, just as science can concern anything that interests a scientist. The difference is in the kinds of understanding they are pursuing: in the questions they ask, the kinds of answers they seek and in how they are expressed. An important common factor is aesthetic appreciation. In aesthetic awareness we respond to the sensory or formal qualities of an experience: to such qualities as harmony, tone, line, symmetry and colour. A feel for aesthetics can be a driving force in creative processes in any field including scientific research. Scientists typically speak of the beauty of ideas and experiments, of the elegance of a theory or proof. In mathematics, aesthetics can be an important test of validity.

Primitive Streak

Between fertilisation and the appearance of the recognisable human form, a single cell (the fertilised egg) divides many times to produce millions of cells. Unchecked cell proliferation leads to cancer, but the regulation of cell production and differentiation during embryonic development ensures that the right kind of cells form in the right place at the right time. Exactly how this happens is one of the most important questions in biology today. In developing the Primitive Streak project, the fashion designer Prof. Helen Storey and the developmental biologist Dr. Kate Storey worked together as artist and scientist in producing a fashion collection chronicling the first 1000 hours of human embryonic life. Their work challenged the commonly held belief that science and art are unable to communicate with each other. The exhibition was attended by many school groups. Helen Storey emphasised that: "perhaps most notable is the diversity of people it has touched; young and old (aged 7-70), the academic and the ignorant, those with a love of the arts, those with a life dedicated to science and almost anyone in between. The work, now on an international tour, has opened doors towards education; it is being used as a model project for both primary and secondary school students and fashion and science graduates alike."

129 There are important continuities and differences of this sort between disciplines. These provide one basis for arguing for a new balance in the curriculum. But the need for balance is also based on the growing interaction between various disciplines and fields. School science, for example, has been traditionally divided into physics, chemistry and biology. As scientific knowledge continues to grow, these categories have blurred and new disciplines have emerged: for example, bio-chemistry and bio-physics. On the way, previously clear distinctions between pure and applied science have begun to dissolve. New theoretical insights now interact almost immediately with possible applications and feed into applied research. These are accelerating most obviously in bio-genetics and in the cognitive sciences: in studies into the brain and the physical correlations of consciousness and psychological states. Another important example is the overlap between the social sciences and the arts and humanities. There is an increasing use in the social sciences of qualitative research to complement statistical evidence with more descriptive forms of inquiry. Some social researchers make use of narrative techniques in developing and presenting their findings. In these and other ways the social sciences are drawing on techniques in the arts and humanities.

> ### *Literacy, Science and Technology*
> STARburst is a completely new tool for primary school teachers. It helps develop literacy by using stories and poems for the teaching of Science and Technology. The aim is to help children develop an imaginative and inquiring response to stories and poems, to enable them to use scientific concepts and technical language and — most important — to allow them to gain confidence in their understanding of the natural and designed world. STARburst, is based on a partnership between the Design Council, Esso, the Royal Society of Chemistry and the Institute of Physics.
>
> *Information supplied by the Design Council*

Hierarchy

130 In the existing National Curriculum there is an explicit hierarchy of subjects. From the outset, the foundation subjects were by definition of lower status than the core subjects. In the revisions to the National Curriculum since 1988, the requirements for the arts and humanities have been progressively reduced. Since the National Curriculum is also a framework for managing resources, there have been implications for the whole pattern of related funding. The message to schools is that they are less important than the core subjects. A longitudinal study (Pollard et al, 1994) on the effects of the introduction of the National Curriculum indicates that primary schools have reduced the provision for art, while increasing time for science and technology. Heads and teachers involved in the study expressed concerns about the impact of the National Curriculum on creative activities for young children. These concerns have come through clearly in our own consultations.

131 The real effect of the existing distinction between the core and foundation subjects now needs to be carefully assessed in the light of ten years' experience. It appears to have reduced the status of the arts and humanities and their effective impact in the school curriculum. Moreover there is no clear evidence that the current distinction between core and foundation subjects has increased the number and quality of our young science students or the level of scientific awareness of the general population. We accept the case for a priority to be given to the teaching of literacy and numeracy in the primary school. Beyond that, it is not clear that the present distinction between core and foundation subjects, and the implications which have followed for the allocation of time and other resources, have benefited the teaching of science nor of the foundation subjects in the arts and humanities.

132 The majority of children learn the basics of literacy and numeracy by the end of primary education. A significant minority of children do need additional help with literacy and numeracy beyond this stage, but the needs of the few should not shape the curriculum for everybody. All pupils should study English and mathematics throughout secondary school. This should not mean that English and mathematics are set apart from the rest of the curriculum, nor that their roles in the whole curriculum should be dominated by the need to establish basic skills in the primary school.

133 We have emphasised the necessity of science education as one of the key learning areas for all children. Within the case we have presented for creative and cultural education, we see no basis for distinguishing in value between sciences, arts, humanities, technological education and physical education. Education in each of these has fundamental roles in meeting the challenges we have identified. In our view, the curriculum should be restructured to raise the esteem of the non-sciences and promote cultural parity between them. This restructuring should include reconsidering the present distinctions between core and foundation subjects in the National Curriculum. Science education has vital roles in meeting the challenges of the future. But it will not fulfil them in isolation.

134 The economy needs scientists and technologists with a broad understanding of cultural and social processes, and lawyers, civil servants and others with a good understanding of science. This argues for other key areas of the curriculum to be given equal status with science. A certain level of basic understanding of scientific method is properly part of basic numeracy. Indeed the word 'numeracy' was coined by a British Educational Committee in 1959 to include 'some understanding of scientific method' (Ministry of Education 1959). This basic understanding provides the same building blocks for creative work in science as learning to read and write does for creative work in the arts and in the humanities. There is no logical nor practical reason for not treating more in-depth study of the creative and cultural aspects of science as being precisely equivalent to similar tasks of creative and cultural study in the arts and humanities.

> *There are different routes of entry into each child's mind. It is amazing how much can be taught when subject boundaries are taken away.*
>
> **Professor Helen Storey**

> *Creativity is not only an outcome of a good education, but a means of achieving a good education.*
>
> **Professor Michael Barber, Standards and Effectiveness Unit, DfEE**

> *Science is continually bringing forth new technologies... but science also brings forth new thinking.*
>
> **Lord Stone of Blackheath**

135 There are two arguments against removing the distinction between core and foundation subjects. First, that it would disadvantage science teaching. We see three questions here. First, would fewer pupils take science in Key Stages 1-4? We think not, since science would continue to be compulsory. Second, would it lead to less time for science in the National Curriculum? This is a possibility, but the opportunities remain for individual schools to develop additional science programmes within the whole curriculum. Third, would it lead to lower standards in science education? There is no reason to suppose this. For reasons we develop later, there would be opportunities for greater specialisation in science courses in Key Stage 4. Clearly any change must ensure that the next generation is adequately equipped to survive in a twenty-first century that will be even more dominated by science and technology than the present. Our primary concern is a culturally and creatively balanced curriculum which actively promotes synergistic interaction between science and technology on the one hand and the arts and humanities on the other.

> "
> The core and founda-
> tion distinction is wrong
> — you either have
> areas that you value or
> not.
> "
>
> *Lindsey Wharmby,*
> *Teacher, Lawnswood*
> *School*

136 The second argument is that there is no need to change because under the present arrangements individual schools are free, if they want to, to increase provision for the arts and humanities. This is not the point. One of the purposes of a National Curriculum is to identify core values and priorities in state education. The existing orders for the National Curriculum do allow schools to promote and maintain the non-core subjects. But in the view of many of those we have consulted, the general ethos of policy militates against this. Implicitly and explicitly, the message of the current National Curriculum is that the arts and humanities are lower priority. This message conflicts with the purposes that the National Curriculum is intended to promote. Either the aims or the structure of the National Curriculum should be changed so that the present contradiction can be resolved. If a balanced education is important, the message should be clear, and the provision consistent.

Development

137 The original conception of Key Stages was to mark points of assessment between children of the same age, ie. at seven, eleven, fourteen and sixteen. In practice they have come to refer the periods between them: ie. as key *phases*. The implication is that they correspond to phases in the development of children. If this is the purpose of Key Stages, there is a case for reviewing them.

Early Years

138 There is a strong case for a more developed provision for creative and cultural education in early years education. Studies into the development of the brain suggest that the new-born and infant child have enormous latent capacities. The extent to which these are encouraged in the first years of life has a crucial bearing on the development of the brain itself. Children brought up in bilingual or multilingual households, for example, will normally become competent in all the languages they use. Children brought up in monolingual households normally master that language only. This is not a matter of capacity but of exposure. If these capacities are not exercised, the neurological patterning, the hard wiring of the brain, is allocated to other purposes. The same applies in other areas of development, including, for example, music. Children who are involved in music making from an early age establish musical competencies, which provide an invaluable foundation for subsequent development. If these capacities are not used, they are put to other uses. Teenagers and adults often have greater difficulty than young children do in learning an instrument, or a second language. Because early development provides a foundation for all subsequent learning, opportunities lost in the first years of life are difficult, if not impossible, to regain. Consequently the nature of early years education is as important as the fact of it. In our terms, it is particularly important in the early years to encourage imaginative play and discovery learning as essential processes of intellectual, social and emotional development.

Key Stage 1 and 2

139 In January 1998, the Secretary of State for Education and Employment announced that for two years schools would not be required to teach the full National Curriculum in the foundation subjects. This announcement was intended to ease the pressure on schools and allow them to concentrate on raising standards in literacy and numeracy. We accept the need for a sustained strategy for literacy and numeracy, but it is vital that this emphasis in Key Stages 1 and 2 should not marginalise other areas of intellectual and personal development, which are equally important in the early years and during primary school. There is some evidence that this is happening. A questionnaire survey carried out by the *Times Educational Supplement* following the Secretary of State's announcement, found that about a fifth of the head teachers questioned intended to reduce time for music in the school year 1998-99. National orchestras report that they have received virtually no requests from primary schools to participate in educational projects this year. In our view, the requirement to teach the arts and humanities on an equal basis with the existing 'core' curriculum must be reinstated.

140 Doing so will have benefits for all areas of young people's achievement. For example, there is evidence that literacy and numeracy are best promoted through a broad and balanced curriculum, which includes, rather than excludes, the arts and humanities. Forty of the most disadvantaged primary schools with the best results in literacy were recently studied by OFSTED. The common factor was that they had strong arts programmes[1]. HMI said: 'There is a positive correlation between good provision/performance in the arts in schools and higher standards of performance in literacy and numeracy according to OFSTED inspection statistics[2].' OFSTED data on pupil response to learning indicates drama to be at the very top in motivating learning[3]. Such data underlines the value of a broad and balanced curriculum that incorporates opportunities for

"
Music has played a big part in my life and I want youngsters to have access to the enormous benefits it can bring. Learning an instrument, singing, or simply enjoying the music of others, can help develop the awareness of the spiritual dimension of life. So I want all children to have the opportunity to be enthused by the range of musical experiences which should be available to us all. **"**

David Blunkett MP, Secretary of State for Education and Employment

"
I want to emphasise this Government's belief that the arts play a vitally important part in our education system... time spent on the arts is not peripheral, it is absolutely fundamental to all that we are trying to achieve. **"**

Rt. Hon Chris Smith MP, Secretary of State for Culture, Media and Sport

pupils to learn within and through arts subjects, and within and through focused creative and cultural contexts.

141 The literacy hour is a new departure in that it sets out in detail the content and suggested methods of teaching for schools. The National Literacy Strategy Framework sets out objectives for each term in each year of primary education; at the levels of the word, the sentence and the text. The majority of the text-level objectives refer to the reading and writing of fiction and poetry: teachers are encouraged to work with their pupils to develop a critical awareness of the techniques writers use and the effects these have on the reader. Many of the teaching objectives, particularly at the upper end of Key Stage 2, demand a high level of both textual analysis and creative writing. The *Framework for Teaching* (DfEE 1998a) also specifies the range of texts which should be used and expects that challenging texts will be explored.

Stories that Sing

Over the 1998 Summer term, Children's Music Workshop ran a pilot for a three-year project to explore ways of using creative class music to enhance Key Stage 2 children's understanding of the use of language. The pilot, in three Tower Hamlets primary schools, combined composition, songwriting, storytelling and performance, and encouraged teachers to link the work with the literacy programme. Two of the schools have a 99.9 per cent Bengali intake and the third school has an 80 per cent Bengali intake. The children in each of the schools were alert, attentive, and highly motivated by the project. All of them participated, often to the surprise of their teachers, throwing themselves into the work with real enthusiasm. The pilot began with a workshop for the class teachers, to give a taste of the work that would be done by the children. This was followed by eight weekly sessions with each class, culminating in a performance by each class to the rest of the school. To stimulate the children's imaginations, the projects focused on wishes, a drawing, a 'magic' hat and mat. The children worked in small groups to create poems, verses and stories which they developed into whole-class songs and instrumental pieces. There were considerable differences between the schools and the teachers in terms of their experience and attitude to music, although all of them embraced the project with energy and enthusiasm. The pilot was considered by the teachers, headteachers and musicians to have been very successful. All the teachers want to continue to be involved, the children are hugely enthusiastic, and the musicians found it exciting and stimulating.

Information supplied by Children's Music Workshop

142 Some schools complain that the literacy hour has a dominating effect on the school day and is squeezing even further the opportunities for creative and cultural education. There are numbers of teachers who are uneasy about what they see as an imposition of teaching methods and the consequent reduction in their own freedom and professionalism. The extent of these concerns and their impact will need to be monitored both locally and nationally. But there are schools and teachers who have used the literacy hour as a starting point for a wide range of creative activities in reading, writing, drama and in the other arts. We see great value in integrating the objectives of high standards of literacy with those of high standards of creative achievement and cultural experience. Similar opportunities may be generated for science and technology by the introduction of the numeracy hour. To ensure this it would be of value to many schools to have access to materials, ideas and strategies in the imaginative implementation of these strategies.

Key Stage 3

143 There is evidence from OFSTED and QCA that many students become bored, disaffected and disruptive during this period. With a three-year programme and a fairly low-key external assessment, which covers only English, mathematics and science, the pace of teaching and the students' sense of urgency have been further diminished. According to OFSTED, the general quality of teaching observed at Key Stage 3 is lower than at Key Stage 4. When students arrive in secondary school, they are excited at having specialist teachers. This diminishes over the next three years. Schools using base-line testing and CATS data linked to internal examination are aware of significant numbers under-achieving by year 8, only one year into their secondary education. By year 9, many students, boys in particular, have found the school curriculum boring and undemanding and an important minority has become disaffected, disruptive and truanting. We see a particular case for revising the structure and length of Key Stage 3. External assessment at the end of two years instead of three would generate greater pace and accountability for students and teachers at this stage. This could increase motivation and achievement.

Face 2 Face

Hampstead School has been involved in the development and introduction of financial literacy and numeracy initiatives during 1997 and 1998. Two projects from the NatWest *Face 2 Face with Finance* package have been completed. Both of the activities were targeted at Key Stage 3 and 4 pupils and featured much role-play, creativity and the use and development of vocabulary. Pupils were invited in groups to simulate various roles, where they were either an adult or a young person planning a bid to put on an event, eg. a celebratory dinner. Alternatively they are someone who is lending or borrowing money. In the course of these activities a lot of basic numeracy is covered, but the opportunity to create bridges with other areas of the curriculum and gain fresh insights through discussion and role play is very effective. They are looking to include some materials produced by Personal Finance and Education Group in our lessons this year and courses for the future.

David Monks, Head of Mathematics, Hampstead School

Key Stage 4

144   We are concerned too that children in Key Stage 4 are able to drop subjects such as arts and humanities, and then sacrifice breadth in favour of specialisation. There is a need to increase depth of study as young people develop, but at present they specialise too much and too soon. More time at Key Stage 4 would increase opportunities to consolidate basic skills; to provide extension activities for gifted students; and to provide time for students' choices of study areas and more integrated work experience, without reducing breadth and balance. There would also be valuable opportunities to extend the base of creative activities. On this basis, we believe that all seven curriculum areas we have discussed should be available to all pupils throughout key stages 1-4 as a matter of entitlement.

Prescription

145 In her analysis of over 1,000 lessons, Montgomery (1999) found that 70 per cent of periods was taken up by the teacher talking, while only 1 per cent involved cognitive challenges where pupils worked things out for themselves. She believes that this is partly the fault of an overloaded curriculum which leaves little time for creative thought. During the last ten years there have been repeated efforts to thin it out, but the pressures of over-prescription remain. These problems are greatest in primary schools. Consequently, many primary schools welcomed the Secretary of State for Education and Employment's announcement, relaxing the full requirements of the National Curriculum, partly, we suspect, from a sense of relief.

146 We welcome the Government's commitment to reduce the content of the National Curriculum and to allow schools more flexibility and freedom. But many schools are also worried about the impact on the breadth and balance of the curriculum, and particularly on the status of the foundation subjects. The problem as we see it is that in practice the relaxation has been in the interest of concentrating on the core subjects, rather than promoting increased flexibility across the whole curriculum. Our argument for greater flexibility is not to reduce provision in arts and humanities, but to allow more freedom for them to flourish on an equal footing with the existing core subjects. Greater flexibility is important to allow schools more freedom to innovate within the requirements of the National Curriculum, but it will be counter-productive if it is seen as an encouragement to drop or neglect vital areas of children's education.

147 The national requirement of a public education system is that there should be:

- an agreed rationale and targets for the performance of schools;

- a systematic framework for comparing standards of achievement between pupils;

- a systematic framework of inspection which supports schools in meeting targets and which ensures that they are accountable in doing so.

Since 1988, there has been a transformation in the culture of education in schools. The principal instruments of change have been the National Curriculum; delegated budgets and local management of schools; the national framework for school inspection; the publication of school league tables; and the introduction of national standards in initial teacher training. The original engine of change was the introduction of the National Curriculum. It was through this that the involvement of Government in setting and monitoring standards in other ways became accepted. During the past ten years these other measures have become firmly established. We think it essential now to ease the pressure of the prescribed curriculum to allow schools more flexibility in devising their own programmes of work.

148 There would be four benefits from this change in relation to creative and cultural education.

a. It would raise the morale of teachers by affirming confidence in their professional competence.

b. It would allow more time and opportunity for schools to develop imaginative forms of teaching and learning.

c. It would allow schools greater flexibility in developing programmes which meet the needs of their own pupils and which take account of the local and regional circumstances in which they work.

d. It would allow all schools to develop their own particular strengths and profiles within any given area of the statutory curriculum: sciences, arts, humanities, physical education or technology.

> " The more prescriptive a curriculum, the greater the need to be explicit about creativity and not leave it to chance. "
>
> *Design Council*

> " We are throwing out the baby with the bathwater in this country if, in an attempt to have a standardised and demanding curriculum, we leave no room for teachers to exercise a little judgement and imagination in an excursion of the academic piste. If they are so focused on a fixed curriculum, so rigid that there is no time, literally, for anything as important as the human mind, then we are in for a very sorry future society. It could also be argued that the teachers themselves would benefit from a broader view. Surely a teacher who has become excited, and learnt a new angle on a subject, will import renewed enthusiasm and vigour back to the class. "
>
> *Professor Susan Greenfield*

149 The revised National Curriculum should be based on six principles:

- *Breadth*
  The National Curriculum for each pupil should be broad as a whole and in its various parts.

- *Balance*
  Each area of the curriculum should have the time and resources to enable it to make its specific contribution, but should not squeeze out other essential areas. This balance need not be the same throughout the 5 to 16 years age range.

- *Relevance*
  The programmes of study should be clearly related to the individual pupil's current needs, to the requirements of the next phase of education and to the health and wealth of the nation.

- *Parity*
  There should be parity of esteem between the different components of the National Curriculum. While, at different stages of a pupil's development, some components might be more important than others, it should not be necessary for any area to be dropped from the curriculum or become optional for individuals or groups of pupils.

- *Entitlement*
  All children are entitled to an education in schools, which addresses fully and appropriately the declarations of the National Curriculum. This entitlement should not be contingent on geographical or social factors.

- *Access*
  All children should have access to the experiences, people and resources necessary to realise their potential in education.

150 There is no one best way of planning the curriculum or organising timetables. There are many examples of innovative curriculum models and of timetables that promote creative and cultural education. Schools of many different kinds, in very different circumstances have found their own solution. Often what works in one school does not directly transfer to another. But the principles of provision may have wider application. The QCA should promote good practice and disseminate a wide range of approaches and models for schools to draw on in planning their own curriculum.

Redefining the School Day

151 Schools of the future will have to provide for the curriculum in very different ways. There is considerable evidence that the present day and term structures adopted by most schools in the maintained sector do not support sustained learning and quality teaching. Nor do they ensure achievement for important groups such as disaffected boys. Through the New Opportunities Fund and the DfEE's Study Support Programme, the Government, is making a significant investment in after school clubs. These initiatives could open the way for an extended school day, offering more opportunities for creative and cultural activities.

152 An earlier start, for example, would allow teaching and learning to be concentrated during the mornings when students and teachers are most alert. This would open up afternoon and twilight sessions for supporting independent study, ensuring that the large group of students who find it impossible to do homework because of lack of key skills or parental support, can catch up on those who have every advantage. This opens up huge opportunities for extension and creativity, for developments such as competitive sports between schools, for the arts and for schemes like Birmingham's University of the First Age. There can also be greater flexibility at this time and more use of adults other than teachers.

153 Staff INSET, particularly for the use of ICT, team meetings and links with industry and commerce, with all the disruption this can cause, can also take place during the afternoon and twilight sessions without removing teachers from their teaching of the National Curriculum. For the students, their days would be far more varied; they would have completed homework or independent and extended work assignments and greater access to creative activities. Clearly there would be implications and possible difficulties for working parents. These need to be addressed and the disadvantages weighed against the benefits of new patterns of education. By making such a structure an entitlement, the time for learning would be considerably extended and could lead to greater enjoyment and achievement.

Redefining the School Year

154 We have become used to the pattern of three school terms and three long holidays of different length. This has some inherent difficulties for education. Internationally, successful models have four or five terms with breaks between which prevent the huge discontinuity of a five and a half week summer break. This is a particular problem between Key Stages 2 and 3, as children are not being taught at the same pace after SATs in May until September — a break of three months. The exhaustion of keeping up quality teaching and learning through the very long fifteen/sixteen week Autumn term would also be removed. East Sussex LEA is embarking on a five-term year model and some other authorities are currently discussing similar possibilities. We want to urge a thorough evaluation of these initiatives to help inform the debate on a possible redefinition of the school year.

" In the United Kingdom, the Millennium Commission has awarded £41.3 million to Bristol 2000 and a further £27 million to the International Centre for Life in Newcastle and, to these figures, can be added the grant of £23m from the Heritage Lottery Fund to the National Museum of Science and Industry and countless other and recurrent sums spent by industry, government and by radio and television companies in an attempt to engage the public with scientific ideas. Science and technology 'weeks', 'fairs', 'Olympiads' and competitions are now commonplace and the boundaries between education and entertainment have become sufficiently blurred to sustain 'edutainment' as a neologism. There is ample evidence that many young people and many adults are interested in science but on selective and critical basis. This interest needs to be set alongside the relative unpopularity of the sciences, especially the physical sciences, as subjects for study beyond the age of 16. "

Professor Edgar Jenkins

Summer Schools

155 Currently, the long summer holidays are filled by a wide range of summer schools. Many of these focus on the improvement of literacy and numeracy skills. There would be value in extending the range and type of summer schools to include opportunities for creative and cultural development. These opportunities could be hosted in collaboration with cultural organisations and businesses. We say more about such partnership initiatives in Chapter Eight.

Conclusion

156 The changes we propose to the curriculum are intended to create the conditions in which creative abilities and cultural understanding can be formed more effectively. Changes to the curriculum in themselves will not do this. Nonetheless, we believe that the changes we propose here to the priorities, structure and organisation of the National Curriculum are essential to creating the circumstances in which the creative and cultural education of young people can flourish. Within each curriculum area, teachers will need to:

- require young people to think creatively by setting appropriate assignments;

- offer practical support and guidance in the processes of creativity;

- promote the four roles of cultural education we identified in Chapter Three.

In the next chapter we look at the implications for teaching and learning and for school policies.

Recommendations

157 We recommend that:

i. The rationale for the revised National Curriculum from 2000 should make explicit reference to the necessity of promoting the creative and cultural education of all young people. In relation to creative and cultural education it should specify:

a. the knowledge, skills and values which young people should acquire;

b. the principles of organisation of the National Curriculum to facilitate these outcomes;

c. the principles of teaching and learning through which they will be realised.

ii. The DfEE should put in place a more fundamental review of the structure and balance of the National Curriculum beyond 2000. Within this review full consideration should be given to achieving parity between the following discipline areas throughout key stages 1-4 as a matter of entitlement:

> **"**
> We cannot afford poverty of vision, let alone poverty of aspiration. There are always risks in changing, but the risk of failing to change is much greater.
> **"**
> *Valerie Bayliss, 1998, Redefining Schooling, RSA*

- language and literacy;

- mathematics and numeracy;

- science education;

- arts education;

- humanities education;

- physical education;

- technological education.

iii.   In order to achieve parity, the existing distinction between core and foundation subjects should be removed.

iv.   Provision for creative and cultural education in early years education should be further developed, in particular through provision for the arts.

v.   The structure of Key Stages 3 and 4 should be reviewed. Reducing Key Stage 3 to two years (11-13) and increasing Key Stage 4 to three (13-16) would increase the vitality of Key Stage 3 and the opportunities for depth of study and choice in Key Stage 4. The curriculum of Key Stage 4 should be designed to maintain breadth and avoid narrow specialisation.

vi.   The pressures on schools should be reduced by ensuring that the National Curriculum programmes of study, and the requirements for assessment and reporting can be accommodated within 80 per cent of the ordinary school timetable. The statutory requirements should specify the entitlement of young people in each of the subject areas, and the criteria for attainment and assessment. Schools should have increased freedom to devise patterns of curriculum provision to meet these requirements.

vii. In its overall structure and in the specific programmes of study and attainment targets, the revised National Curriculum should be based on six principles: breadth, balance, relevance, parity, entitlement and access. The Government should reinstate the requirement to follow the full National Curriculum in the core and foundation subjects in Key Stage 1 and 2.

viii. The QCA should disseminate successful models of curriculum organisation and timetabling that promote creative and cultural development within and between the main subject areas. These materials should be made available on the National Grid for Learning and through other media.

ix.   Head teachers should conduct an audit of the quality and nature of opportunities for creative and cultural education for all the pupils in their schools, including the balance of the curriculum in all Key Stages.

x.   A thorough investigation should be undertaken into possible redefinition of the school day and year.

6 Teaching and Learning

Introduction

158 In this chapter we look at the implications of our arguments for teaching and learning and at the processes that are involved. We look first at issues in creative education and go on to relate them to our view of cultural education.

'Only Connect'

159 We want to make some preliminary points. First we began this report by arguing that developing creative and cultural education raised systemic issues: that it involves all aspects of education including styles of teaching and assessment and the ethos and values of individual schools and of more general educational provision. We believe this is true and in later sections we look at these wider issues. But the heart of education is the relationship between teachers and learners, and by extension the relationships that also develop between learners — young people themselves. Creative and cultural education require and make possible particularly rewarding relationships between all of them.

160 Second, creative and cultural education are not subjects in the curriculum: they are general functions of education. They can and should be promoted in all areas of the curriculum and not just through so called 'creative subjects'. Different areas of the curriculum do contribute to creative and cultural education in different ways. The opportunities and the focus in the arts, for example, are not identical with those of the sciences and humanities, nor with physical education. Each of these broad areas contributes in different ways to a balanced education as we suggested in the last Chapter. But there is also considerable overlap and potential synergy between different curriculum areas as we implied in discussing the dynamics of intelligence and of culture in Chapters Two and Three. Not least, there are similarities in the processes of teaching and learning.

161 There is a further point to emphasise. There is much debate about methods of teaching in schools, and in particular about the effectiveness of 'progressive' teaching methods. These include methods that encourage exploratory learning activities; group work and 'learning from experience'. These methods are often associated with promoting creativity, freedom and self-expression. Some critics of progressive education see a link between these and a lack of rigour and authority in schools, and with low standards. They prefer more 'traditional' methods of teaching: those associated with formal instruction of specific skills and content. In these terms, the debate on teaching and learning seems to some to involve a choice between creativity or rigour, freedom or authority.

162 In our view, there is a balance in all good teaching between formal instruction of content and of skills, and giving young people the freedom to inquire, question, experiment and to express their own thoughts and ideas. In creative and cultural education, this balance is a matter of necessity. Genuine creative achievement, for example, draws from skills, knowledge and understanding. These are sometimes taught best through formal instruction. But formal instruction alone will not encourage creativity and may even stifle it. In thinking about the nature of creative and cultural education in schools it is vital to move beyond divisive stereotypes of traditional or progressive teaching, and to see the need for elements of both. Creative education and cultural education are not the same, but they are intimately related. We want now to look a little closer at some of the principles and processes involved. We begin with creative education.

Teaching Creatively and Teaching For Creativity

163

There is an obvious sense in which children cannot be 'taught' creativity in the way that they can be taught the times tables. Creative processes do draw from knowledge and practical skills. It is also the case that there are various techniques to facilitate creative thinking. But this does not mean that children are taught creativity by direct instruction. We define creative teaching in two ways: first, teaching creatively, and second, teaching *for* creativity. Many teachers see creative teaching in terms of the first (NFER 1998:31). Our terms of reference imply a primary concern with the second. By teaching creatively we mean teachers using imaginative approaches to make learning more interesting, exciting and effective. Teachers can be highly creative in developing materials and approaches that fire children's interests and motivate their learning. This is a necessary part of all good teaching.

> **The Present**
> Capturing young children's attention, making an activity attractive and exciting, takes imagination and creativity on the part of the teacher. Some aspects of the curriculum appear difficult to introduce in an imaginative way: for example, that living things need air, water and food. In this approach the teacher captured the children's interest and challenged them to think and make sense of the experience. Children sat on the carpet area and watched as the teacher brought out a box covered in brightly coloured paper with a big bow on top. The teacher explained: "A friend of mine has sent me a present, doesn't it look lovely? She says that it is a very important present and I couldn't live without it. I wonder what is inside?"; she gave the box a gentle shake, but the children couldn't hear anything and wondered if there was anything inside. When the box was opened, it was empty and the children gasped. "Oh dear!" said the teacher, "There's nothing in the box. Why would my friend say there was something in the box which I needed to be able to live?" The children offered ideas until one child made the connection and exclaimed: "It's air, it's air in the box!"
>
> *Information provided by Julia Kelly, Dudley Infant School, Hastings*

By teaching *for* creativity we mean forms of teaching that are intended to develop young people's own creative thinking or behaviour.

> " To me the essence of creative and cultural education is that individuals, in this case young people, find their own creative/cultural 'voice', develop skills to service this, engage with the creativity and work of others with a view to participating in society. It has to be an active engagement. When it is, it is an answer to other problems: social exclusion, disaffection, etc. But the creative act — whether it is an arts activity or another creative endeavour — has to empower the individual child. At best it critiques and challenges past and current practice and leads to renewal of the individual and the society. "
>
> *Pauline Tambling, Director of Education and Training, Arts Council of England*

> " Creative thinking skills can promote quality and coherence in education and training in the interests of industry, the economy and society. "
>
> *Design Council*

Teaching for Creativity

164 Teaching for creativity involves teaching creatively. Young people's creative abilities are most likely to be developed in an atmosphere in which the teacher's creative abilities are properly engaged. To put it another way, teachers cannot develop the creative abilities of their pupils if their own creative abilities are suppressed. This too has implications for the curriculum — and in particular for the type and amount of national prescription of what is taught and how, and for teacher training. Teaching for creativity is a demanding process which cannot be made routine. However, it is possible to identify some general principles. There are three related tasks in teaching for creativity: *encouraging, identifying* and *fostering.*

Encouraging

165 Highly creative people in any field are often driven by a strong self-belief in their abilities in that field. Having a positive self-image as a creative person can be fundamental to developing creative performance[1]. Many young people and adults do not think of themselves as creative and lack the confidence to take even the first steps. Consequently, the first task in teaching for creativity in any field is to encourage young people to believe in their creative potential, to engage their sense of possibility and to give them the confidence to try[2]. These are the most simple steps but they can be the most important for stimulating creative performance. Other attitudes are important for creative achievement; these include high motivation and independence of judgement, willingness to take risks and be enterprising, to be persistent and to be resilient in the face of adversity and failure. These attitudes can be encouraged and nourished to varying extents in all young people, particularly if they are linked with the development of self-directed learning. We come back to this idea later.

Identifying

166 All young people have different creative capacities. A creative musician is not necessarily a creative scientist, a creative writer is not necessarily a creative mathematician. An essential task for education is to help young people to discover their own creative strengths. Creative achievement is often driven by a person's love of a particular instrument, for the feel of the material, for the excitement of a style of work that catches the imagination. Identifying young people's creative abilities includes helping them to find their creative strengths — to be in their element. This too has implications for the range and balance of the curriculum.

Fostering

167 Creativity draws from many ordinary abilities and skills rather than one special gift or talent. Thus the development of many common capacities and sensitivities can help to foster creativity — for example, curiosity can be stimulated, memory can be trained and awareness can be enhanced.

Recognising and becoming more knowledgeable about the creative process can also help foster creative development; teaching for creativity helps young people in understanding what is involved in being creative and becoming more sensitive to their own creative processes. Creative ability is best enhanced in the process of being creative. This 'learning by doing' can be further developed and enriched by working with personal models and mentors who are prepared to share their experience[3]. We come back to this in Chapter Eight.

168 In teaching for creativity, teachers aim to:

- allow for both broad and narrowly focused experimental activity, but always specifying and explaining the purpose of such activity. Those involved have to feel prepared and secure enough to be willing to take risks and make mistakes in a non threatening atmosphere that challenges but reassures. Such work has to be carefully tuned to the appropriate level of development;

- encourage an appropriate attitude towards imaginative activity — a sense of excitement, respect, hope and wonder at the potential for transformative power that is involved, accompanied by a sense of delayed scepticism and distance;

- assist in the understanding of the room that has to be given to generative thought, free from immediate criticism by the learner or others before ideas are subject to rigorous critical evaluation and further development;

- encourage self expression that is oriented towards a given task;

- convey an appreciation of the phases in creative activity and the importance of time — including the ways in which time away from a problem may facilitate its solution;

- assist in developing an awareness of the differing contexts in which ideas may occur and of the roles of intuition, unconscious mental processes and non-directed thought in creative thinking;

- encourage and stimulate learners in periods of free play with ideas and conjecture about possibilities, but complement this with critical evaluation in testing out ideas;

- emphasise the use of the imagination, originality, curiosity and questioning, the offer of choice, and the encouragement of the personal attributes that facilitate creativity.

169 Teaching for creativity aims at encouraging:

- *autonomy* on both sides: a feeling of ownership and control over the ideas that are being offered (Woods 1995:3);

- *authenticity* in initiatives and responses, deciding for oneself on the basis of one's own judgement;

> " A lot of people find themselves being creative despite their social standing. You're the kid who's smart, so all your mates listen to your counsel. You're the kid who's funny, so they look to you for a laugh. You're the great dancer at the local disco. You're the one who's good at building stuff. You're the one who's been practising the guitar in your bedroom since you were nine. You're the one who's good at problem solving. I think it's a teacher's job to spot these kids and give them a nudge in the right direction – encourage the smart one to get smarter; encourage the funny one to read books, look at the history of comedy, organise his thoughts, write stuff down; encourage the dancer to practice, look at videos, see shows, etc. I know there are some schools that do this, but there are a lot that don't. It is not just about numeracy and literacy... it's about vigilance, kindness, empathy and creativity. "
>
> *Lenny Henry*

- *openness* to new and unusual ideas, and to a variety of methods and approaches;

- *respect* for each other and for the ideas that emerge;

- *fulfilment:* from each a feeling of anticipation, satisfaction, involvement and enjoyment of the creative relationship.

Above all there has to be a relationship of *trust*. Teaching for creativity aims to encourage self-confidence, independence of mind, and the capacity to think for oneself. Such teaching is compatible with a wide range of teaching methods and approaches in all areas of the school curriculum. The aim is to enable young people to be more effective in handling future problems and objectives; to deepen and broaden awareness of the self as well as the world; and to encourage openness and reflexivity as creative learners.

Self-directed Learning

"
The ability to think about your own thinking (metacognition) is essential in a world of continuous change. **"**

John Abbott

170 Encouraging self-monitoring, reflection upon their own performance and progress, and thinking about their own thinking — metacognition — can enhance young people's control over creative activity and the development of their best practice[4]. In these ways the aim is to encourage the development of the self-directed learner. Teaching for creativity encourages a sense of responsibility for learning. It aims at a growing autonomy involving goal-setting and planning, and the capacity for self-monitoring self-assessment and self-management. In principle, the earlier self-directed learning is internalised, the better, but again this aspect of teaching for creativity must be sensitive to the appropriate stage of the learner's development. It must be recognised that it will be in the secondary school where self-directed learning is more likely to move in tune with the development of young people's growing maturity, the flow of their need for independence, and their growing proficiency in forms of information technology.

"
Learning involves going beyond simply acquiring new information and adding it to our existing knowledge. It involves us in making sense of new information by using our existing knowledge and modifying, updating and rethinking our own ideas in the light of this new information. **"**

Scottish Consultative Council on the Curriculum 1996

171 Creativity is itself a mode of learning. It is distinctive in the combination of three features:

a. It involves a thoughtful playfulness — learning through experimental 'play'. It is serious play conjuring up, exploring and developing possibilities and then critically evaluating and testing them.

b. It involves a special flexibility in which there may be a conscious attempt to challenge the assumptions and preconceptions of the self — an unusual activity in which there is an active effort to unlearn in order to learn afresh.

c. This process is driven by the need to find, introduce, construct or reconstruct something new. It seeks actively to expand the possibilities of any situation. In this sense the learning of creative thought is not neutral; it has a bias towards the innovative.

For these reasons creative activity can itself be regarded as a form of learning particularly suited to the testing and complex conditions and which will face us all in the twenty-first century and which we outlined in Chapter One.

A Creative and Visionary Teacher

A north Leeds comprehensive, Harehills Middle School, and its accompanying youth group Harehills Youth Dance, produced virtually a whole generation of UK contemporary dancers in the 1970s and 80s. In 1972, Nadine Senior became the physical education teacher at the school, situated in a vibrant but run-down multi-ethnic area in north Leeds. Gurmit Hukam, now Artistic Director of the Northern School of Contemporary Dance says, "We began to explore different movements, usually based on imaginative themes given to us by Nadine — simple ideas, involving partner and group work. I guess it first dawned on us that it was 'dance' when we had our first performance, and Nadine asked us whether we wanted to wear tights and a T-shirt or tights and a leotard — we decided on the tights and a T-shirt as the lesser of two evils!" Nadine Senior always demanded the highest standards of artistic integrity, but the criteria were as much decided by the children. There was no external imposition of artistic ideas or ideals; this was rather developed from the child's own imaginative responses. Allowed to express themselves, Nadine's pupils became 'artists' in the deepest sense, and carried this quality into their later work and careers.

Information obtained from animated

Lifelong Learning

172 Increasingly, teaching has to promote the skills and attitudes appropriate to the encouragement of lifelong learning. But the encouragement to 'learning' in itself tells us nothing about the capacity for, or orientation towards, change or action. We believe that the habit of learning has to be complemented by the disposition to be creative. Vital as it is in economic, social and personal terms, regular task-oriented retraining will often not be enough. Adult learning will in future take place in a world where flexibility and adaptability are required in the face of new, strange, complex, risky and changing situations; where there are diminishing numbers of precedents and models to follow; where we have to work on the possibilities as we go along. In this changing world, old assumptions and old directions as to the routes forward can be a useful asset but they can also become an encumbrance. We will often find ourselves seeking entrances after emerging through unexpected exits. This is where creativity is of special importance and where the attitudes and abilities it entails come into their own.

> **"**
> Setting out to embed the concepts of creativity deeply in the educational establishment is the greatest challenge, offering the greatest prize of all. That prize would be the realisation of an ethos of creativity, rather than a compartment of creativity.
> **"**
>
> *CAPE UK*

173 In various ways there are important links between lifelong learning and creativity. Learning and creativity are enhanced and sustained by a range of abilities, attributes and activities common to both — including intrinsic motivation, enterprise, persistence and resilience, curiosity, questioning and reflecting, assessing and testing, moving from problems to solutions and back to new problems —understanding and using failures on the road to success. A prerequisite for effective lifelong learning is sustained motivation towards self-improvement. This motivation is at its most powerful when it involves both love of learning and the desire for personal growth, realising the potential of the individual in some form of creative activity.

Creativity and Information Technology

174 Teaching for creativity must take account of the new opportunities presented by information technology. Information technologies provide for new forms of creative practice, through, for example, computer graphics, animation, and sound production. They are also making available new ways of working within traditional forms of creative practice: in design, choreography and musical composition, for example. Information technology can also revolutionise forms of teaching and learning through providing easier and fuller access to information, ideas and people. Information technology is one of the easiest ways of encouraging the urge to learn in a child. It offers them some control over their learning and it lets them interact with the "tools" in such a way that they can make a difference through their own actions. It is not only important to consider when and when not to use information and communication technology in the classroom, but also how best to use them to stimulate learning.

Art and IT in Practice

Art departments in schools are beginning to develop their use of IT alongside traditional art room practice in order to provide opportunities for the exploration of new forms of visual communication.. Artists have always used new tools and materials to express their ideas and feelings about the world around them. Pupils today have an ever-increasing range of environments and possibilities in which to create art. As a visual medium the computer has a rightful place within the art curriculum, both as a tool and a means of expression. As part of a Year 7 project designed to give them experience in using a variety of materials, processes and techniques, pupils looked at stimulus material on Indian art and culture so they could design their own T-shirt motifs. Starting with their own drawings, these were scanned and students then experimented with different colourways and repeat patterns. Their chosen design was then printed on transfer paper and applied to a white T-shirt. As part of a study of colour mixing, Year 8 students had been asked to examine the work of Lionel Feininger and create a painting in which they divided the picture's surface into different colour ranges. In this part of the work, they were able to use a computer package to recreate the same image but this time using flood-fill. This introduced a project looking at Seurat and the Pointillists.

Information obtained from BECTA (formerly NCET)

Creative Teachers

175 Teaching with creativity and teaching for creativity include all the characteristics of good teaching. These include strong motivation, high expectations, the ability to communicate and listen and the ability to interest and to inspire. Creative teachers need expertise in their particular fields. Creative teaching in mathematics involves a command of mathematical ideas and principles: creative teaching in music involves a knowledge of musical forms and possibilities. But creative teachers need more than this. They need techniques that stimulate curiosity and raise self-esteem and confidence. They must recognise when encouragement is needed and confidence threatened. They must balance structured learning with opportunities for self-direction; and the management of groups with attention to individuals. They must judge the kinds of questions appropriate to different purposes and the kinds of solutions it is appropriate to expect.

176 There is a distinction for example between closed questions where there is one generally agreed solution, and open questions where there can be more than one. Both may be taught creatively but the open questions offer greater opportunity for creative activity on the part of the learner. Creative activity often involves both open and closed questions. The evidence is that too often our education activities are focused on closed questions with their reliance on linear processes and logical reasoning.

> *Teaching is not to be regarded as a static accomplishment like riding a bicycle or keeping a ledger: it is, like all arts of high ambition, a strategy in the face of an impossible task.*
>
> *Lawrence Stenhouse, Education and Emancipation Authority*

What If?

One of the most powerful prompts to creative thinking is the asking of open-ended questions. Some answers will be better than others, but none is likely to be 'wrong'. Set out an odd number of counters on a table. Explain that you will need four volunteers, forming two teams of two: the rest of the group choose to support one or other team. Ask the teams and their supporters to gather at either side of the table. Stand between the two teams and explain that you'll ask a *What If?* question. Immediately the two teams will begin having answers. The team to your right may speak at normal volume into your right ear; the team to your left at normal volume into your left ear, simultaneously. Team supporters must not speak to you directly, but can relay their answers by *whispering* them to their team members. For each reasonable answer you receive, that team will get a point in the form of a counter. When all the counters have been distributed, the game has thirty seconds left to run. During that time, good answers will win points *from the opposing team's store of counters*. After thirty seconds blow a whistle to signal the end of the round. Take care to explain that although one of the teams has accumulated more points than the other, they've all won because:
You've proved that everyone can have lots of ideas if the circumstances are right (and you need to have lots of ideas in order to have good ideas). You now have lots of ideas, and therefore some good ones you can look at in more detail.

From Imagine That *by Stephen Bowkett*

177 Teaching for creativity is not an easy option, but it can be enjoyable and deeply fulfilling. It can involve more time and planning to generate and develop ideas and to evaluate whether they have worked. It involves confidence to improvise and take detours, to pick up unexpected opportunities for learning; to live with uncertainty and to risk admitting that an idea led nowhere. Creative teachers are always willing to experiment but they recognise the need to learn from experience. All of this requires more, not less, expertise of teachers. Creative teachers need confidence in their disciplines and in themselves. There are many highly creative teachers in our schools and many schools where creative approaches to teaching and learning are encouraged. But many teachers and schools will want practical support and guidance in developing these approaches. Consequently there are important issues of staff development to address and we come to these in more detail in Chapter Ten. But there are also issues of opportunity.

178 It is important to reduce or eliminate the factors which inhibit the creative activity of teachers and learners and give priority to those that encourage it. There are now in education unusually high levels of prescription in relation to content and teaching methods. There are risks here of de-skilling teachers and of encouraging conformity and passivity in some. At a national level we believe that there are actions that the Government should take to reduce these risks and to promote higher levels of teacher autonomy and of creativity in teaching and learning. But there is also much that schools can do to review their own approaches to teaching and learning and the balance of the whole curriculum. We come back to this later.

Cultural Education

179 Teaching for creativity is not a single method or technique. It can involve a wide range of methods and approaches. It is possible and desirable to teach for creativity in all areas of the curriculum. Throughout this report we link together creative and cultural education. First, creative processes draw from the cultural contexts in which they take place; second, human culture is the outcome of human creativity in all of its forms. Different areas of the curriculum lead young people into different forms of enquiry and provide different opportunities to develop their cultural knowledge and understanding.

180 Schools are involved in cultural development on two broad fronts. First, they embody and promote particular values and ways of behaving in the kinds of institutions they are. Implicitly and explicitly the culture of a school is conveyed to young people every day and in many ways: in the structure and content of the curriculum; in the relationships between teachers and learners; in the methods and criteria of assessment; in how the school is managed and in its links or lack of them with the wider community. The ethos of the school and the values it expresses have a direct bearing on the attitudes and values of young people — to education itself and to each other. It is for this reason among the others we have given that we describe the issues facing creative and cultural education as systemic. Second, the core business of schools is cultural education. The primary purposes of formal education are to develop in young people the knowledge, understanding and abilities they need to make their way in the world. These include combating ignorance, extending and deepening cultural knowledge and understanding and encouraging curiosity, questioning and informed critical thought and action. All education involves a selection. Schools cannot teach everything. The National Curriculum identifies which subjects are to be taught — and what counts as a subject — and what aspects of those subjects are to be included. In those ways, national policy sets a cultural agenda for education. Schools add or subtract from this in the choices and emphasese they bring to teaching and learning. This process of selection is inevitable and desirable: but it must be done with care and wisdom if schools are to fulfil the four roles of cultural education identified earlier.

181 *To enable young people to recognise, explore and understand their own cultural values and assumptions.*

As we said in Chapter Three, young people do not develop their ideas and values in isolation. This is true of all of us. How we think, feel and behave is influenced by the cultural environments we live in, by the communities we are part of, and by our own histories and backgrounds. Sometimes we recognise consciously the values we hold and the ideas we espouse. As often, we are not conscious of them. They form part of our taken-for-granted view of the way things are. They occur to us as common sense — until we encounter others whose common sense view of the world is strikingly different. Attitudes to the roles of men and women, or of the place and station of children and young people are good examples of views that vary greatly between cultures — and over time — but which tend to be taken for granted within them and at the time. There are many others.

182 Teaching and learning should provide opportunities for young people to explore and recognise what their own assumptions and values actually are, and how they have been formed. This is not necessarily a process of challenging cultural values but of recognising and understanding them. The arts and humanities provide important opportunities for such exploration and powerful techniques. Drama, for example is essentially concerned with exploring social behaviour and the values that underpin it.

Through improvised drama, and through work on texts young people can investigate a wide range of real and imagined social issues through the safety of assumed roles or situations. This process can generate powerful insights into the values and dynamics of groups and communities.

> ### Drama Provides Equal Opportunities
> Equal Voice focuses on new ways of resolving conflicts with special regard to individual self-esteem. Some of the work was undertaken at Crusoe House, a school for children with emotional and behavioural difficulties (EBD). Often pupils remain at EBD schools for many years and some are never reintegrated into mainstream schools. The work improves a child's ability to be emotionally articulate, gives them a voice and raises their self-esteem so that they can begin to take responsibility for their own behaviour. This small change in attitude is often enough for a child to be able to return to mainstream education and modify the behaviour that has caused, and been reinforced by, the stigma of exclusion and low achievement. Irene Flynn, head at Crusoe House said of Equal Voice: "Drama provides opportunities to explore and release a variety of emotions in a safe environment. This encourages our pupils to experiment with different ways of behaving — increasing their repertoire of acceptable responses. The majority of our pupils have low self-esteem, often feel under attack and will over-react in a confrontational and sometimes aggressive manner. The drama programme was of real benefit to pupils. It encouraged positive interaction and group work. The environment created by the drama workshops was non-threatening and dispelled much of the everyday hostility. Staff also benefited from observing how their pupils responded to the expertise and techniques used by the Equal Voice leaders."
>
> *Information provided by Pop-Up Theatre*

183 *To enable young people to embrace and understand cultural diversity by bringing them into contact with the attitudes, values and traditions of other cultures.*

We see two priorities here for schools. The first is to develop processes which help young people to understand cultures that are different from their own. The second is to ensure that young people's own cultural experiences and traditions are valued and validated. This is especially

important for young people from minority cultures who may be faced with complex issues of identity at home and at school.

184 Teachers and school need to create opportunities for children and young people from different cultural backgrounds to work together and to learn to respect each others' ways of living. This is not just a matter of learning factual information about other cultures and times: the real task is to enable young people, as far as possible, to understand other cultures from the inside. Seen from their own cultural perspectives, the ideas and patterns of behaviour of other cultures can seem strange. Young people need to have insight into other ways of living and understand the ideas that give them meaning and significance. To achieve this, it is important to provide opportunities for pupils to work with and listen to people from other cultural backgrounds: hearing their stories, listening to their language, music and backgrounds, seeing the images and designs that move them. Where possible this can be done through direct face to face contact: meeting and working with people from many different backgrounds and cultures in the school itself and through outside projects and events.

185 In Chapter Eight we looked at the need to establish networks and links with individuals, groups and communities beyond the school. One reason for this is to extend the cultural experience of young people. But a variety of other strategies are also available involving visits, exchanges, residential weekends, and now video conferencing and the Internet. These can be inexpensive and convenient ways to broaden experience and to learn about different cultural values and perspectives. In many areas of the curriculum these purposes can be met through practical projects: for example, local history projects; reminiscence projects — talking with older pupils about their lives and times; and through cultural festivals and exchanges.

Celebrating Diversity

At City Infant School a diversity of cultures is in evidence both in assemblies and in the wall displays around the school. One assembly began with the head greeting the children in Irish Gaelic, followed by a discussion, at an appropriate level for their age phase, on how they had worked out what she had been saying through context, routine and paralinguistic features. Recently a Muslim staff member had taken an assembly explaining the meaning of Eid and showing the children some of the customs of that festival. There were multilingual displays around the school. Wall displays of stories included one labelled 'We heard Mr. Gumpy in English and Turkish', with Turkish-English bilingual labels below the pictures, another big collage display on the book 'The Village of Round and Square Houses' was labelled 'Cameroons, West Africa'. A model of a mosque used in a recent assembly had been kept standing in the hall. The Head's office too, reflected the school's diversity; including Chinese pottery; African batik, statues and masks; South American and Russian dolls; a book of Greek myths; examples of Gaelic script and postcards of Ireland.

Information from Blair et al 1998

186 *To encourage an historical perspective by relating contemporary values to the processes and events that have shaped them.*

The humanities and especially history have central roles in helping young people to understand the ideas and values of those removed from themselves in time and culture. But the lived experience and cultures of societies are intricate and overlapping. Science, technology, political events, geography, religion and the rest affect each other and the course of development of cultural communities. Teaching and learning in all disciplines should contribute to a sense of historical perspective and understanding. World science has been deeply affected by intellectual innovations in many cultures: in geometry, mathematics, and modes of calculation — from China, India, the Middle East and from Europe. It is a world culture with a multicultural history. One of the most vivid ways of feeling the sensibility of a cultural community or period is to listen to its music or poetry and to understand the circumstances that helped to form them. It is important to encourage young people, and teachers, to make connections between disciplines in the curriculum; and to recognise that the dynamic, interactive nature of culture is a fact, not a theory, which is at the heart of cultural change and evolution.

187 *To enable young people to understand the evolutionary nature of culture and the processes and potential for change.*

On of the three principles of balance we are proposing is between freedom and tradition. We mean by this that it is important, for all the reasons that we have given, that young people learn about the histories, traditions and established ways of thinking in different disciplines and cultures. But they also need to know that these are evolutionary, sometimes revolutionary processes which are prone to rapid and fundamental change. The driving force of change is human imagination and creativity in our responses to the demands of living and force of circumstances; and the impelling pressures of curiosity and inquiry. Young people are part of this process — and can and will be at its leading edges. In all teaching they need to be enabled to see the importance of, and the opportunities for, innovation, and the processes by which they can contribute to it. One way of achieving this is to encourage dialogue and debate rather than passivity and acceptance; to encourage the exchange of ideas from a range of perspectives; to set puzzles and problems, before providing solutions and answers; and to balance closed questions with open ones.

188 In teaching for cultural understanding teachers aim to:

- promote a sense of inclusion and respect between the different cultural communities and traditions in the school and the classroom;

- deepen understanding of the meanings and values that underpin different cultural perspectives and ways of behaving;

- point to the contribution of different local and national cultures to global culture;

- convey an understanding of the complex interactions — artistic, scientific, technological and others — between as well as within cultures;

- encourage an understanding of the different ways in which human ingenuity and creativity have shaped and are shaping the nature and diversity of human culture.

Cultural Understanding

At playtime at Sunning Hill primary, white children yomping round the playground are outnumbered by pupils from families originally from India, Pakistan and Bangladesh. Paul Read, head teacher for 10 years, wants to ensure that the children who grow up in the tolerant community he has created in a poorer part of Bolton stay tolerant when they leave at the end of each day. He is a pragmatic man, with an ethnically diverse staff and an approach to racism based on experience rather than theory. He sees ethnic divisions being blurred by inter-marriage and suggests religion can be more important as a defining factor than colour. "It's mindsets that we have to address. We have to concentrate on what we can do here. We cannot change what goes on at home."

"It's difficult to change attitudes given to children for more than four years before we see them. And we have them for only 25 hours a week," said Janet Marland, Mr Read's deputy. "When there is an argument during a football game, language can be used which has been ingrained in the children since they learned to speak. ...If children respect a teacher, you are more likely to be able to check their behaviour, if not change their thought processes." If problems continue Mr Read will call in a child's parents and make them aware of behaviour that will not be tolerated at school. There are assemblies of a broadly Muslim and a broadly Christian character; and children are free to opt out of RE lessons on religious grounds. Sunning Hill has to follow the National Curriculum, and the Macpherson report recommends it should be amended to stress the value of cultural diversity. Ms Marland suggests a start might be made with art, music and history.

Abeda Manjra, a teacher at the school, grew up in south Manchester and studied at Leicester and Leeds universities. She defines herself as a British, Indian, Muslim, Gujerati-speaking woman who on any day can feel any one of those characteristics more strongly than another. In the classroom there can be petty feuds and name calling, and white children too can be on the receiving end of racism. Ms Manjra takes the same pragmatic line as the head. 'The process has to start in the home. I feel I have made an impression with some children. They will go home and perhaps make a difference there. But sometimes we feel as if we are educating parents as much as their children.'

David Ward, The Guardian, Friday February 26, 1999 School Policy

189 Promoting creative and cultural development should involve a commitment from the whole school. Creative and cultural education can flourish in adversity and under growing constraints. There are examples of this happening. But the best conditions for creative and cultural education include that:

a. the school culture is characterised by a willingness to question assumptions, an emphasis on mobility of ideas and flexibility of perspective, and a constant raising of new possibilities;

b. the personal attributes significant in creative behaviour are strongly encouraged;

c. there are opportunities for reflective time, mental play and self-development by teachers and the space and time appropriate to creative activities and personal styles are available to the learner;

d. bureaucratic burdens are reduced to increase time for reflective preparation and experimentation;

e. there is an inclusive policy towards the different cultural traditions and communities represented in the school and a positive strategy of multicultural education in the content of the curriculum and in methods and values of teaching.

The Roles of the Head Teacher

190 The key figure in every school is the headteacher Headteachers can raise the priority they give to creative and cultural education, engendering an ethos in which they are valued and encouraged. Characteristics of outstanding headteachers include their passionate conviction; their ability and determination to use challenges as opportunities; their drive to seek out resources and links which will allow them to achieve their shared vision for their students and the schools. Such headteachers are creative, risk-takers. They value and use creativity in their own thinking, in management, in teaching and learning and in the curriculum. They hold fast to their conviction that creativity in all its forms must significantly affect the children and teachers in their schools and their futures. They are confident that the important core skills of literacy and numeracy can be developed and enhanced using creative approaches.

A School Action Plan

191 Headteachers always set the tone of their schools. We believe they should give a lead in the development of an action plan for creative and cultural education: a plan which involves teachers, pupils and the wider community. Such a plan might involve the following elements.

a. *Auditing Provision*
A necessary first step is to take stock of existing provision and opportunities for creative and cultural education. To be effective and comprehensive this audit should involve all partners — teachers, students, parents and the communities.

> It has often been said that schools 'cannot go it alone' against the forces of racial inequality, prejudice and social exclusion that are outside their gates but reach into the classroom. While that may be true, and offer some comfort to those schools who feel they are constantly battling against the odds, it must not become an excuse for failure to take action, because if schools do not take a stand, what hope is there for breaking the vicious circle of these corrosive forces which exist in society at large? Indeed, the best schools more often than not combine a drive for high achievement with a strong community programme which both promotes, and benefits from, good race relations.

Information from Ofsted 1999 a

b. *Creating Opportunities*

School policies should aim to encourage creative approaches to teaching and learning; in literacy, numeracy, the arts, sciences, humanities, physical education and technology, equally within the whole curriculum, and establish timetable patterns and flexibility to ensure all areas of the curriculum can be enhanced, both within and outside formal education.

c. *Valuing Diversity*

Diversity should be seen and celebrated as being valuable and enriching to the school environment: not as a problem but as a strength or asset. Children need to be comfortable and empowered in their own cultures. This may mean giving young people responsibility for managing how they interact with other cultures — with teachers supporting the process: for how the school operates and to develop anti-racist, anti-bullying strategies, and so on.

d. *Monitoring Progress*

The school might establish monitoring systems which identify and encourage students' creative talents and develop praise systems or a rewards policy to celebrate achievement and which monitor in particular progress and achievement by children from ethnic minorities. Such ethnic monitoring is vital in order to determine whether all ethnic groups have access to the same opportunities; problem areas can be identified and solutions developed based on ethnic monitoring.

e. *Developing Networks*

The school could establish networks which bring in expertise and funding for creative and cultural projects and events. It could develop links between schools in different areas — even between countries — to combat parochialism and to widen experience of pupils outside the immediate environment of the school. It is essential in these and other ways to widen children's experiences to raise achievement

f. *Involving Parents*

It is always important to involve parents in the working life of the school. Children bring an immense amount of cultural baggage with them to school each day — from parents and social circumstances within community. Some parents are suspicious of institutions. others are very involved, competitive and demanding. Regular meetings and events can be vital in enriching the creative and cultural life of the school and in strengthening their support for it. The agenda for teaching and learning we have offered here will require schools to give parents full information and understanding of what is involved — and, perhaps crucially, what is not involved. Parents will need reassurance that the school priorities are right. The more they are involved, the more likely it is that learners will be able to respond fully to this agenda. In Chapter Eight we make a range of suggestions for how this involvement might be further developed.

❝ Following an analysis by ethnicity of National Curriculum results in one primary school, concern about black underachievement and low self-esteem led to a focus on the culture of Black African pupils, even though they were few in number in this predominantly British Asian school. African influenced art and craft work was developed as part of a curriculum initiative in history where Benin was chosen as a unit of study. Work of outstanding quality, supported by stimulating and carefully chosen artefacts, was much in evidence in the school. The response of all the pupils was enthusiastic. The progress and behaviour of the black pupils have improved. **❞**

Information from Ofsted 1999 a

g. *The Ethos of the School*

Multicultural education should be institutionalised into school life as an attitude or value. Values stay with children far longer than items of specific information about different cultures. But both are needed. The starting point for creating a positive multicultural school ethos is to create a safe, friendly and welcoming environment with which all the children can identify, regardless of race, class, gender, language or culture. All young people need to feel secure, safe, respected and allowed to achieve and succeed. Children should feel confident to share their own cultural traditions without fear of being persecuted for them. The school environment can play a critical role, for example displays of children's creative work in a range of forms. Giving children responsibility for their environment through school councils and other formal and informal structures can be a vital foundation.

Headteachers cannot act alone in this. They must involve all the staff, and they must provide for staff development to enable their plans to be put into practice. We come to these issues in Chapter Ten.

Every Subject a Creative Subject

Malbank School and Sixth Form Centre in Cheshire has been identified as one of a number of vastly improving schools. The headteacher attributes their success to creative and cultural education: "Visitors are invariably struck by a range of creative, purposeful activity taking place throughout the school. They see evidence of a lively cultural life, which values creative and cultural education for its own sake, for what it contributes to young people's achievements and to the success of a school. Virtually everyone gains good GCSE and four good A levels is the norm at the sixth form of some 400. We regard every subject as a creative subject, in which youngsters are encouraged to think creatively and work creatively. They create aesthetically pleasing, useful 'things' alongside interesting and stimulating images and ideas; they tackle problems requiring imaginative solutions; they participate in events and celebrations which enhance the school's 'learning culture' and they experience something of the traditions and cultures of people in other times and in other societies. This 'sort' of education, institutionalised through agreed curriculum principles and entitlements, monitoring, review and development, develops students' key skills and motivates them to participate actively, to take pride in their work, to want to learn more. Creative and cultural education contributes to their having the means and the will to achieve success. OFSTED found that 'teaching, learning and academic standards are of a very high order'; 'quality standards', 'high achievement' in a 'good school which is determined to become even better'. This is not despite our putting thought, time and energy into the creative and cultural dimensions of the curriculum. It is a product of our doing so."

Allan Kettleday, Headteacher, Malbank School

Advice and Materials

192 The QCA is developing non-statutory guidance for schools in a number of National Curriculum subjects. The case we have presented for creative and cultural education, and the approaches to teaching, learning and assessment that are required, call for careful programmes of curriculum and staff development. The QCA should support this process with guidance for all areas of the National Curriculum. Such guidance should be supported by training opportunities provided through the Standards Fund and other sources. We will return to this in Chapter Ten.

193 There are a number of distinctive systems and approaches to creative thinking, including problem-solving. These systems make available specific techniques for generating ideas, by individuals and groups, and for evaluating them critically. Often they are based on ways of distinguishing the different phases and tasks in creative thinking. Among the best-known of these are:

- the work of *Edward de Bono* in promoting 'lateral thinking' and his techniques of group creativity through the 'Six Hats' method;

- the *Synectics* method which promotes the use of metaphor and analogy;

- *Accelerated Learning* which uses techniques of association and visualisation to improve memory and make creative connections;

- *Thinking Skills* which promotes a number of techniques, particularly in raising attainment in mathematics and science;

- *Mind Mapping*, a technique developed by Dr. Tony Buzan for recording information and seeing patterns in ideas.

These and other techniques are being taken up by business, industry and, increasingly, by public institutions as ways of fostering creativity in the workforce. We see considerable potential for their use in education, to enable teachers and pupils alike to tap into their own process of creative thinking. It has not been within our remit or resources to evaluate the efficacy of particular techniques or programmes. But we think that this should now be done by the QCA in association with others, and that advice, materials and impartial information should be made available to schools.

Conclusion

194 In this chapter we have looked at what is involved in teaching for creativity and cultural development. In the next chapter we look at what is involved in assessing

> **"**
> The education system should be aware of different ways of thinking and not be restrictive.
> **"**
> *Professor Sir Harold Kroto*

> **"**
> It is our job to determine what makes a creative child a creative adult.
> **"**
> *Sir Claus Moser*

these processes of teaching and training. Appropriate forms of assessment and accountability are essential to raising standards in schools and to sustaining the strategy for improvement that we propose. Inappropriate forms of both will have the opposite effects. Changes to the curriculum must be supported by developments in the national systems of assessment and inspection.

Recommendations

195 We recommend that:

i. Head teachers and teachers raise the priority they give to creative and cultural education; to promoting the creative development of pupils and encouraging an ethos in which cultural diversity is valued and supported.

ii. The QCA should:

    a. undertake an evaluation of existing techniques and programmes promoting creative thinking skills and creative problem solving;

    b. establish pilot projects to develop practical programmes and techniques for promoting creative thinking in primary and secondary schools, and formulate advice to schools;

    c. develop non-statutory guidance for creative teaching and learning for each subject and attainment target of the National Curriculum;

    d. collate examples and curricular materials of positive uses of the literacy and numeracy strategies in creative and cultural education in primary schools.

These materials should be made available on the National Grid for Learning and through other media.

iii. School plans for staff development should include specific provision to improve teachers' expertise in creative and cultural education.

7 Raising Standards

Introduction

196 Assessment and inspection have vital roles in raising and maintaining standards of achievement in schools. Methods of assessment must be appropriate to different types of learning if they are to encourage and not inhibit the creative and cultural development of young people. In this section we discuss the need for assessment and identify a number of difficulties in current approaches. We argue that there is a need to restore a proper balance between different types of attainment target, and between the different forms of assessment that are needed. On this basis we make proposals for the development of assessment methods, and for related developments in the national framework for school inspection.

The Need for Assessment

197 Our consultations have revealed many concerns about the effects of current processes of national assessment on creative and cultural education. Assessment is the process of judging pupils' progress and attainment. Reliable and systematic assessment is essential in all areas of the curriculum, to improve the quality of teaching and learning and to raise standards of achievement. This is as true of children's creative and cultural education as for all other areas of education. But how assessment is done must take account of what is being assessed. For many people, this is where the problem lies. As they see it, education is increasingly dominated by methods and criteria of assessment which, at best, take little account of creative teaching and learning, and which, at worst, militate directly against them.

198 The problem for creative and cultural education is not the need for assessment, but the nature of it. In principle, assessment should support children's learning and report on their achievements. In practice, the process of assessment itself can determine the priorities of education in general. Our consultations suggest four related problems: first, a growing emphasis on summative assessment; second, the related emphasis on measurable outcomes; third, the difficulties of assessing creativity; fourth, the growing pressures of national assessment on teachers and schools. Each of these need to be addressed if national assessment is to support rather than inhibit creative and cultural education.

Methods and Functions of Assessment

199 Methods of assessment can take many forms: from informal judgements in the classroom, to written or practical assignments, to formal public examinations. They can draw on many forms of evidence: from children's attitudes and participation in class, to portfolios of course work, to formal

> *"*
> The present assessment arrangements need to be scrutinised to determine the extent to which they support the teaching of science as a creative and imaginative activity. There is a growing body of evidence, for example, that the teacher-conducted assessment of 'scientific investigations' at Key Stage 4 reduces science to little more than an algorithmic variable-handling exercise.
> *"*
>
> *Professor Edgar Jenkins*

assignments in writing or other media, to conventional essays and examination scripts. All of the work that children do can provide evidence for three distinct but related functions of assessment.

- *Diagnostic*
  To analyse pupils' capabilities and aptitudes as a basis for planning.

- *Formative*
  To gather evidence about the pupils' progress to influence teaching methods and priorities.

- *Summative*
  To judge pupils' achievements at the end of a programme of work.

All three functions of assessment are important in schools. In practice, national assessment puts the strongest emphasis on summative assessment.

High Stakes Assessment

200 Summative assessment has two distinct purposes. The first is certification: summative assessments are the basis of school leaving certificates and of the judgements about pupils which are passed from one stage of schooling to the next. These are so called 'high stakes' assessments. The second is accountability: summative assessments are used to judge how well the school itself is doing overall and how the performances of different schools compare. The outcomes of these assessments are linked to the public status of schools, to their funding and, ultimately, to their survival. Since 1992, the DfEE has published data on school performance and rate of pupil absence. This information is used by the national press to compile league tables to rank schools publicly. The DfEE publishes a whole range of performance measures; the press tends to use the information selectively: for example, by putting emphasis on the number of students attaining five or more GCSE grades A*-C. The DfEE aims to publish more information on achievement to steer public attention away from crude league tables, and is moving towards the publication of value-added performance tables. As it is, poor performance in these 'high stakes' assessments can affect the recruitment of pupils, associated funding, and the long-term viability of a school. As a result, summative assessments have a powerful influence on the ethos and priorities of schools.

> **"**
> Because behaviourist objectives had to be observable, attainment had become the only educational yardstick, thereby excluding concepts like creativity and understanding.
> **"**
>
> *Professor John MacBeath, Director of the Quality in Education Centre, University of Strathclyde*

Measurable Outcomes

201 The comparative use of summative assessments to rank pupils, schools and local education authorities, puts considerable emphasis on 'objective' testing and on 'measurable outcomes'. Such testing tends to concentrate on testing pupils' recall of factual knowledge and skills which can be measured comparatively. It generally takes little account of experimentation, original thinking and innovation: processes which are essential to creative and cultural development. Evidence from QCA monitoring indicates that national testing of 11-year olds has changed the way nearly eight out of ten primary schools plan their curriculum. Out of 400 primary schools surveyed, the majority reported that national testing had changed their focus of curriculum delivery. Almost one in four primary schools said they 'taught to the tests' while fewer than half said it was possible to cover the curriculum satisfactorily in the teaching time allowed. Only 47 per cent of schools said they had time to teach outside the National Curriculum. Three out of five schools said geography had lost the most teaching time, while 60 per cent of teachers said five to seven-year-olds were losing out on time for art. A survey of 370 secondary schools revealed that Key Stage 3 tests had had a similar impact on teaching strategies.

202 The programmes of study and attainment targets of the National Curriculum are broad and balanced. But some subjects, some attainment targets, and some types of learning outcome are now self-evidently more important than others. Some areas of achievement are tested objectively and validated externally: others are left to teacher assessment. Only the former are used in judging the effectiveness of schools, and only these are monitored. The focus of teaching narrows, and so does children's learning and achievement. Some areas of the curriculum, especially arts and humanities; some forms of teaching and learning, including questioning, exploring and debating, and some aspects of particular subjects are neglected. The understandable tendency among pupils, parents and teachers is to respond to what the assessment system values most: and for education as a whole to fulfil MacNamara's Fallacy: 'the tendency to make the measurable important rather than the important measurable' (Rowntree 1977). This is not the intention of the National Curriculum, but many schools and teachers see it as the practical effect.

Assessing Creative Development

203 A further problem is that assessing creative and cultural development is more difficult than testing factual knowledge. In the first place, conventional assessment tends to focus on products or outcomes. We noted earlier that creative outcomes have to be both original and of value. But there are different types and degrees of originality. Moreover, judging value depends on a sense of clear and relevant criteria. Teachers are often unclear about the criteria to apply to children's creative work and lack confidence in their own judgement. Second, we have also argued that creative practises often

> *Although assessment on its own cannot change approaches to learning, we know that assessment is a powerful device to help gear teaching and curriculum. In order to encourage the teaching and development of higher-order skills, thinking processes and problem-solving, we must use assessment which directly reflects these processes.*
>
> *Professor Caroline Gipps, Kingston University*

> Active learning does not mean that learners have to 'discover' things for themselves but that they must be actively thinking for themselves.
>
> *Harlen and James 1997*

depend and build on 'failure' and successive attempts to reach a solution. Much of the value of creative work in education is inherent in this process, and not only, in the final product. Assessing creative development in education has to take account of the value of the process, and of children's learning and achievement through it, as well as of the qualities of the public products that result.

204 In these ways, judging children's creative development does require expert judgement and teachers do need help and advice on how this should be done. Insensitive assessment can damage children's creativity. Marilyn Fryer (1996) notes that formally assessing all the work children produce can be inhibiting. Torrance has found that children are monitored so much that they hardly make the leap in their thinking for fear of criticism. This forces them to take the safe option, avoiding experimentation and never learning how to find and correct their mistakes. In Project 1000 (Fryer 1996) a geography teacher described how insensitive marking encouraged children to play safe, writing only what they know to be correct. Renfrow shares this view, maintaining that excessive emphasis on accuracy is counter productive — it discourages experimentation and risk-taking by pupils. A deputy head who took part in Project 1000 described how he worked hard to build children's self confidence but he feared that this would be completely undone by an excessive emphasis on testing. Another teacher described how some children felt unable to make a mark on the paper because of distressing past experiences of assessment[1].

205 Children need periods where they can experiment, make mistakes and test various approaches without fear of failure. Immediate assessment can overlook aspects of creative development which only become visible in the longer term. There are also issues of comparability. How should young people's creative work be compared between schools or regions? The difficulties of assessing creative development can be overcome and there is much research, experience and expertise to draw from. The problem is that tackling these issues is not yet a priority nationally, nor in schools. For these and the other reasons we have indicated, the emphasis in national assessment remains on factual knowledge and on 'objective' testing of skills. The net effect is to increase the emphasis on some forms of learning and to lower the status of others.

Everybody can be somebody

I have yet to meet a young person who does not want to do well. They want to be recognised for their achievements. They want to show that they too have something to offer. They want to feel they are somebody. We want standards to rise, but sideline that very area of learning where many students can excel. It is not uncommon for parents to make it clear that they would prefer their child to drop art, dance, drama and, if need be, music, to make way for 'more important' subjects. The arts can build confidence in the student, release talent in their learning, and act as a lightening conductor for achievement in other subjects. Some schools greatly value expressive subjects in their own right, and as a vehicle capable of driving higher standards in other areas of learning. In these schools, framed art work proudly displayed shouts out, from every wall, how good individual student work can be. The fact that this framed work survives undamaged makes a powerful comment about pride and personal discipline. The same is true of music, dance and drama. These learners can demonstrate ability greater than that of the teachers. Not many subjects can boast this. And it is a degree of relative excellence that motivates. All can succeed. All it takes is a self-belief and the motivation to make it work. Everybody can be somebody.

Steven Andrews, Greenwich Education Directorate Secretariat

The Pressures of Assessment

206

There is a further problem. Teachers and schools now spend considerable time on the administration of assessment, collecting, analysing and submitting information for national testing and spending proportionately less time in developing courses, teaching materials and strategies. They have to record and report in detail the basis of their assessments and subject them to time consuming processes of national checks and balances. Teachers complain that their own judgements are neither trusted nor valued. Clearly, there must be national moderation of pupil assessment to ensure fairness to individuals and comparability between schools. But the strong sense we have from our consultations is that the present levels of administration have become counter productive. Teachers are willing to accept greater responsibility for assessment as part of their professional duties. With appropriate support and training, we believe they should. This is desirable in general terms. It is also necessary to enable teachers to create the conditions for creative and cultural education which we have set out. We strongly support the need for reliable forms of assessment. But the methods and styles of assessment must be appropriate to the tasks in hand. What actions are needed?

> **"**
> More responsibility should be given back to teachers. They can't stimulate creativity if they feel powerless themselves. It is essential to have pressure on schools through inspection, but it should go hand-in-hand with support. **"**
>
> *William Atkinson, Head, Phoenix High School*

Proposals for Development

207

The programmes of study and assessment targets of the National Curriculum emphasise the need for breadth and balance. In some subjects there are specific attainment targets that relate to exploratory and creative work. For example: Mathematics Attainment Target 1: Using and Applying Mathematics; Science Attainment Target 1: Experimental and Investigative Science; Art Attainment Target 1: Investigating and Making. If these areas of learning matter, as the National Curriculum Orders proclaim, they must be assessed and assessed appropriately. Assessing all desired outcomes in the National Curriculum will involve external testing and internal teacher assessments; pencil and paper and practical tasks; demonstrations and coursework assessments. The findings of those varied assessments should be used to influence teaching and learning; to describe or accredit individual performance, and for school and system accountability. The alternative is a drift from the official National Curriculum to a de facto National Curriculum, which is set not by statute but by the practical pressures of assessment.

208 If schools are to make serious attempts to develop and assess creative development, they will need guidance in developing appropriate methods and criteria. There is a considerable literature, and a good deal of research expertise, in the assessment of creative capacities and achievement. Some of this research is focused on particular disciplines, some on more general processes. As part of its role in supporting curriculum development, the QCA is well placed to provide guidance to schools based on an independent review of international experience in the assessment of creativity.

209 By trying to use summative forms of assessment for all purposes, the education system downgrades the importance of formative assessment. Yet formative assessment, properly done, has been shown to promote higher standards of achievement. Formative assessment is particularly important in supporting creative teaching and learning. The findings from a review of over 250 separate studies of the link between assessment and learning, which was conducted by Professor Paul Black and Dr. Dylan William (1998) of King's College London, give a clear message: that initiatives designed to enhance the effectiveness of the way assessment is used in the classroom to promote learning can raise student achievement by the equivalent of between one or two grades at GCSE for an individual — and, for England as a whole, they would have raised the country's position in the recent Third International Mathematics and Science Study from the middle of the 41 countries involved to the top five. The gain for lower-achieving students is likely to be even more substantial. To be effective, formative assessment must conform to four principles:

- it must be built into the design of the teaching programme as an integral element rather than added on to it;

- pupils should be actively involved in the processes of assessment and contribute to them;

- it must be focused on the development of each individual: i.e., it must be criterion referenced rather than norm referenced;

> "
> There are now tremendously high stakes involved - for both individual teachers and for schools - in the current system of assessment, especially in the core subjects. This context militates against innovation, and encourages teachers to play safe. We need an assessment framework which supports creativity, without compromising rigour.
> "
>
> *Valerie Hannon*

- the evidence it provides must be acted on if teaching is to be tuned to the range of pupils' individual developments.

210 Summative and formative assessment both have essential roles in encouraging a wide range of teaching and learning; in improving the quality of achievement; and in ensuring a healthy balance between factual knowledge and more open-ended styles of learning, all of which are necessary to creative and cultural education. Achieving a greater role for formative assessment, carried out by teachers with proper moderation, would do much to increase curricular and subject flexibility; and to reinstate the proper importance of areas of the curriculum such as the arts and humanities. It would emphasise the necessity of inquiry, questioning and experimentation in all areas of the curriculum, and enhance the professionalism and accountability of teachers. It would reduce curricular prescription and overload. It would encourage and enable teachers to devise their own routes to agreed goals and call them to account on the basis of how effectively they achieve them, rather than on the fine detail of their methodology.

211 The amount of compulsory recording currently required of teachers is considerable. The DfEE has started to address this issue in the circular *Reducing the Bureaucratic Burden on Teachers* (DfEE 1998e) and asked the QCA to produce guidance to schools on the recording of assessment information. Teachers' own diligence makes the recording of assessment data an even heavier load to bear. The teaching profession feels that it is sometimes the amount of assessment and recording that causes subjects to crystallise as separate entities, rather than the structure of the National Curriculum. In our view, teacher judgements should be trusted without having to show every detail of their workings. Confident teachers should then be allowed to take creative risks, without adding to the burden of other teachers.

School Inspection

212 The national system of school inspection is an essential element of national educational provision. It makes fundamental contributions to the processes of:

- *Public Accountability:* to ensure that the enormous national investment in education is effective and gives value for money.

> **"**
> Teachers are caught up in a culture of diligence. The recording of assessment data has become a burden because teachers do it so well.
>
> **"**
> *Carol Adams, Chief Education Officer, Shropshire County Education Office*

- *Transparency:* to ensure that politicians and administrators; teachers, head teachers and governors; pupils and students; parents and guardians; local communities and the nation at large know the state of the education service, its strengths and weaknesses and what needs to be done to improve shortcomings and promote good practice.

The inspection system influences what schools do and how they do it. This happens as a result of what and how it inspects; on what and to whom it reports; and what happens as a result. In a very short time, OFSTED has established an effective national system of school inspection that has achieved a great deal and has much to commend it. Against the background of these achievements, we have been made aware repeatedly of a number of specific concerns about the effects of the inspection system on opportunities for creative and cultural education.

Flexibility

213 OFSTED's inspections are now delegated to teams of independent inspectors. These teams necessarily have varied experience in different areas of the school curriculum. To ensure comparability and reliability in the findings of its many inspection teams, OFSTED has had to develop a framework for inspection that can be applied in all circumstances. As a check list for all that the school should consider about itself, the framework is better than average. But it has significant shortcomings in relation to our concerns. OFSTED inspection has to do more than work to an a priori inspection framework. Given the inspectorate it has available, there are limitations on the flexibility that OFSTED can allow them if reliability and credibility are not to suffer. Without flexibility, inspection teams can become insensitive to the qualities and nuances of work in individual schools. School inspections need to be nationally comparable, but in our view they must ease up somewhat to allow inspections to reflect particular strengths and characteristics, and to pick up early signs of promising developments or concerns. That might mean pre-inspection work, identifying what, if any, special characteristics of a school should be reflected in the make-up of the inspection team. A framework which is too rigid, or which is applied too rigidly will not allow the unique characteristics of individual schools to emerge.

> " It is the nature of this kind of inspection that teachers will over-prepare because the outcome has such high stakes. "
>
> *John Bangs,*
> *Secretary, National*
> *Union of Teachers*

Specialist Knowledge

214 We have heard many concerns about the ability of inspection teams to provide authoritative judgements about specialist subjects, such as the arts, and about particular aspects of educational provision. Inspection teams do not necessarily include inspectors who are specialists in all the subjects taught in the school. In consequence it is difficult to gauge the soundness of the judgements that are put forward. Specialist inspectors are essential to ensure the reliability of inspection findings, and to contribute in expert ways to raising standards in all areas of the curriculum. The reduction in the number of HMI, and the kind of work that they now do within OFSTED, has removed the national teams of specialist HMI which were so well-informed about standards in their fields and able to carry out national inspections of particular activities with a high degree of authority. HMI have essential roles as expert judges of standards and quality, and in relation not only to school inspection, but in the broader processes of policy inspection.

Policy Inspection

215 Inspectors can only comment on what is going on in the school at the time of their visit. While in many ways this is wholly defensible, it does mean that what is inspected can be unrepresentative. OFSTED has come to have an important influence on national educational policy. Yet the national programme of school inspection is not now designed to provide a broad base of evidence on how particular policy initiatives are working out in practice. The absence of such advice can create an information vacuum for policy-makers. Inspection should be able to inform policy-makers, schools and teachers about the state of the education service so as to point to what needs to be done by whom to speed good practice and minimise shortcomings. That requires more iterative inspections, carried out by expert inspectors in relation to specific themes and issues. A particular case is the effect of the current emphasis on the core curriculum on provision for non-core subjects, and the impact on the broader curriculum of the literacy and numeracy hours.

The Whole Curriculum

216 Effective and appropriate systems of pupil assessment and of school inspection are vital to the quality of education and to raising standards. We see them as of special importance in raising standards in creative and cultural education and in making these functions of education as effective and accountable as the rest. The problems as we see them now derive from the fact that assessment and inspection are not primarily focused on the kinds of development we are advocating. The effects of this are not neutral. The practical effect is to discourage and inhibit creativity in teachers and in students. For example, following the Secretary of State's announcement, suspending the programmes of study for art, music, PE and humanities in Key Stages 1 and 2, OFSTED wrote to primary schools

In Nottinghamshire, out of 170 OFSTED reports in 1996, only three primary schools and no secondary school reports mention dance. OFSTED inspectors do not always report on everything happening in schools (eg. dance activities). Non-specialist inspectors always comment positively on dance classes where they are found, even if it is bad teaching. This is because they do not know how to assess them. The result is a limited development of dance as an art form. Dance specialists should inspect dance lessons.

Nottinghamshire Local Education Authority

to say that inspections would no longer take account of the extent to which schools followed the National Curriculum in these subjects. Some primary schools seem to have concluded that they need no longer spend much, if any, time on these subjects. Yet these processes are of vital importance from the earliest years of education if the Government's intention to promote the creative abilities of all young people are to be realised at any stage of education. The general danger we see is that an inflexible inspection framework and a prescriptive system of assessment can combine to encourage schools to play safe. As one primary head has put it to us, the tendency now is 'to keep your head above water and just below the parapet'.

Conclusion

217 Pupil assessment and school inspection have essential roles in raising standards throughout the school curriculum. Current priorities, methods and criteria now need to be sophisticated to take account of the nature and roles of creative and cultural education in raising standards. Doing so will help to create a virtuous circle in which the benefits of creative and cultural education will be more effectively realised by being more publicly recognised.

Recommendations

218 We recommend that:

i. All of the desired outcomes of the National Curriculum should be assessed in appropriate ways, including those that relate to creative and cultural education. The results should all contribute to the profile of young people's achievements and of the school's performance.

ii. There should be a greater emphasis in schools on formative assessment: ie. assessment that is intended to improve the day-to-day quality of teaching and learning.

iii. The DfEE should arrange to ease present pressures of assessment by:

  a. reducing the detail required of schools in support of assessment;

  b. training teachers to conduct formative and summative assessments supported by a national sampling scheme.

iv. The QCA should:

  a. collate existing knowledge and expertise in assessing children's creative development in each of the main areas of the curriculum, and issue practical guidance to schools;

  b. develop advice to teachers on approaches to formative assessment, particularly in relation to creative teaching and learning;

  c. develop a system of national moderation of formative assessment based on appropriate methods of sampling.

v.   The OFSTED framework for school inspection should be further developed to take fuller account of creative and cultural education and of the processes of teaching, learning and assessment it involves.

vi. OFSTED should develop its capacity to ensure that specialist areas of the curriculum, such as the arts, are inspected by specialists. In particular, there should be a greater number of specialist HMI in OFSTED to offer expert advice on specialist teaching, provision and standards.

vii. On the basis of wide-ranging inspection, OFSTED should provide the Government with the inspection-based information and professional advice it needs to develop and carry out its policies for education; to know how those policies are working out in practice and ensure a constructive link between school and policy-related inspections.

viii. OFSTED should reaffirm its commitment to inspect all areas of the curriculum, including the arts and humanities throughout compulsory education.

Part Three:
Beyond the School

8 Developing Partnerships

Introduction

219 Partnerships between schools and outside organisations and individuals are essential to the kinds of educational development we are advocating. They are not additional luxuries. Such partnerships enrich and extend the experiences of young people and support teaching and training. In both ways they can help directly to raise standards of achievement. In this chapter we identify the benefits of partnerships and the conditions for successful development.

The Opportunity

220 The National Curriculum was built on the assumption of what schools can achieve with the help of outside providers, including LEA support. Schools cannot achieve the required standards on their own. It is crucial to build on existing good practice to develop a national strategy of partnerships to support schools. Every child should have a basic entitlement to a range of partnership activities in school. This should not depend only on geographical location or the personal enthusiasms of individual teachers. The work of schools can be supported by a wide network of other partners and providers, including community groups, business, industry, and cultural organisations. By 'cultural organisations' we mean museums of all kinds - for the arts, sciences and humanities - galleries, performing arts organisations, sports organisations and other subject-based or youth organisations. There is room for a huge range of partnerships and joint projects with such organisations. Some offer one-off events to schools; others provide long-term projects or residencies. Over the last twenty years there has been an extraordinary expansion in education work by cultural organisations.

221 At the beginning of this report, we noted the rapid growth in the UK of the creative industries. There is a second area of development which is of equal significance. This is the work of artists and of other creative organisations in education and the community. This sector includes artist-in-residence schemes, children's theatre, theatre in education, education liaison programmes of major cultural organisations and community-led projects which are based in the arts and cultural activities. The UK has a leading international reputation for such work and its significance is now increasingly recognised though research and policy. The creative industries are often quoted in support of the economic case of the arts. This broader field of community education and outreach work is evidence of its social significance. We attach great importance to these programmes and initiatives and see vital roles for them in achieving the objectives set out in this report.

> " Good schools alone will never be good enough — we need communities that think differently, work differently and are even designed and built differently. Such communities would make for a better, more exciting world in which living, working, and learning come together again and recreate vibrant, self-sustaining communities. I would love to live in such a world. "
>
> *John Abbott 1997*

> " It is important that partnerships between schools, artists and galleries give access to and act as a catalyst for creative learning for young people in their transition from school to further and higher education and into independent life. "
>
> *Lindsey Fryer*

Life Options

Opt for Art is the flagship project of Engage, the National Association for Gallery Education. Whereas art galleries had succeeded in attracting large numbers of primary schools to visit exhibitions, very few pupils at Key Stage 3 were visiting galleries as an organised part of the curriculum in secondary schools. A pilot scheme was organised in eight schools in 1995 that aimed to give pupils in Year 9 an inspirational experience of art to coincide with discussions they would be having with parents and teachers about their option choices at Key Stage 4 and GCSE. The experience of art was to include a visit to an art gallery and work with an artist. Between 1998 and 2000 it will work with pupils in Year 8 and Year 9 in ninety schools. The project hopes to generate special, hopefully inspirational, experiences of real art and artists outside of school and, in doing so, promote art as a valuable life option for young teenagers. Possibly as many as 18,000 pupils will benefit directly from Opt for Art in the current phase of work. The project has thus far been developed in Wales, but is now being extended to England.

Information provided by Opt for Art

222 The roles of schools in partnerships are twofold. First, the ethos of the school itself can be enormously enriched through the involvement of the wider community. Second, schools' own resources can be of tremendous benefit to the community at large. Schools have much to offer in terms of the experience and expertise of staff and their own specialist facilities and resources, including laboratories, sports halls and performing arts facilities. Creative schools can contribute significantly to the social and economic development of the whole community. Significant sums of public money are invested in schools. The return on this investment is less than it might be because many schools are closed more than they are open. Creative partnerships between school, business and the wider community are already taking place in many areas. We need to identify and build on existing good practice to develop a national strategy of creative partnerships.

" The wealth and expertise and well-founded perspectives available within the community and beyond can be harnessed for education. Conversely, the wealth of expertise and well-founded perspectives in schools can be made available to the wider community. As a result, new syntheses of ideas and experiences can take place. *"*

CAPE UK

The Benefits of Partnerships

223 Partnerships offer different, but mutual benefits to schools, including staff and pupils, and to everyone they work with.

Benefits to Schools

Curriculum Development

224 Effective partnerships can:

* raise school morale by bringing staff together to work to shared goals, promoting collaboration in curriculum development;

* promote and develop innovative working methods;

* provide an opportunity for cross-curricular links throughout the school which demonstrate that each specialism can affect the development of others;

"
I used to think that today's art was just an excuse not to do any serious work, but now I believe it forces the person to try to understand by using their imagination.
"

Pupil after Opt for Art project

- provide opportunities for issue-based work which offers a broader perspective on current affairs and on cultural development; for example equal opportunities, gender, and cultural diversity.

The School in the Community

225 Effective partnerships can:

- strengthen the school's relationship with its community through sharing skills, expertise and resources;

- strengthen the relationships between schools in the same area through cross-phase or cross-disciplinary projects;

- raise the profile of the school and the part it plays in the social, cultural and economic life within the community;

- develop the school itself as a community by building strong and supportive relationships between students, staff, parents and governors.

The 'Poor' School's Creative Professionals in Residence Scheme
The National School's Playwright Commissioning Group consists of twenty schools around the country pulling resources together to commission a leading playwright and composer to write a play suitable for these schools to perform with music, adaptable to different musical talents and the different circumstances of the schools. By collaborating and contributing £1000 a year for two years, the schools have exclusive rights to a play and the music that they have commissioned themselves, and contributed to, through a series of cluster workshops with teachers, students and the writer and composer. Local and regional theatres give support in kind. The play is published. This scheme could be easily replicated by others and in other disciplines.

Information provided by Hampstead School, London

Staff Development

226 Effective partnerships can help teachers to:

- learn new skills and techniques for use in the classroom;

- develop professional relationships with a wide variety of other skilled adults beyond the school;

- develop and promote a wider understanding of their subject from different social and cultural perspectives;

- deepen their understanding of pupils in different social and cultural situations;

"
School life is enriched by working with these artists, who are practising in their own right, and bring a different focus. Expectations are raised and they bring tremendous energy to the work.
"

Kathy Halpenny, Headteacher, Blue Gate Fields Junior School

"
The project was very productive and I have been trying to work in a similar way — giving short bursts of quality teaching time.
"

Ruth Aplin, Rhyl School, Camden

- develop their understanding of different disciplines and how they can interact with each other;

- try out new teaching strategies.

Science Fair

Robert Smyth School, at Market Harborough, held a Science Fair in 1997 — it developed into a large event. The fair was described in the local paper, which carried a four-page supplement. This was sponsored by advertising from a number of local companies, many with a scientific basis to their operations. After seeing it in the paper, companies that did not take part at the first fair immediately asked to sign up for the next one in 1998. Judith Green, a teacher at the school and one of the prime movers for the fairs writes: "What a week! You could buy minerals or a gyroscope in the science shop, you might bump into Marie Curie or Isaac Newton, you could make slime or a hot air balloon, visit the science road show, try on the fire brigade's full protective clothing or have a go at particle physics with Leicester University. As if all that wasn't enough, how about a visit to the Science Museum, an in-house lecture on Light and Luminosity full of spectacular demonstrations — and the double-page pull-out in the local paper?"

Information obtained from the August 1997 issue of Prism.

For Pupils

227 Effective partnerships can help pupils to:

- develop their understanding of the wider community, and their roles within it;

- develop skills and techniques for creative work through contact with skilled adults;

- deepen their understanding of different disciplines and their practical application;

- develop their understanding of the key skills and how they apply to 'real-life' situations;

- deepen their understanding of, and practical experience, in the creative process, including imaginative thought, problem-solving, research, technical skills, editing, risk-taking, reflection, presentation and dialogue;

- experience working as part of a team;

- build self-confidence and self-esteem in learning new skills, meeting new people, sharing ideas;

- increase confidence and expertise in making judgements and evaluating experience with a wider range of people.

"
When I first had a try, my very first one, I was rubbish, but I got a lot better. Thank you for showing me I can play a xylophone.
"

Tracy at All Souls' School

Benefits for Outside Partners

228 There are benefits, too, for the organisations and individuals who work with schools in these ways. These include:

- sharing skills and expertise with young people and adults in a variety of new contexts;

- developing their own knowledge and skills;

- developing and reflecting on their own work and methods in new contexts;

- developing communication and teaching skills with young people and adults;

- finding stimulation for their own creative work through partnerships with other professionals and young people;

- working collaboratively with professionals in other disciplines.

> **"**
> The players have found this work not only immensely stimulating, but also beneficial to their playing in general concert work. **"**
>
> *David Pickard,*
> *General Manager,*
> *Orchestra of the Age*
> *of Enlightenment*

> **The Very Young**
> A team of artists and twenty-six Birmingham nursery schools have collaborated to produce original works of public art. This has created an exciting trail of interactive artwork around the city. Each artwork is the result of the skill of an artist in incorporating ideas of children, teachers, parents and community into works that engage the school but can also be enjoyed by the general public. An annual open day will be held on the second Friday in July each year to view these artworks, but works can also be viewed individually.
>
> *Information provided by Birmingham City Council Education Department*

Improving Partnerships

229 There are five factors that affect the quality of partnerships:

- status and priorities;

- information and liaison;

- quality assurance;

- resources;

- training and development.

We discuss the first three of these here. We look at resources in Chapter Nine and training in Chapter Ten.

Status and Priorities

230 Developing creative partnerships does not yet have high enough priority in many schools. Some have many contacts with outside organisations: others have little or none. Successful partnerships are often the result of the personal enthusiasms of particular staff. According to a MORI survey in secondary schools in 1995 (O'Brian 1996), in the five months prior to the survey:

- 50 per cent of the students had not been to a play;

- 80 per cent had not been to a museum, gallery or concert;

- fewer than one in ten had been to a dance or opera performance;

- of those who had the opportunity to go, 97 per cent enjoyed it.

All children are entitled to access to the opportunities provided by working with external professionals during each year of formal schooling. Schools should be required to make explicit provision for such opportunities in their development plans, and to allocate appropriate resources. Schools could also try to ensure that a member of the governing body is responsible for policies relating to creative and cultural education, and for ensuring that all children have such opportunities. One way of raising status is to give this work public recognition. The QCA, RSA, Arts Council, DCMS and others are developing criteria for a possible Artsmark scheme for schools and for arts organisations as a way of celebrating good practice and raising the status of arts education work. Schools or cultural organisations would be awarded the Artsmark for arts education work that is of high importance and integral to the rest of their work. This scheme has a lot to recommend it and should be taken forward.

Opportunities for All

In May 1999, Warwickshire Education Authority launched the Warwickshire Education Arts Action Zone. The roles of the Zone are:

- to co-ordinate, support and publicise existing good practice, based on the themes of creativity, additionality and inclusiveness;

- research and development to promote and extend good practice, celebrate and spread success, defend and enhance the arts in the curriculum in their own right as creative contributors to other areas and subjects;

- to inspire a programme of extended continuing professional development;

- to link with the creative ideas and aspirations of other phases in education, other agencies in public service, and other institutions;

- to enhance extra-curricular opportunities in the arts;

- to promote capital investment in the arts;

- to seek partnership funding for the arts in the authority;

- to promote partnerships in the management of the project.

A Year 5 pupil will receive a badge and certificate as a member of the Zone, and an Arts Action Pack, based on the reading programme agreed between the Education and Library services, and a programme of activities, including community outreach and networking opportunities.

Parents will learn about the Zone's work through leaflets, exhibitions and performances, county-scale publicised events, and through after-school clubs.

Information provided by Warwickshire Education Arts Action Zone

Information and Liaison

231
Effective communication is essential to successful partnerships to ensure that the needs and the expertise of different partners are compatible. The interests of the various partners are mutual but not always identical. Each partner has different contributions to make and each will gain differently in terms of skills, understanding and experience. The success of partnerships lies as much in the quality of preparation and follow-up work as in the event itself. Consequently, partnership projects must include enough time for research, planning, evaluation and dissemination. Young people too should be involved in planning and preparation. They have much to gain through this process, and much to give.

232
Many schools are simply not aware of the opportunities available. A national audit of current standards in, and provision for, creative and cultural education in schools is needed to provide a clear picture of

“
TIE is valuable in that it is a process that happens with children . . . not for them. The experience often creates a sort of tension which takes the child close enough to the precipice so that it catches a glimpse of the reality of the situation, but at a level with which it can cope. A very important part in the process of bringing the inner child out. That is education.

Bryn Davies,
Secretary of the
Powys Association of
Primary Schools
”

“
The organisation AXIS has compiled a national central registry of contemporary visual artists and craftspeople, which is available free of charge and stored on a computer database.
”

available opportunities and of specific gaps in provision. This audit should identify strengths and weaknesses in current provision, in each area of the curriculum; in different areas of the country; and in the existing patterns of partnership between schools and other providers. It should be updated on a bi-annual basis to provide a comprehensive and accumulating body of evidence to inform future policy-making. The information should be distributed on the National Grid for Learning. This could provide the basis for a regional register of opportunities to help providers and users in all sectors to make informed judgements and have clear expectations.

Young Tate, Liverpool

Whether a museum sees itself as an agent in social regeneration or as a service provider, working with young people can pay great dividends. It institutes a more responsive and outward-looking approach; broadens understanding of the contemporary significance of collections and exhibitions; and sustains the awareness of the necessity of meeting the needs and interests of a new audience. In 1993 the Tate Gallery, Liverpool formed a consultative group made up of young people. This group became known as Young Tate and it helps to advise on ways of making the gallery and its exhibitions more accessible to young people. Apart from its advisory role, one of the strengths of the Young Tate programme is the development of peer education. Young Tate members are paid a fee for leading workshops and projects for other young people in the gallery. They are introduced to the display or exhibition at planning meetings and then presented with ideas for the workshop which have been drafted in advance by the artist facilitator and the Young Tate co-ordinator. Further ideas and suggestions are then explored. At present, training for this peer-led work is informal, but work is underway to establish a more formal training programme, drawing on models of good practice within the voluntary and statutory youth services.

Information provided by The Museums Association

233 This should cover all areas of the curriculum and a variety of schemes, including one-off performances and workshops to longer-term projects and residencies. The register could be co-ordinated by the proposed Regional Cultural Agencies or by the Regional Arts Boards. One possible model is as follows:

- Outside organisations, individuals or performing groups apply to be put on the register and pay a fee to do so.

- For registration, each group or individual would put on a performance, project or session to a volunteer host school, to be assessed by a panel of the headteachers, students, teachers and the local community. The school would receive the performance, project or session free.

- The panels would assess the event according to agreed criteria and produce a short report and recommendation.

- The panel could be guided in these criteria by a regional co-ordinator.

- Groups or individuals that are accepted would be included on the annual register which is sent to all schools and onto a database on the internet.

- Groups or individuals would be reviewed every two years by a different panel.

- All schools would be asked to evaluate the project when they have a visit to their school. These evaluations would be shared with the groups and individuals.

- All groups and individuals would be expected to provide preparatory and follow-up materials.

Quality Assurance and Evaluation

234 Appropriate quality assurance systems for visiting professionals and cultural organisations are essential. The work of creative partnerships is often not thoroughly evaluated because of lack of time, funding or expertise within arts organisations and schools. The Arts Council of England has commissioned a research study to identify effective approaches to evaluation. The aim is to produce an innovative, accessible and flexible evaluation resource for use by arts organisations, individual artists, youth, education and community sectors. Once this has been developed, training courses will be provided on the use of the evaluation materials. This study could make a valuable contribution to improving creative and cultural education through partnerships. Agreed quality criteria are needed so that all partners have clear expectations, and informed judgements can be made to improve practice. The DCMS has established a new unit to evaluate and monitor educational provision by funded organisations. We welcome this development and the serious commitment to education within the DCMS that it suggests.

The Roles of Different Partners

235 In its Comprehensive Spending Review the DCMS proposed bringing together regional arts boards, arts agencies, local authorities, business concerns and other interested parties, in regional cultural partnerships. It would be possible to include local sub-structures within such partnerships to include, among others, groups of schools and LEAs, arts agencies, artists and local businesses. Each partner would have something to gain and something to give: continued active involvement with schools for LEAs; the involvement of arts and education in community development and good relations for businesses. Each partner could contribute funding and other resources, and the total activity would contribute to the vitality of education and cultural life in the locality. More importantly, such partnerships might begin to fill the gap that resulted from the decline in the involvement of local authorities in such activities. New working partnerships are now needed involving schools, higher and further education, local education authorities, local authorities more widely,

> **"** Partnerships are potentially one of the most powerful tools in securing the development of creativity in education. **"**
>
> *CAPE UK*

cultural organisations and local commerce. Such partnerships would be characterised by a mixture of altruism and self-interest that could ensure the development of activities that, to be done well, need to involve more than single or groups of schools.

Involving the Community

Based in Ulverston, Cumbria for over twenty years, Welfare State International have been developing a close relationship with their community and local schools, so that now the creativity of children, artists and townspeople are closely integrated. For example, the annual Lantern Festival each September involves scores of families who make elaborate sculptural candlelit lanterns with willow and tissue paper. The Sir John Barrow primary school makes eight gift lanterns for the town's unsung heroines and heroes and the art teacher at the Victoria High school can incorporate innovative lanterns into an A level Design and Technology course. The May Flag Festival is designed by primary school children. They invent unconventional and freely drawn images for town shops (such as sticky cakes for the bakers and wriggling worms for the anglers, or even lipstick on the collar for a gent's outfitters). Working with artists, these are sewn onto large silk banners, making Ulverston a joyous patchwork on the celebration scale between Matisse and Beano. Following a £1 million arts lottery award, WSI artists have refurbished their Victorian school headquarters to create 'Lanternhouse', a training centre in Ulverston. Here, artists, teachers and administrators may escape to recharge. Creativity is encouraged in a non-competitive and non-institutional shelter. People from many disciplines connect over conversation and coffee, and research lateral solutions. If you want to make a musical weather vane or a sand painting of giant dragon flies, sing, for the first time, play drums or mythologise the quicksands of Morecambe Bay, Lanternhouse is the place. During the building process, primary school children created a 30-metre painted hoarding round the site. Like a contemporary cartoon Bayeaux tapestry, this depicted wild street bands on stilts and even levitating welders. Children are central to Lanternhouse. Provision has been made for a créche and for a storytelling garden, and an IT and communications studio where the fast forward generation can teach adults how to go electronic.

John Fox, Welfare State International

Central Government

236 The creative and cultural development of young people is of concern to several government departments. The DfEE, DCMS, Home Office, the Social Exclusion Unit and other Government departments or agencies all include in their remit cultural activities by young people. The Department for Trade and Industry has a particular role to play, in collaboration with the DfEE, in promoting the creative and cultural development of young people through science activities. There is a need for greater co-ordination between these departments in order to promote a more coherent pattern of provision, and a more strategic use of existing resources.

Local Education Authorities

237   Since the introduction of local management at schools (LMS) the roles and services provided by LEAs have been greatly reduced. We look in more detail at the implications of this in Chapter Nine. But local education authorities still have statutory duties to ensure that schools in their area meet the terms and requirements of the National Curriculum and to improve standards and quality in education. Schools can not achieve the required standards on their own, and need to work in partnership with a variety of agencies, organisations and individuals. LEA advisory services are well-placed to facilitate dissemination of effective practice between schools. They have a key role as catalysts in establishing partnerships and encouraging relationships between schools and outside organisations and individuals. The future roles of LEAs will relate to the new settlement of the School Standards and Framework Act. In it, LEAs are charged with the new general duty 'to promote high standards'. We are arguing for an inclusive definition of high standards to include creative and cultural education.

The Youth Service

238   In recent years, both the voluntary and statutory youth service sectors have become increasingly active in promoting and supporting creative and cultural programmes for young people. These are important areas of development. The Youth Service reaches out to young people beyond the formal education sector in a wide range of different contexts: through youth clubs, community projects, festivals and visits. In many instances they do this in partnership with a variety of funding and organisational partners. Young people themselves are often closely involved in the planning and organisation of events and initiatives. We see great value in the work of the Youth Service and commend the growing variety of initiatives of partnerships that are now developing. Inevitably, provision is uneven nationally. The need now is to disseminate good practice, and to address related issues of training. We return to this issue in Chapter Ten.

Joint Arts Policy

The councils of Bournemouth, Poole and Christchurch have joined together to produce the first arts policy for the whole conurbation. It grew out of the strong conviction that the cultural needs and aspirations of residents and visitors to Bournemouth, Poole and Christchurch could best be met by the councils working together. One of the aims of the policy is to promote the role of the arts in formal and informal education with subsidiary aims such as:

- to promote education and outreach work as an integral part of programming by all arts deliverers and as an important tool for audience development;

- to raise the quality of arts education in the conurbation through recognising and promoting best practice;

- to collaborate with education services to provide arts training and resources.

The aims and objective of the Joint Arts Policy are ambitious but achievable. It provides a clear framework for the development of the arts and gives a strong incentive for a collective approach, while allowing the councils to work in individual ways where appropriate.

Information provided by the councils of Bournemouth,
Poole and Christchurch

Cultural Organisations

239 We noted earlier the extraordinary growth of interest in cultural organisations over the past twenty years or so in developing work with education. In recent years, national and regional funding policies in the arts have strongly encouraged this development. According to a survey by the Arts Council of England (Hogarth et al 1997), 78 per cent of all publicly funded arts organisations are involved with education work and 63 per cent have a dedicated education officer. There is a wide variety of models of organisation and of types of practice. These range from dedicated arts education organisations, such as theatre-in-education, to the appointment of a single education officer to an established arts organisation. At best education is fully integrated into the life and work of arts organisations, and is seen as a core function. At worst it is a reluctant add-on: a minimal provision to meet funding requirements. As often education is seen as important but peripheral to the main business of the organisation.

240 The term education itself is sometimes unhelpful in these contexts. It can carry with it connotations of worthiness and civic duty which feels at odds for some artists with the excitement that drives them. This is a pity and if the term education itself prompts a listless commitment it should be dropped. The fact is that arts organisations do not need two separate policies — an artistic policy and an educational policy. They need one: a co-ordinated and unified cultural policy. That is, they need to find ways to engage people in their work, to deepen their understanding of it; and to promote the creative response and potential of others. This is what education programmes should be for. These should be seen as core functions, not extras, whatever they are called.

241 As partners in the creative and cultural development of young people, arts organisations that are publicly funded should integrate their artistic and educational policies. The policy and development plan should clearly state what the relationships are between artists, artistic programmes, formal and informal education work with and for young people. The plan should also set targets for developing these relationships and for the development of partnerships with others including schools and colleges, youth and community agencies, training agencies and funding partners in the locality. All organisations in receipt of public funds, whatever the source, should be held accountable to deliver their educational objectives.

242 Sports clubs and organisations have important roles in the creative and cultural education of young people. The diversity and range of physical activity and sport provides pupils with many opportunities to develop a variety of skills. PE and sport are inextricably linked to cultural values and traditions. Sport also provides challenging opportunities for pupils to develop their problem-solving abilities, creative thinking, social skills, and physical prowess as part of their continued development. Sport clubs and organisations can support schools in promoting these particular skills in children and should be regarded as important allies in promoting the creative and cultural development of all young people in schools.

Arts Education Agencies

243 With the contraction of local education authorities, a number of alternative systems of provision and support for the arts in schools has begun to emerge. For example, a wide range of arts education agencies are working with schools around the country. They operate through a range of different types of partnerships between national funding bodies, regional arts boards, city council arts development units, LEAs, schools and college courses, artist and arts organisations. They vary greatly in their requirements for quality assurance and training and in the quality of services they provide themselves. It is important that the DCMS and DfEE should both monitor and support the development of these agencies through combined funding strategies, quality assurance and evaluation guidelines in order to secure quality work in schools, resource material for schools, the dissemination of good practice, project development and the training of practitioners to work in schools.

Business and Industry

244 Business and industry are valuable resources to education in a variety of ways. There is a wealth of experience and expertise within business.

II
Promoting the 'public understanding of science' has become big business. Across the world traditional science museums are reducing their historic curatorial function and vying for custom with the newer science centres set up to engage paying members of the public in a variety of investigative and 'hands-on' science-based activities. *II*

Professor Edgar Jenkins

II
The arts are important in education because they give young people access to the ideas, values and beliefs of others and contribute to all aspects of a child's development. They have been shown to feed the creative imagination and improve cognitive and academic skills. *II*

Create the Future, the Labour Party's pre-election cultural manifesto

Industry must be encouraged to share this through active engagement in education. This investment will be mutually beneficial. Ways of involving business in education include:

- experts from business and industry should be encouraged to visit schools and share their experience of the professional world with children and teachers;

- work experience placements could be provided for pupils and teachers;

- business can become involved in mentoring programmes at schools;

- members of staff from business can undertake placements in schools;

- business can share equipment with schools or to donate old stock;

- cash donations can be made to support specific creative projects of schools.

The focus here is not only on big businesses, but on medium and small businesses that could donate an hour a week to link with schools. Successful partnerships exist between some schools and private ICT firms. The firms provide the schools with up-to-date ICT equipment and training for teachers in return for the use of the facilities out of school hours to provide adult courses.

245 The organisation Arts and Business (formerly ABSA) has long experience of promoting partnerships between business and the arts in all of their forms. It has now established the Creative Forum for Culture and the Economy. This is an initiative which brings together key figures from some of the UK's leading businesses to explore ways of unlocking the latent creativity in British business. The forum in particular, and Arts and Business more generally, has important roles in taking forward the arguments and recommendations of this report in developing the roles of business partnerships in creative and cultural education.

Visiting Professionals

246 Visiting professionals in all subject areas should be encouraged to visit schools to share their experience of the world of work and to enthuse children about their chosen fields. There are many examples of professional artists visiting schools. These are important but people from many other areas of work have much to offer too. The joint DCMS/DfEE initiative, the Sporting Ambassadors Scheme, was successfully piloted during 1997-98 and is now being introduced to all the English Sports Council regions. The scheme provides opportunities for successful sports men and women of all ages to visit schools to enthuse young people about the benefits of physical activity and a healthy lifestyle. We commend this project and hope that it will be extended to other areas of creative and cultural education.

"
It is only through business partnerships that education can keep up with the development of new technologies.
"

Dame Tamsyn Imison

Aiming High

In 1995, Stoke-on-Trent Community Partnership initiated a major project to raise the aspirations and ambitions of young people in North Staffordshire. The project, called Aiming High, has involved over 5,000 students each year in a series of inspirational activities with the hope of encouraging them to achieve their full potential, whatever their abilities. The project targets Year 9 students and involves approximately thirty schools in a cross-curricular programme of events, centred around talks by inspirational speakers and a combined music and visual arts project in association with the BBC Philharmonic Orchestra. Previous speakers in the project have included Helen Sharman, Britain's first astronaut, astronomer Patrick Moore, polar explorer Dr. Mike Stroud, explorer and author Benedict Allen, and Britain's first woman to climb Mount Everest, Rebecca Stephens. The aim of these speakers is to enthuse and motivate young people to achieve their ambitions whatever their background or social upbringing. The raising of personal aspirations is considered to be of major importance in achieving a significant change to the social and cultural environment of North Staffordshire, thus contributing to long-term economic regeneration in an area that has suffered from a sharp decline in traditional industry and low staying-on rates in schools. Furthermore, bringing together local businesses and schools in a major campaign to raise awareness of the potential of young people, is aimed towards the restoration of a new pride in the city of Stoke-on-Trent.

Information provided by the BBC Philharmonic Orchestra

247 The National Endowment for Science, Technology and the Arts (NESTA) was established by the Department for Culture, Media and Sport in 1998. It will be involved in three broad activities:

a. helping talented individuals in the fields of science, technology and the arts to achieve their full potential;

b. helping turn inventions and ideas into products and services which can be effectively exploited;

c. contributing to public knowledge and awareness of science, technology and the arts.

In meeting the first objective, NESTA is about to introduce a fellowship programme, involving mentoring. It is also considering further research on approaches to mentoring. The introduction of co-ordinated mentoring programmes to young people in schools could have tremendous benefits. We strongly endorse NESTA's intentions in these fields. There is great scope to develop a mentoring programme in particular in association with other relevant agencies including the QCA.

100 Black Men is an organisation of black businessmen in the Birmingham area who go into schools to act as mentors to black youths with behavioural problems. The opportunity for these children to identify with successful black role models help improve their attitudes, behaviour and expectations in life.

Specialist Schools

248 We support the Government's initiative to identify specialist schools as centres of excellence in the specialities of arts, languages, technology or sport. Investment should be made in these centres to ensure balance across each LEA. The expertise, knowledge and facilities at specialist schools should also be made available to other schools in the area. Specialist schools already have a role to play in sharing their expertise with their local communities; this could be co-ordinated further by LEAs and the DfEE on regional and national levels.

Further and Higher Education

249 There is a huge wealth of expertise in further and higher education in all disciplines. Successful links can be forged between schools and further and higher education to support the work of the National Curriculum, to provide teacher training and to enrich opportunities for creative and cultural education. Many good examples of such links already exist. The National Grid for Learning also offers opportunities to increase access to such partnerships, as it is less resource-intensive. Virtual links should not replace real visits, but they can be used as an additional partnership opportunity.

Professional Associations

250 Many professional teacher and subject associations play key roles in supporting and enriching the school curriculum and teacher training across a range of disciplines. In art and design, for example, the National Society for Education in Art and Design is the largest provider of continuing professional development to teachers. We strongly encourage such initiatives. Professional teacher associations and subject associations also have key roles in disseminating this report and in promoting creative and cultural development through the partnerships we recommend.

Parents

251 Partnerships should be created with parents by encouraging them to share their different talents, knowledge and expertise with the school. Children need to relate their learning to the adult world in terms of work and leisure opportunities. Parents can help children to make these links by sharing information and experience in a structured way. Parents could also help teachers with pastoral care duties. Children can benefit immensely by involving parents more actively in their education. Schools could hold open weeks for parents to share their experience of the adult world and to help them understand daily school life. This serves to educate parents about the lives of their children and the processes of their education. Parents who are involved in the education of their children in a practical way will be better able to support the creative and artistic activities of their children.

> **"**
> According to a study by Barber (1995), about a third of parents said they would like more information about the curriculum and extra-curricular activities. **"**
>
> *Sharp & Cato 1998*

> **"**
> We need to make sure that parents know that they are needed as a vital component to the success of their child's education. In middle class households this is taken as a given, but it's a different story elsewhere. **"**
>
> *Lenny Henry*

Parents as Partners

As part of an initiative to promote careers education among people from varying ethnic backgrounds in Manchester, the Progress Trust publicises career opportunities at public events in a variety of locations. Action Factory conducted interviews at a careers convention at the Manchester G-Mex centre in October 1997 which were edited to create a resource for use with parents from Asian, African-Caribbean and Chinese communities. As it is considered that the biggest influence on young people's career choices comes from their parents, the Careers Service was interested to record the thoughts of parents who are struggling to make sense of the increasing variety of training and education options that are now available to young people. Parents were asked to talk about what they find difficult, what support they and their children need and to say something about the difference between their experience of choosing a career and that of their children. The resulting video, translated into Chinese by the Manchester Translation Service, was shown at an event held for members of the Chinese community. A short booklet has also been written to accompany the video.

Information provided by the Progress Trust

Conclusion

252 Schools need no longer be sole traders in education. We all have an interest in the quality of education and many people can contribute from different fields of expertise. We see these partnerships in education not as luxuries but as essential to the kind of education all young people now need. They do not happen without planning, and they often have implications for resources. In the next chapter we look at the different ways in which resources can be found.

Recommendations

253 We recommend that:

i. The development plans of schools should make explicit reference to provision for creative and cultural education, including: the patterns of provision in the formal and informal curriculum; the opportunities for contact with outside specialists, and with the community and cultural organisations.

ii. Schools should explore practical ways of developing the use of their facilities for creative and cultural education; to enrich the experience of pupils and of the wider community.

iii. Where possible, school governing bodies should designate a member to have responsibility for encouraging links between the school and cultural organisations and to have an overview of the school's policies and programmes for creative and cultural education.

iv. The DCMS in collaboration with the Arts Council and the QCA should develop:

   a. guidance on the factors that contribute to successful partnerships between schools and outside organisations or individuals;

   b. a national arts education award scheme for schools and arts organisations centred on supporting and encouraging schools and cultural organisations to improve and extend their arts education provision.

v. OFSTED and the QCA should collaborate in a national baseline audit of current standards in, and provision for, creative and cultural education in schools.

vi. The DCMS should:

   a. undertake an audit of provision for creative and cultural education in publicly funded cultural organisations;

   b. co-ordinate the development of a quality assurance system for partnerships between artists, arts organisations and the formal and informal education sectors.

vii. LEAs should specify support for school improvement in creative and cultural education in their Education Development Plans and consider making creative and cultural education one of the priorities.

viii.   All cultural organisations should develop policies and programmes which relate their work to formal and informal education. Such policies should not separate education from the main objectives of the organisation, but should recognise the need to engage with the wider community as a core objective.

ix.   NESTA should undertake research on approaches to mentoring. This work should be disseminated in collaboration with the QCA for adaptation to and widespread implementation in schools.

x.   LEAs should encourage the exchange of knowledge, expertise and facilities between specialist schools and other schools in the area.

xi.   Professional teacher associations and subject associations should:

    a.   provide opportunities to discuss the full implications of this report with their members and the ways that it will impact on teaching, learning and teacher training;

    b.   give guidance to their members on how to respond to this report in positive ways by improving creative and cultural education through their teaching and/or particular subject areas.

9 Funding and Resources

Introduction

254 In this chapter we look at the new patterns of educational funding and resources that are emerging locally and nationally. We identify problems and opportunities for the kinds of provision we are advocating.

LEA Services

255 In the past, local education authorities had wide-ranging roles in the promotion and support of young people's creative and cultural activities. The provisions of LMS have eliminated the key services in these fields that LEAs once provided. There is widespread uncertainty about the extent of available services within LEAs. An audit should be undertaken by OFSTED to address this problem. It is known, for example, that advisory services have all but disappeared in many local education authorities; peripatetic music and instrumental services have been dismantled; and provision for a wide range of essential cultural activities has gone, including support for youth theatres, orchestras and dance companies. Many LEAs have only one, if any, specialist providing educational leadership in the arts. According to a survey conducted by the Royal Society of Arts in 1995 (Rogers 1995) one third of arts advisory posts had been abolished since 1990. While posts were reduced in all curriculum areas, there was a disproportionate loss of advisers in music, PE and art. At the time of the survey, nearly a third of LEAs had no specialist advisers for music and a quarter had none for PE or art. The fourth survey of LEA Advisory and Inspection Services by NFER in 1998 (Hendy) showed that the majority of the remaining advisory staff now have a general brief, with subject specialists becoming 'an increasingly rare breed'. Of 87 LEAs responding, about one third indicated that specialist support for arts and performing arts was 'poor or barely adequate'. Co-ordinated action is needed to establish new structures of funding and resources to provide these services in new and imaginative ways. An essential starting point is to create new patterns of partnership between the government departments and funding agencies with an interest in creative and cultural education, so as to make more effective use of resources in the long term.

256 Some LEAs maintain networks for primary and secondary teachers in various subjects. Teachers value these meetings because they provide them with an opportunity to share ideas, issues and practice with colleagues from other schools. There is considerable concern that this valuable networking could be under threat from the Government's proposals for 100 per cent delegated funding of curriculum support services to schools. The DfEE should enable LEAs to employ co-ordinators or curriculum advisers for creative and cultural education, to work with schools, to ensure access to specialist advice; liaison with community

> " Curriculum work in music, dance and drama has been devastated by delegation of monies to schools and is a shadow of its former self. "
>
> *Peter Baker, Head of Arts in Education Service for Leicestershire*

groups; and co-ordination with other services provided by local government through other departments. These co-ordinators should be accountable to head teacher boards. This provision should enable active participation in creative and cultural activities as well as the opportunity to see performances, exhibitions and events and support for theatre in education and youth music groups.

> **Funding through Partnership**
>
> Twelve schoolgirls at the Stonehenge School, Amesbury produced a stage show, Communicate, to highlight issues such as bullying, racism, drug and alcohol abuse. They have been given £500 by Wiltshire Crimebeat so they can take their show to a wider audience. The cash will enable them to pay the production costs of the show and a video, which can be distributed to schools and other audiences. Production spokesman Nigel Mansfield said parents who saw the girls perform at the Salisbury Arts Centre were so impressed with the message it put across, they felt the production should be seen by as many schoolchildren as possible. The success of this project is due to partnerships with a variety of organisations from the arts, education, health and social services sector: Frontline Theatre, Amesbury Young Women's Drama Group, Artswork, Wiltshire Youth & Community Service, Salisbury District Council's Arts Unit, Southern Arts, Salisbury District Community Safety Partnership, Crimebeat, the police, social services, the probation service and county councillors.
>
> *Information provided by Artswork and The Journal*

"This partnership with LEAs should see the return to a level of provision where every child has access to the support they need."

*David Blunkett MP
Secretary of State for Education and Employment*

Music Services

257 It is important to distinguish provision for general music education within the school curriculum from provision for specialist instrumental and vocal teaching. Peripatetic music teachers are vital in the music education of young people. In order to restore music services, instrumental/vocal music teachers should have access to secure and long-term employment with opportunities for development. There are currently no quality assurance mechanisms in place to monitor and evaluate the quality of peripatetic instrumental/vocal music provision. The Federation of Music Services and the National Association of Music Educators have developed a national framework to form the basis of an instrumental/vocal curriculum. This framework aims to complement the requirements of the National Curriculum while ensuring coherence, consistency, continuity, progression and parity of esteem in instrumental and vocal tuition. Based on the National Curriculum model, it includes five programmes of study, at different levels, within which teachers can develop their own specific schemes of work. In each programme of study, statements are provided of what pupils should be taught and of what pupils should be able to do. These statements are helpful in:

- planning schemes of work for particular instruments/voice;

- identifying the focus of teaching and learning for particular lessons;

- identifying criteria for assessment; and

- providing appropriate information to pupils, parents, colleagues and schools.

The guiding principle should not be that every child should have to play a musical instrument, but that every child should have the opportunity to do so as a basic entitlement.

258 The Federation of Music Services and the National Association of Music Educators has estimated that national non-delegated funding for music services over the last ten years has declined from a level of £100 million per annum to less than £40 million per annum. The devolving of budgets may be a good thing in some areas; for music, it has had disastrous results in many parts of the country. Over the last 30 years, the LEAs had built up sophisticated services for music, all, by their nature, linked. If even a small number of schools choose to use their money for subjects other than music, as is their right, then LEA music services collapse, if not completely, then in breadth and expertise. This has happened throughout the country. The effects in many areas have included the abolition of peripatetic music posts.

259 The 1988 Education Reform Act ruled that schools could charge parents for individual lessons. The 1993 Education Act adjusted the situation by allowing schools to charge parents for group instrumental lessons, providing the group was not more than four in number. The result was that some schools absorbed the full cost and continued to offer instrumental teaching free to all pupils; others passed on part of the charge, while a few expected parents to pay the full cost. The evidence is that the trend is growing for schools to pass on a substantial part of the cost. We welcome the steps that Government is taking to address this situation. The DfEE has made £150 million available and the DCMS has offered £30 million towards the improvement of music services. Through new arrangements announced in January 1999, existing music services are to be protected, and new music services encouraged by the availability of grants through the Standards Fund. This acknowledgement of the importance of instrumental music education is very important, as is the recognition that delegation to schools is not the solution.

> Even as a middle-class kid, I could not have become a musician without the huge, varied infrastructure of music services provided by Liverpool in the 1960s.

Sir Simon Rattle

260

The arrangements introduced in 1999 have been welcomed with relief by the music education community. But some serious problems remain. First, in areas where music services have not been financed by local education authorities, grants will only be available if the authority can find 50 per cent matched funding. Second, there will remain marked disparities across the country. According to the DfEE (1999), 88 per cent of LEAs have applied to the Standards Fund on the basis that they currently run some music provision. But 'some provision' could mean a notional contribution to supporting ensemble work for example. It cannot be deduced that 88 per cent of LEAs across the country sustain significant or adequate music services since there is no complete picture of the extent, reach or quality of different services. Third, although the terms of the grants under the Standards Fund require improvements in equality of access to music services, no basic principle of entitlement to access has yet been established.

261

In addition to the action taken by the DfEE, the DCMS has established the National Foundation for Youth Music (formerly Youth Music Trust), using money from the National Lottery. The purpose of the Trust is to assist areas where music services do not exist or need to be built up. To ensure the continued survival of music services, all these strands should be brought together. Government has at last given the lead by affirming

> *"*
> 75 per cent of orchestral players would not be playing today if there wasn't free instrumental provision.
> *"*
>
> **Sir Simon Rattle**

> *"*
> Music is a vital part of every child's education and plays an important role in this country's culture. Years of underfunding have left some children without access to musical instruments or the tuition they desperately need to develop their talents. The Government is determined to reverse that decline.
> *"*
>
> **David Blunkett MP**
> **Secretary of State for**
> **Education and**
> **Employment**

the importance of musical education. This is a tremendous step forward. What is now needed is a vision of how disparate funding strands, uneven geographical coverage and standards, and differing fee structures can be made coherent and fair. We believe that in the longer term, these two departmental initiatives should be unified to create a co-ordinated, coherent system of supported musical education across the country. This could involve the formation of a national body, solely charged with the administration and funding of music services. The desire to play an instrument or sing is as strong as ever. Music has always been the pride of our nation. We need to establish firm foundations for its growth.

> ### *National Platform for Young Performers*
> Ruth Wilson, aged six, from Swansmere Primary School in Surrey played her own composition in front of an audience of 2,700 people at the Royal Festival Hall in London — twice . . . thanks to Music for Youth. An estimated 500,000 schoolchildren are actively involved in instrumental and vocal music lessons in schools. Music for Youth, working closely with all the major music teaching organisations, provides a national platform for around 10 per cent of this number each year. The number taking part in Music for Youth activities has increased from 25,000 in 1992 to 40,000 in 1997, and demand continues to grow.
>
> *Information provided by Music for Youth*

Choral Projects

262 There is growing interest in revitalising the tradition in this country of choral music. Not all children have or can play instruments, but they do have voices and they can sing with increasing pleasure and skill — with help and enthusiasm. These schemes have enormous benefits for children and their communities and, in expert hands, can help to raise standards and motivation as well. The DCMS and the DfEE could take an important lead, perhaps in association with the National Foundation for Youth Music in part-funding and initiating local choral schemes involving schools and the wider community.

Choral Singing Raises Morale

In Tower Hamlets, with an 80 per cent pupil population of Asian origin — predominantly Bangladeshi, the project ended with a singing event in Canary Wharf involving 300 pupils. This had gradually built up over three years through smaller group performances with the involvement of the Spitalfields Festival, a dynamic local permanent community arts organisation. This was another important contributor to the debates about quality. The pupils sang in up to four parts, as a whole choir and in individual school groups, sometimes unaccompanied, sometimes with a jazz orchestra. The songs were taken from many cultures, and demanded different vocal effects. The event was impressive in many ways. But the bedrock achievement for those of us privileged to have seen the progress over time lay in the fact that most of these children had effectively been non-singers before they started three years before. Standards and quality of singing are only a part of the overall intentions of singing performance. The children had an experience that was transparently unforgettable and so did the audience. They knew what they had achieved. Their teachers were enthused with their success, and were explicit about the overall benefits that had come to the children in their learning more generally. But that is not the end. The LEA is taking the singing work forward to higher standards by employing from its own resources a tutor for singing at its Saturday morning music school. It has also used the lessons of this animation project to part-fund another singing project which is explicitly linked to the LEA literacy strategy. There is a connection between all these achievements, and the challenging and mutually supportive debate about standards.

Information provided by the National Foundation for Youth Music

Funding Opportunities

263 The opportunity to visit cultural organisations - like museums, science centres or galleries - or to bring professional organisations or individuals in to school should be part of the basic entitlement of all children. A strong creative and cultural life is the key to a healthy society. Youth orchestras, youth theatres and other creative activities play a vital role in the wider community, but it is often difficult to find funding for such projects. A survey by the National Campaign for the Arts (NCA 1997) found that the average subsidy for theatre in education companies had fallen by 22 per cent in real terms over the last 10 years. 10 per cent of companies had closed. A further 20 per cent of the companies surveyed had closed by the time the research was published in 1997. Funding is required for a variety of services, including access to specialist advice, liaison with community groups, co-ordination with other services in local government, artist or scientist in residence schemes, visits to or from cultural organisations or merely for the busses to transport children to and from an event.

"I am sure my parents are thankful too that it was music and the youth orchestra which helped steer us through our teenage years so enthusiastically and safely. "

Ex-youth orchestra player

264 There is a variety of funding opportunities available to support creative and cultural education in schools and other organisations. However, these opportunities are not co-ordinated and can cause widespread inequality of access. Moreover, many funding schemes are short term whereas the problems and opportunities are long term. Schools are often not aware of all the funding opportunities available to them, not just through recent government initiatives. This problem could be eased by developing a directory of funding opportunities available to schools. This directory should be distributed to all schools in printed format and it should be made available and updated regularly on the National Grid for Learning.

Successful Funding Strategies

265 Many successful strategies are currently in place in schools and cultural organisations to raise funds or share resources. These examples should be collated and disseminated by the DfEE and DCMS. Some of the best examples include:

- self-help groups of teachers who share facilities, exchange examples of good practice and offer mutual support;

- industrial sponsorship of increased technical support and access to consumable materials in schools;

- corporate membership schemes to loan museum and gallery exhibits to businesses in exchange for funding;

- arts liaison officers in businesses who link with schools or arts organisations to offer business expertise or funding;

- a Young Person's Performance Pass which offers discounted ticketing to schools for arts events;

- arts miles schemes where schools or individual pupils get credit for attending arts events;

- trusts who give money to pupils to attend cultural events rather than giving the money to the organisations to put on the events;

- partnership schemes to cover the costs of transport for pupils to visit cultural organisations.

National Lottery

266 The Government has secured reform to the National Lottery and put significant amounts of new public money into the arts. We commend these actions. There is still scope for further action. It is still much easier to secure funding for specific projects that for longer-term developmental work. A lot of time and resources are wasted on repetitive bidding processes. A coherent system is needed that will improve sustainability and development within schools and funded organisations. The funding system should ensure that cultural organisations allocate core funds to the development of partnerships with the formal and informal education sectors and that the use of funding allocated for education work is monitored. There are many examples of successful funding schemes and strategies involving partnerships with education. These need to be widely disseminated and made accessible to other cultural organisations.

Lottery Initiatives

Many children and young people have enjoyed creative activity through Lottery awards from the Arts Council. Projects that turn scrap materials into art; create a sculpture trail in the school grounds; encourage creative use of the internet; or provide much-needed new instruments for school bands are just a few examples. The Lottery has generated enthusiasm, helped inspiration to blossom and given fun to children and young people across the country. An Arts for England (A4E) grant enabled 5-11 year-olds in Richard Atkins Primary School in Lambeth to use photography, storytelling and multi-media activities on the internet. At London Fields Schools in Hackney, a barren playground space has been transformed into a stimulating environment with sculptures and play structures, all made with the children's help.

Information provided by the Arts Council of England

---

267 Many arts organisations now only receive their grants in return for added educational components. Many feel that they are constantly being asked to produce more with less support. For those companies who see education as part of their fundamental purpose, there is a real problem. Without exception, these educational components came from idealistic impulses within the companies, provided on a shoestring out of concern for the long-term health of the arts. Whatever funds could be put aside are. But it all still costs money. Now that even the present insufficient grants will be predicated on an increased educational output, often the original function of the company can be lost sight of. In an orchestra, for instance, 75 per cent of the turnover goes on salaries — the only way to make meaningful savings is to sack the musicians, who provide the *raison d'être* of the orchestra, and who are also the in-built educational team. They cannot perform fewer concerts, without losing more revenue. The arts need to grow, not merely struggle to survive — the amount of energy spent in simply trying to survive is now the major factor in an arts organisation's life. There is a noticeable drift towards safety, the mediocre middle-road which can be a death-knell for arts. If this happens, or the central activities are weakened, badly-prepared or simply shelved, how can the educational activities supply the necessary vitamins for our children?

268 The New Opportunities Fund is investing £180 million for out-of-school-hours activities and £20 million for combined out-of-school-hours activities/childcare. The NOF is not able to enter into long-term funding arrangements, like all Lottery distribution bodies. But it is keen to support local and regional partnerships in establishing its healthy living centres, child care, and after-school programmes. It is possible for local

❚❚ No arts funding system can be complete, or even credible, without a clear line on education and training and clear ideas about how they can deliver. ❚❚

Professor Christopher Frayling, Arts Council member

❚❚ It is a great irony that, at the moment and from my perspective, much of the exciting thinking about children and creativity is being channelled towards study support clubs and out-of-hours activities rather than mainstream schooling. ❚❚

Patricia Lankester, Director, The Paul Hamlyn Foundation

partnerships which satisfy NOF criteria to gain funding for up to three years, to establish local networks that can provide for the sustainability, as well as the quality of the work. We welcome these steps, as after school clubs can provide curriculum enrichment and extension opportunities in creative and cultural development. The findings of this initiative should be disseminated and good practice exemplified so that all schools can learn from the experience of these leading after school clubs and holiday facilities. This could be a valuable opportunity for improving creative and cultural education. The DfEE document *Extending Opportunity: A National Framework for Study Support* (DfEE 1998a) provides a number of short case studies of projects. The department is also funding a three year longitudinal research project on study support. We are encouraged by these initiatives and hope that these projects will further focus on the creative and cultural development of young people.

269 Plural funding could be the answer to ancillary funds. Other partners cannot be expected to fund the basic entitlement of all children, but extra activities can be resourced through business partners, trusts, or other sources of funding. Education Action Zones involve business partners in the education of young people. Education Action Zones are test-beds for innovation; they are obviously an important - and rare - opportunity to gauge alternative approaches. There are now a number of Education Action Zones in operation and in prospect. These will need to be fully evaluated to identify new patterns of provision and the most effective models for change. Arts and Business encourages business to sponsor the arts, including arts education. A national scheme, introduced by the Government, could co-ordinate and regulate all business sponsorship of education initiatives. The feasibility of a tax incentive scheme to encourage business to provide expertise and funds for the development of creative and cultural education should also be examined.

270 From the industrialists' viewpoint, a key driving force for initiating change in education is the requirement for appropriately-trained staff for the

future. To this end, the strengthening of the links between schools and industry are vital. Industry should play a key role in both promoting the opportunities for careers in technology, and in the training of new and established teachers. Both government and industry should contribute resources to drive these initiatives. This would include not only financial provision, but providing appropriate equipment and teaching aids, and a role in co-ordinating initiatives nationally.

271 There is a clear gap in understanding between industrialists and teachers over the requirements of industry for our trained technology students. Some industrialists do not understand the scope of what can be achieved in schools. It is critical that the technology syllabus is accurate, up to date and relevant to current industry practices. In order for teachers to teach technology creatively, they must keep up-to-date with developments in industrial technology. While some schools do have excellent links with local industry, the fact that these are locally driven and funded dilutes their national effectiveness. A number of initiatives are needed to bridge the gap. These should be locally organised, but centrally funded and directed through government. They could include attachments from schools to industry and vice versa, 'Teach the Teacher' schemes, Partnership Centres, resident specialists, and so on.

New Technologies

272 Schools have to be in a position to access fully the new interactive television services that will become available this year on all three digital television platforms and the internet. The DfEE are about to award a major contract to a broadcaster to deliver around 1,000 hours of GCSE-linked programming from September. Pupils and teachers will need the digital equipment, television and computer, to access this new channel and the BBC Learning Channel. The BBC has developed the Learning Channel as a broad-based learning service which would embrace life-long learning, skills training and some schools' programming. The corporation has said that if it were successful, it could incorporate programmes on English, French, mathematics, geography, science and history within existing plans. In the very near future, convergence will offer teachers a genuine opportunity to harness the information revolution to both inform and inspire pupils. We want to encourage all schools to take full advantage of these materials. It

is important that these technologies are made available and used as a medium of expression and communication in schools. We are therefore encouraged by the Government's drive to connect all schools to the National Grid for Learning.

273 We need to build on existing knowledge to make the best use of technology for creative and cultural purposes. The implementation of the National Grid for Learning is a step in the right direction, but it will not necessarily lead to creative uses of the technology. The potential value of technological advances is not just in using the devices and applications themselves, but also in creating new ways of learning and working where the technology is a catalyst for innovative thinking as well as a medium for communicating and developing new ideas and artefacts. The contribution of the creative media industries to creative and cultural education could have many positive implications in schools. This too will need to be co-ordinated nationally. Organisations like BECTA could play a leading role in this process.

274 Growing numbers of children now have access to a computer at home; our schools must not lag behind. Computer literacy is vital for anyone now entering the world of work and preparing for individual life. Lack of basic computer skills will condemn young people to be deprived, both of vital information and of new forms of art and entertainment that will, in future, be delivered by television and the internet. We commend the partnership initiative between schools and business recently announced by the Tools for Schools charity[1] and hope that this work will be taken forward. This new organisation plans to supply thousands of new and refurbished PCs to all state schools at a nominal price. All computers will be Year 2000 compatible.

Conclusion

275 The introduction of local management of schools has radically effected systems of support for creative and cultural education. Patterns of provision now vary widely throughout the country. New forms of partnership are needed, with support and advice from central Government, including more strategic use of new funding, information on good practice and guidance on quality assurance.

Recommendations

276 We recommend that:

i. OFSTED should conduct an audit of LEA provision for creative and cultural development, including advisory support, music services, youth music groups and theatre in education.

ii. The DfEE should enable LEAs through the Standards Fund to employ co-ordinators /curriculum advisers for creative and cultural education, accountable to head teacher boards, to work with schools, to ensure access to specialist advice; liaison with community groups; and

---

> **"**
> Technology is a bridge to content, not a destination.
> **"**
>
> *Lord Puttnam of Queensgate*

co-ordination with other services provided by local government through other departments.

iii. The DCMS and DfEE should establish a mechanism and formula to:

  a. provide all schools with dedicated funds for creative and cultural programmes and activities;

  b. to provide local education authorities with dedicated funds to co-ordinate provision for creative and cultural programmes and activities.

iv. The model framework developed by the Federation of Music Services and the National Association of Music Educators should be taken as the basis for a national strategy to ensure coherence, consistency and progression in instrumental and vocal music tuition.

v. The DfEE and the DCMS should take action to ensure long-term provision of a single national system of music services after the interim arrangements of the Standards Fund. This system should provide:

  a. peripatetic music services which are available to all young people on the same payment basis with remission for those on low incomes;

  b. local services to create and update stores of instruments for loan.

The Youth Music Trust should be developed to complement this national system.

vi. The Government in association with the Youth Music Trust should initiate and part-fund local schemes for choral music involving schools and the wider community.

vii. The DfEE and the DCMS should develop a directory of funding opportunities available to schools, and collate and disseminate examples of successful funding strategies. This information should be printed and made available on the National Grid for Learning.

viii. The DCMS should extend the funding programmes for the development of the creative industries to support partnerships and joint projects with education.

ix. The DCMS should:

  a. establish a coherent system for long-term funding for the development of education programmes by cultural organisations;

  b. ensure that cultural organisations allocate core funds to the development of partnerships with the formal and informal education sectors;

  c. ensure that the use of funding allocated to cultural organisations for education work is monitored.

x. Good practice in after school clubs should be disseminated by LEAs to encourage all schools to consider the opportunities for creative and cultural development of pupils as part of their extended provision.

xi.   The Government should examine the feasibility of a tax incentive scheme to encourage business to provide expertise and/or direct funds for the development of creative and cultural education.

xii.   The Government should:

   a. explicitly encourage the creative uses of new technology through The National Grid for Learning;

   b. support traditional libraries with a virtual library in every school, with access to dedicated databases and general information banks;

   c. set as its goal not just the provision of a computer and an internet/intranet connection in every school, but the provision of a PC to every pupil and teacher's desk;

   d. provide hardware and software to ensure that every pupil leaving school has had opportunities to explore the creative possibilities of new technologies.

xiii.   Existing national programmes for the development of computer software to support creative and cultural education should be co-ordinated in such a way as to support the wider needs of education in all sectors.

10 Training People

Introduction

277 Teachers are the most important resources in education. They must be well trained and motivated. The new arrangements for initial teacher education and the existing priorities for continuing professional development present some serious difficulties for creative and cultural education. In this chapter we look at the implications of our arguments for the training of teachers and of other professionals involved in creative and cultural education.

"
Teachers affect eternity; no-one knows where their influence stops.
"

Anon

Initial Teacher Training

278 The Government has in hand a wide-ranging programme to raise the quality of initial teacher training (ITT). There are four central elements to the current policy: a national curriculum for initial teacher training, national standards, school-based teaching and the national framework for inspection. We strongly support the drive to raise overall standards of teacher training, and to promote closer relationships between the profession and the training institutions. The national standards bring clarity to the task of teacher education and set out systematic criteria for student development and assessment. We strongly support the need for extensive school-based experience as part of teacher training programmes, and the involvement of classroom teachers as mentors to students in training. But these new arrangements do present some serious difficulties for the promotion of creative and cultural education of student teachers, and, by implication, of the children they eventually teach. As with the National Curriculum for schools, the ITT National Curriculum is likely to prove over-full and congested. Providers of teacher education, like teachers in schools, are increasingly required to teach to the test and have little room for dialogue, debate and creative work with students. If the creative potential of student teachers is ignored, it is unlikely that they will be able to promote the creative and cultural development of pupils

National Standards

279 In 1997, the Government introduced national standards for initial teacher training. These standards relate to new course requirements for teacher training and, for the first time, to a prescribed National Curriculum for initial teacher training in English, mathematics, science and information technology. Trainee teachers are now required to cover, in detail, the National Curriculum for these subjects. Primary trainees are also required to identify a specialist subject. This could be one of the existing core subjects. For the reasons we have given throughout, it is essential that English, mathematics and science should contribute to creative and cultural education and that teachers should be trained accordingly. As it is the standards make only passing references to promoting children's creative and cultural development.

"
Problems exist where teachers are not educated in the cultural and creative arts. The potential of the child is overlooked. Children's abilities are underestimated.
"

Mildred Dodds, teacher

280 There is a further problem. In the existing standards there are no detailed requirements relating to the arts and humanities at all. Unless students choose an arts or humanities subject as their specialist study, they need not study the arts and humanities in any detail at all during initial teacher training. The prospect is that future generations of primary school teachers can qualify to work in schools with only a minimal understanding of the arts and humanities in education. These disciplines are at risk in schools from all the pressures we have identified. The new danger is that the National Curriculum for teacher education threatens even the supply of teachers in these disciplines.

Extending Teacher Training

Some children's potential is only limited by our own expertise. As a musician I can encourage/develop children's potential, resulting in our school orchestra of over fifty children — of whom most reach grade 3, 4 or 5 on their instruments. Unfortunately I had no training in dance — I don't know where to start — my staff is similarly untrained! Primary schools need the resources to employ experts. What bliss it would be to have sufficient funding to employ an expert for half a day a week for the arts — a mere £4,500 would do. All of our extra resources support special needs children which has to take priority. Too much funding goes on special projects. The experts are often drawn in for a short-term project and yes, they create a splash. But after they've gone the staff is really none the wiser, the children certainly cannot cope without guidance, and the standard of work reverts to type. We need in-depth staff training not the occasional day here and there. Let my school teach to its strengths. Until the day comes when I have a staff equally qualified in all ten areas of the curriculum let us teach to our strengths, do it well and enable children to reach their potential. We object to the power of inspectors telling us that our expertise in certain areas of the curriculum is deficient. Was it my fault that in my own education I was deprived of dance? I hope the committee remembers that teachers are a very willing group of people. We really want to do our best for the children in our charge but we cannot lead children where we have never been ourselves.

Judith Graydon, Parish C of E Primary School

281 A study published in November 1998 by the Royal Society for Arts on the arts in teacher training (Rogers 1998) says that there is widespread evidence that teacher training institutions are:

- abandoning specialisms in arts subjects;
- cutting back the hours allocated to the arts;
- losing access to vital resources such as facilities, equipment and staffing.

Institutions report that they have five major challenges:

a. avoiding further cuts in time for specialisms in the arts;

b. coping with inadequate staffing and other resources;

c. finding suitable placements for students in schools which have good arts provision;

d. ensuring good quality mentoring for students while in schools;

e. providing teachers with opportunities for in-service training in the arts.

282 The national picture is mixed, both by region and by discipline. The problems are more acute in primary training than in secondary, since secondary training is based more on subject specialisms. According to the RSA study, students on primary teaching courses often receive little or no experience of the arts. Nine out of ten surveyed felt that they spend too little time on the arts during training. Over half the student teachers do not teach dance during their school placements, over a third do not teach music. The majority of students feel the teachers they work with in schools lack experience, subject knowledge and confidence in teaching the arts. Many newly qualified primary teachers have little confidence in teaching the arts, especially in drama and music. A declining minority of institutions offer specialist training in one or more of the art subjects — art, music, dance and drama. On current Government plans, only 14 per cent of newly qualified primary teachers will have specialised in an arts subject. Provision for arts teaching is thus facing severe adversity.

> **"** Any course option which gives a high priority or profile to the arts is likely to run against the grain of the national prescription and will require an act of commitment by the university to see it through. **"**
>
> *Departmental head at HEI*

The specialist PGCE music course for primary school teachers at the University of East Anglia will no longer run after this academic year. East Anglia is a rural area. The PGCE music students brought activities into schools that they had not hitherto experienced. The University of East Anglia's education department brought in outside artists to work with students, and while there, these artists gave open lunchtime performances, which were enjoyed by students of other disciplines. The artists sometimes visited local schools, teachers became enthused by these musical influences and started to think about training to be recognised as subject specialists under the TTA's new scheme. Had this cycle continued, it could have perpetuated a musical culture in the schools where the students were placed. That cycle is now broken and the cultural impetus is gone.

283 Like schools, teacher training institutions are free to provide more comprehensive programmes in the arts and humanities if they wish. But they are faced with a complex equation of providing for the existing standards, teaching the National Curriculum for the core subjects, and preparing the students for school experience in 50 per cent of the course time available. Moreover, if the institutions are judged by OFSTED inspections not to be meeting the standards, they risk being de-accredited. In these circumstances, as in schools, the pressure is to play safe: to do what is required but no more. As with the National Curriculum, the standards focus on the core subjects. There must be compatibility between the two National Curricula if the one is not to frustrate the other. It can also not be reasonably expected of newly qualified teachers to teach the arts and humanities with insufficient training in these areas. Many generalist teachers shy away from teaching arts subjects like music, because of a lack of confidence. Appropriate modules in these subject areas during teacher training could bolster teachers' confidence to teach all areas of the curriculum well.

Developing Teachers' Own Creativity

In 1997, a teachers' and artists' collaborative was established, driven by the conviction that the current intense focus on education, welcome as it must be, does not adequately consider the creative needs of teachers. The acute demands made on teachers by the education system, with its emphasis on grades, performance and league tables, means that there is little time or opportunity for them to realise their creative capacity. Tandem seeks ways in which teachers, working with experienced practitioners, may be afforded space and time for their own self-expressive, creative work. Actual practice of an art is not only a source of infectious excitement, discovery and renewal, but really the only source able to animate and inform with authority and empowering confidence. One teacher who attended a Tandem course summarised this project as follows: "I saw the mention in the TES and rang immediately to check it really was for *me*, and not for 'how to do it' tips [...] if as teachers we aren't creatively and imaginatively alive/enlivened, we can't create, imagine and inspire, i.e. we can't teach. We can deliver, inform, police, but *not teach*. Tandem is the first initiative that I've come across that recognises the centrality of teachers' creativity to their role in education, and then combines that recognition with the understanding that practitioners are the best people to nourish and develop that creativity."

Information provided by the Extension Trust, Tandem Project

School-Based Work

284 All programmes of initial teacher training are now conducted in close partnership with schools and involve classroom teachers as mentors to students in training. Almost half of the initial teacher training programme now takes place in school. There are benefits in this process. But not all schools have the subject expertise nor the skills in enabling creative development that students need if they are to become competent in these areas. Primary schools in particular often lack subject expertise in arts disciplines. This problem is likely to be compounded under the new arrangements. There is no requirement for the higher education institutions to provide courses in arts and humanities: many students will find themselves in schools where mentors feel inexpert in these disciplines. We anticipate a spiral of decline in arts and humanities teaching, driven by the combined effects of the current National Curriculum and the new teacher training standards.

Inspection Framework

285 The new framework for inspecting standards in teacher training relates closely to the structure of the national standards for teacher training and the new course requirements. It identifies clear criteria and a system of grades against which the competence of institutions to provide teacher training is judged and to which their funding and allocation of student numbers is related. The inspection framework makes little reference to the areas of development with which we are concerned.

Recruitment

286 There are particular problems of recruitment to secondary teacher training. Providers are unable, year on year, to recruit to target in secondary science, mathematics, modern foreign languages, music and technology. There are also signs of a downturn in subjects that have traditionally recruited well, such as English, religious education, music and geography. At present only primary teaching and secondary history, art and PE are able to fill their places relatively easy. Student recruitment for arts subjects in secondary schools is worsening. According to the RSA report on teacher training, in 1997/98, art under-recruited by 7 per cent, music by 18 per cent and design and technology by 41 per cent. Final estimates for 1998/99 show further deterioration: art is under target by 18 per cent, music by 18 per cent and design and technology by 46 per cent.

Proposals for Development

287 In the same way that schools have been encouraged to bid for specialist college status on the basis of expertise in different disciplines, teacher training institutions should be invited to bid for specialist status on the basis of their own major expertise. A network of national centres of excellence in the arts, sports, humanities, sciences and technology would provide a focus for resources, for initial training and for continuing professional development. Such centres of excellence could provide a focus for the accreditation of continuing professional development for adults other than teachers.

> **"**
> Nadine Senior, a teacher whose knowledge, encouragement and inspiration motivated a whole generation of young people. Through the teaching of dance she helped shape the lives of many, including my own. Dance provided a medium for us to use our imaginations, communicate, express and devise our own work. We felt we could achieve and that we had something relevant to contribute to our peers, school, community and beyond. Dance gave us a hook upon which to hang the rest of our learning; without it many of her students would not be here to substantiate this story.
> **"**
>
> *Dawn Holgate*

288 Teacher training programmes should include introductory courses on working in partnership with museums, galleries, theatres and other professionals. Many teachers are not aware of the tremendous benefits of working in partnership with outside cultural organisations and artists. We have discussed these benefits to teachers, pupils and schools in Chapter Eight. There is a growing professional network of education officers in cultural organisations and subject associations who could help to provide such courses, and in doing so, promote their own professional development and networks within education. If the doors to these partnership opportunities are not opened for teachers during teacher training, it may remain locked forever, to the detriment of the pupils.

Training of Head Teachers

289 The key figure in any school is the head teacher. The head teacher affects the style, quality, enthusiasm and tone of the whole institution. Where a head teacher is driven by particular enthusiasms, they are reflected in the programmes of work and patterns of achievement in the school as a whole. The Government has rightly identified the need to support the professional development of head teachers at every level. The newly developing qualifications for head teachers will do much to support this process. All head teachers should be made aware of the importance of:

- creative and cultural education;

- methods of curriculum planning;

- timetabling training and resourcing to achieve this.

These requirements should be built into the head teacher's professional training qualification. An inevitable response to such proposals may be a concern about overload. We emphasise our overlying argument in this report that creative and cultural education are not additional requirements that should be attached to the work of schools. They represent a fundamental dynamic in raising standards and improving the effectiveness and quality of education throughout the curriculum. We see them as an integral part of the process of staff development, especially for head teachers.

Continuing Professional Development

290 Before the introduction of local management of schools, local education authorities were able to provide extensive programmes of staff development through the advisory and support services. The introduction of LMS has effectively removed this source of training. Nevertheless, continuing professional development is a vital element in raising overall standards of teaching and achievement in schools. The gap is being filled for the moment by professional and subject associations and other groups The major proportion of government funding for continuing professional development (CPD) is directed to the National Literacy and Numeracy Strategies and to ICT. We have commented elsewhere on the importance of these strategies, but also that they should not overwhelm all other priorities in schools.

291 Programmes of continuing professional development are increasingly being provided by higher education institutions. The credit accumulation transfer scheme enables teachers to accumulate professional qualifications on the basis of stepped programmes of professional development. These initiatives should be built upon and nationally co-ordinated by the DfEE and TTA. Recognition through accreditation for courses completed can improve teacher morale and help to improve standards of creative teaching and learning.

292 Teachers' professional development is a multi-million pound industry. This includes funds from central government, through the TTA to training providers in the higher education and private sectors, and through the DfEE's Standards Fund to LEAs and schools; from Training and Enterprise Councils (TECs); European Commission grants, and independent providers. Some areas of the curriculum are subsidised more than others for continuing professional development.

293 The Standards Fund is the biggest provider of money for continuing professional development of teachers. The total budget of the Standards Fund was £550 million last year and it has been increased to £900 million for 1999-2000. Although not the full amount, a large proportion of money is allocated to in-service teacher training as this is deemed the best way to improve standards. Thirty priorities have been identified for particular grants in 1999-2000 through the Standards Fund. Not one of those priorities are focused on creative and cultural development in general nor on the arts, humanities or creative teaching or thinking skills in particular. The only current priority which is broad enough to encompass these areas is one focused on general school improvement.

294 The TTA has £21.1 million available for award-bearing in-service teacher training. The TTA lists ten priorities for its INSET funding, four of which are general enough to be used for arts-related training — the priorities for specialist teaching in primary schools, for enhanced subject knowledge for primary teachers, and for teaching early years children and 14 to 19 year-

> " The reduction of INSET provision — via LEAs and nationally — is one of the great losses of the past few years. "
>
> *Patricia Lankester, Director, Paul Hamlyn Foundation*

> " Agendas in education are perceived by many to have become very restrictive, too often associated with academic achievement and examination results taking increasing precedence over wider educational needs. This has resulted in a mirrored narrowing of teacher training, both initial and in-service. Teachers teach to the tests: teachers are taught to teach to the tests. "
>
> *CAPE UK*

olds. However, analysis of the funding bids for the three years 1998-1999 to 2000-2001 shows that of the 79 institutions bidding for TTA funds, 33 were successful — of which eight intended to run a range of award-bearing INSET or CPD courses of course modules in the arts. Only about one per cent of the estimated student numbers for all the TTA-funded courses at the 33 institutions are allocated to courses or modules on art, music, dance or drama.

295 Just as schools have a responsibility towards their pupils to provide a broad and balanced school curriculum, headteachers and senior management teams have a responsibility towards their teachers to provide a broad and balanced programme of CPD. We need a teaching force which recognises and promotes creative and cultural education. Earmarked funding through the standards fund for training courses in thinking skills, creative thinking and creative teaching in all subjects would ensure that the importance of creative and cultural education will not be overlooked in the continued professional development of teachers. It is equally essential that initial training and CPD provides fully for training teachers to address issues of multiculturalism and of anti-racism in all disciplines. The arts, in particular, are regularly absent from the categories eligible for grant aid that embraces the professional development of teachers through the Standards Fund and the TTA INSET funds. They have to operate by stealth through other areas.

Adults Other than Teachers

The Training of Artists

296 Visiting artists and others have enriched the curriculum in hundreds of schools, and for thousands of young people. Supporting their involvement in education and providing appropriate training is essential. From a training point of view these programmes are in double jeopardy. The training of primary school teachers no longer carries a requirement for sustained work in the arts. The training of artists does not usually include any reference to education. The training of artists is predominantly focused on particular conceptions of professional practice: the concert platform, the public gallery, the professional stage. Yet in the last twenty-five years, the roles of artists have diversified enormously through work in education, community and social projects of every sort. Artists have many contributions to make to cultural development, and there are many ways in which they can make them: in schools, through community programmes, through placements in industry, through work in institutional settings and special programmes.

297 It is estimated that 80 per cent of all music conservatoire students are involved in education work within two years of graduating, yet their training still does not prepare them sufficiently for this challenge. If a scheme was introduced for artists to spend one year of their training in a variety of educational settings, this problem could be addressed.

Participation in such a scheme should be by application and should carry a stipend and exemption from tuition fees for that year. This will also serve to raise the profile of education work within the arts sector. Some successful schemes are currently in place for linking music conservatoires and teacher training institutions, for example the link between Manchester Metropolitan University and the Royal Northern College of Music and between the Institute of Education (London) and Trinity College London. These initiatives should be closely monitored and expanded.

298 New models of training should be developed for artists in education which offer venue-based practical training, a mixture of accreditation options and residency planning. Current models of collaboration between cultural organisations and HEIs, such as the one between the Birmingham Royal Ballet and West Hill College could be taken forward into the field of continuing professional development, involving partnerships with schools and local authorities. The Birmingham Royal Ballet provides degree-level studies for dancers in the company. The degree programme is modular and was developed jointly with West Hill College of the University of Birmingham, which teaches the course. Over two years members of the company can study for the degree of BPhil Ed and can progress to a masters programme. Good practice in this area should be exemplified and built upon.

299 Our proposed centres of excellence for providers of initial teacher training could involve links with a wide network of cultural organisations, and collaboration with the proposed regional cultural agencies identified in the Department for Culture, Media and Sport's Comprehensive Spending Review. There are many thousands of professional people who could make sustained and expert contributions to the creative and cultural education of young people. These possibilities need to be further investigated through a number of publicly funded pilot projects, involving cultural organisations and education providers to investigate practical ways of training teachers and other professionals to work in partnership.

> **"**
> Artists working, or wishing to work in education, need to learn a lot more about the ways that schools work, how subjects are organised and their teaching and structured evaluation processes.
> **"**
>
> *Kate Burnett, artist*

Accredited Teaching Assistants

300 Given the mounting problems of teacher supply and recruitment, partnership strategies need to be developed to provide Accredited Teaching Assistants in the field of creative and cultural education. These strategies would provide a valuable resource to education while, at the same time, opening up new fields of professional development and fulfilment for very many highly qualified and trained professionals in other fields. It would build on the Government's intentions set out in the 1998 Green Paper on teacher training (DfEE 1998c), to work with LEAs and the relevant agencies to develop an overall training framework for teaching assistants. However, our focus would be particularly on assistance in the area of creative and cultural education.

Youth Workers

301 Creative and cultural activity seldom features in the training of youth workers. It is assumed that those entering training bring with them interests and enthusiasms to which the theory of practice of youth work can then be added. There is considerable scope to develop a more secure training curriculum for youth workers, introducing them to the roles and benefits of creative and cultural activities. Resources could also be shared, by hosting joint training sessions on creative and cultural education for teachers and youth workers.

Peripatetic Teachers

302 In Chapter Nine we argued that peripatetic music teachers should be recognised as equal partners in the music education of young people. There are few accredited training courses for instrumental/vocal music teachers. A post-graduate diploma in music teaching in private practice has been introduced by the University of Reading and the Incorporated Society of Musicians to provide musically-qualified instrumental and vocal teachers with a training in teaching methods. It is a practical, modular 2-4 year distance learning course. Cornwall LEA is also currently running a pilot scheme where by peripatetic music teachers can train for qualified teacher status. Such programmes could provide a model for wider development to improve the educational skills of professionals other than teachers.

Education Officers

303 The increasing involvement of cultural organisations in education has given rise to the need for training in education. There is some training for museum and gallery educators provided through masters courses such as at the University of Leicester, but there is currently no undergraduate training for education officers or managers in cultural organisations. At present, people either come from an arts background or an educational background. Once in the job, they then have to learn about the other dimension of their work. The work of education managers is multi-dimensional, and there is an urgent need for accredited training that gives equal weight to cultural and educational issues. We are encouraged by the actions that the DfEE has taken to start addressing this issue, by giving grants for training opportunities in this area. The scale of this initiative should be extended.

Conclusion

304 The new provisions in initial teacher training pose serious threats to the future development of creative and cultural education in general, and of the arts and humanities in particular. Urgent action is needed to secure a continuing supply of trained teachers in these fields and to raise the standards of expertise among all teachers, both in initial and in service training. New strategies are also needed to draw on the experience and expertise of specialists other than teachers, both through initial training and through new programmes of continuing professional development. New partnerships should be established between higher education and cultural organisations. Action is needed to improve the quality of training for youth workers to promote the creative and cultural development of young people at all levels.

Recommendations

305 We recommend that:

i.   The Teacher Training Agency should develop the course requirements, standards and National Curriculum for initial teacher training:

   a. to promote the importance of creative and cultural education in all disciplines;

   b. to promote parity between the arts, sciences and humanities in the training of primary school teachers.

ii.   All primary students should be required to take substantive courses in all subject areas of the National Curriculum.

iii. The DfEE should take urgent action to assess and remedy the decline in the numbers of teacher training institutions offering specialisms in the arts and humanities in the training of primary school teachers.

iv.   Immediate attention should be given to improving the pool of specialist expertise available to trainee teachers through mentors, higher education institution staff, and through other professionals to ensure that the training they receive in the arts and humanities is equivalent to that for other National Curriculum disciplines.

v.   The DfEE, the TTA and OFSTED should establish a mechanism for providers of initial teacher training to bid to become centres of excellence in different specialisms. This status should be supported by additional funding and facilities.

vi.   The TTA should ensure that The National Professional Qualification for Head Teachers addresses the importance of creative and cultural education, and methods of curriculum development and evaluation.

vii. Continuing professional development offered by higher education institutions should be further developed in collaboration with partner schools. Practice-based research should be encouraged by enabling teachers to enrol on postgraduate and masters degree courses devised for this purpose.

viii. The DfEE through the Standards Fund, and the TTA through its funds should ensure earmarked funding for continued professional development in the following areas by identifying them as priorities for support:

    a. creative teaching and learning;

    b. creative thinking skills;

    c. the arts and humanities;

    d. teaching for cultural understanding.

ix.   The DCMS and the DfEE should:

    a. establish a national programme of advanced in-service training for artists, scientists and other creative professionals to work in partnership with formal and informal education.

    b. fund a number of pilot projects involving cultural organisations and education providers to investigate practical ways of training artists and teachers to work in partnership.

    c. establish a national scheme to allow arts students to take an intercalated year in schools as part of their first degree programme.

x.   Higher education institutions and cultural organisations should develop partnerships to provide accredited programmes of continuing professional development for artists and other specialists working in education.

xi.   Training programmes for professional artists should include courses and placements to prepare students for work in education and community projects.

xii.   The DfEE should establish a new category of Accredited Teaching Assistant to supplement expertise in schools in the field of creative and cultural education. Qualifications should be provided through consortia of higher education institutions and cultural organisations.

xiii.   The training of youth workers should include courses on development and management of creative and cultural programmes.

xiv.   The TTA and the QCA should develop accredited professional qualifications for instrumental/vocal music teachers.

xv.   Further training opportunities need to be developed for arts educators in the museum, gallery and performing arts sector, giving equal weight to cultural and to educational issues.

Part Four:
A National Strategy

Looking Ahead

306 We began this report by welcoming the Government's commitment to the creative and cultural development of all young people. We have argued that these are essential priorities if education is to meet the many challenges it now faces. We have defined our understanding of the roles of creative and cultural education. We have analysed the opportunities and problems in current provision as we see them and as they have been presented to us through our research and consultations. We have emphasised the need for balance in national policy, in the structure of the curriculum, in teaching methods, in assessment, in the relationships between schools and other agencies and in training of people. Overall, we have attempted to think through the implications in principle and practice of a genuine national commitment to realising the creative potential of young people and of developing their cultural knowledge and understanding.

307 Promoting creative and cultural education is not a simple matter. It will involve a gradual review of the styles, purposes and ethos of education at many levels. We believe that this is not an option but a necessity. The world of the twenty-first will be unlike any we have known. If we are serious in our intentions to prepare young people to move confidently in this world, we have to look at it face on. The best we can do is to develop the capacities of young people as fully as possible, so they will be equipped for whatever futures they do meet.

308 In the future, fare more than the past, education will be shared enterprise. It will not stop at 16, or 18 or 21, as it has done for the majority, but will be continuous and open-ended. It will be provided not only by schools and colleges, but by businesses, commercial organisations, new technologies, by artists, scientists, other professionals and the community at large. The Government has a pivotal role in creating a vision for education and in setting a course. For this reason, many of our recommendations are addressed directly to the Government. But education is a collaborative enterprise, and many others must lend their resources and expertise. For that reason, our recommendations are addressed to many other agencies and organisations. Clearly, these proposals cannot all be implemented at once. In relation to the National Curriculum we have indicated those that call for immediate action and those to be implemented in the medium term. But we believe that the case for change is strong, and the need for action is urgent. We began by identifying three general priorities. Our detailed recommendations for each of these are as follows.

Detailed Recommendations

Objective One: The School Curriculum and Assessment

To ensure that the importance of creative and cultural education is explicitly recognised and provided for in schools' policies for the whole curriculum, and in government policy for the National Curriculum.

The Whole Curriculum

Action by Schools

1 Head teachers and teachers should raise the priority they give to creative and cultural education; to promoting the creative development of pupils and encouraging an ethos in which cultural diversity is valued and supported.

2 The development plans of schools should make explicit reference to provision for creative and cultural education, including: the patterns of provision in the formal and informal curriculum; the opportunities for contact with outside specialists, and with the community and cultural organisations.

3 Head teachers should conduct an audit of the quality and nature of opportunities for creative and cultural education for all the pupils in their schools, including the balance of the curriculum in all Key Stages.

4 School plans for staff development should include specific provision to improve teachers' expertise in creative and cultural education.

5 There should be a greater emphasis in schools on formative assessment: ie. assessment that is intended to improve the day-to-day quality of teaching and learning.

6 Option systems at Key Stage 4 should be designed to maintain breadth and to avoid narrow specialisation.

Revising the National Curriculum for September 2000

Action by the DfEE

Rationale

7 The rationale for the revised National Curriculum from 2000 should make explicit reference to the necessity of promoting the creative and cultural education of all young people. In relation to creative and cultural education it should specify:

a. the knowledge, skills and values which young people should acquire;

b. the principles of organisation of the National Curriculum to facilitate these outcomes;

c. the principles of teaching and learning through which they will be realised.

8 In its overall structure and in the specific programmes of study and attainment targets, the revised National Curriculum should be based on six principles: breadth, balance, relevance, parity, entitlement and access. The Government should reinstate the requirement to follow the full National Curriculum in the core and foundation subjects in Key Stage 1 and 2.

Flexibility

9 The pressures on schools should be reduced by ensuring that the National Curriculum programmes of study, and the requirements for assessment and reporting can be accommodated within 80 per cent of the ordinary school timetable. The statutory requirements should specify the entitlement of young people in each of the subject areas, and the criteria for attainment and assessment. Schools should have increased freedom to devise patterns of curriculum provision to meet these requirements.

Assessment

10 All of the desired outcomes of the National Curriculum should be assessed in appropriate ways, including those that relate to creative and cultural education. The results should all contribute to the profile of young people's achievements and of the school's performance.

11 The DfEE should arrange to ease the present pressures of assessment by:

a. reducing the detail required of schools in support of assessment;

b. training teachers to conduct formative and summative assessments supported by a national sampling scheme.

Action by the QCA

Curriculum Development

12 The QCA should:

a. disseminate successful models of curriculum organisation and timetabling that promote creative and cultural development within and between the main subject areas;

b. develop non-statutory guidance for creative teaching and learning for each subject and attainment target of the National Curriculum;

c. ollate examples and curricular materials of positive uses of the literacy and numeracy strategies in creative and cultural education in primary schools.

These materials should be made available on the National Grid for Learning and through other media.

Assessment

13 The QCA should:

a. collate existing knowledge and expertise in assessing children's creative development in each of the main areas of the curriculum, and issue practical guidance to schools;

b. develop advice to teachers on approaches to formative assessment, particularly in relation to creative teaching and learning;

c. develop a system of national moderation of formative assessment based on appropriate methods of sampling.

Creative Thinking

14 The QCA should:

a. undertake an evaluation of existing techniques and programmes promoting creative thinking skills and creative problem solving;

b. establish pilot projects to develop practical programmes and techniques for promoting creative thinking in primary and secondary schools, and formulate advice to schools.

Action by OFSTED

15 OFSTED should reaffirm its commitment to inspect all areas of the curriculum, including the arts and humanities throughout compulsory education.

16 The OFSTED framework for school inspection should be further developed to take fuller account of creative and cultural education and of the processes of teaching, learning and assessment it involves.

17 OFSTED should develop its capacity to ensure that specialist areas of the curriculum, such as the arts, are inspected by specialists. In particular, there should be a greater number of specialist HMI in OFSTED to offer expert advice on specialist teaching and provision and standards.

18 OFSTED and the QCA should collaborate in a national baseline audit of current standards in, and provision for, creative and cultural education in schools.

19 On the basis of wide-ranging inspection, OFSTED should provide the Government with the inspection-based information and professional advice it needs to develop and carry out its policies for education; to know how those policies are working out in practice and ensure a constructive link between school and policy-related inspections.

Revising the National Curriculum beyond September 2000

Action by the DfEE

Structure and Balance

20 The DfEE should put in place a more fundamental review of the structure and balance of the National Curriculum beyond 2000. Within this review full consideration should be given to achieving parity between the following discipline areas throughout key stages 1-4 as a matter of entitlement:

- language and literacy;
- mathematics and numeracy;
- science education;
- arts education;
- humanities education;
- physical education;
- technological education.

In order to achieve parity, the existing distinction between core and foundation subjects should be removed.

21 Provision for creative and cultural education in early years education should be further developed, in particular through provision for the arts.

22 The structure of Key Stages 3 and 4 should be reviewed. Reducing Key Stage 3 to two years (11-13) and increasing Key Stage 4 to three (13-16) would increase the vitality of Key Stage 3 and the opportunities for depth of study and choice in Key Stage 4. The curriculum of Key Stage 4 should be designed to maintain breadth and avoid narrow specialisation.

23 A thorough investigation should be undertaken into possible redefinition of the school day and year.

Objective Two: Teaching and Training

To ensure that teachers and other professionals are encouraged and trained to use methods and materials that facilitate the development of young people's creative abilities and cultural understanding.

Action by Government

24 The DfEE should:

a. take urgent action to assess and remedy the decline in the numbers of teacher training institutions offering specialisms in the arts and humanities in the training of primary school teachers.

b. establish a new category of Accredited Teaching Assistant to supplement expertise in schools in the field of creative and cultural education. Qualifications should be provided through consortia of higher education institutions and cultural organisations;

25 The DCMS and the DfEE should:

a. establish a national programme of advanced in-service training for artists, scientists and other creative professionals to work in partnership with formal and informal education;

b. fund a number of pilot projects involving cultural organisations and education providers to investigate practical ways of training artists and teachers to work in partnership;

c. establish a national scheme to allow arts students to take an intercalated year in schools as part of their first degree programme.

Action by the TTA

26 The Teacher Training Agency should develop the course requirements, standards and National Curriculum for initial teacher training:

a. to promote the importance of creative and cultural education in all disciplines;

b. to promote parity between the arts, sciences and humanities in the training of primary school teachers.

27 The TTA should ensure that The National Professional Qualification for Head Teachers addresses the importance of creative and cultural education, and methods of curriculum development and evaluation.

28 All primary students should be required to take substantive courses in all subject areas of the National Curriculum.

Action by Higher Education Institutions

29 Immediate attention should be given to improving the pool of specialist expertise available to trainee teachers through mentors, higher education institution staff, and through other professionals to ensure that the training they receive in the arts and humanities is equivalent to that for other National Curriculum disciplines.

30 Continuing professional development offered by higher education institutions should be further developed in collaboration with partner schools. Practice-based research should be encouraged by enabling teachers to enrol on postgraduate and masters degree courses devised for this purpose.

31 Higher education institutions and cultural organisations should develop partnerships to provide accredited programmes of continuing professional development for artists and other specialists working in education.

32 Training programmes for professional artists should include courses and placements to prepare students for work in education and community projects.

33 Further training opportunities need to be developed for arts educators in the museum, gallery and performing arts sector, giving equal weight to cultural and to educational issues.

34 The training of youth workers should include courses on development and management of creative and cultural programmes.

Joint Action

35 The DfEE, the TTA and OFSTED should establish a mechanism for providers of initial teacher training to bid to become centres of excellence in different specialisms. This status should be supported by additional funding and facilities.

36 The DfEE through the Standards Fund, and the TTA through its funds should ensure earmarked funding for continued professional development in the following areas by identifying them as priorities for support:

a. creative teaching and learning;

b. creative thinking skills;

c. the arts and humanities;

d. teaching for cultural understanding.

37 The TTA and the QCA should develop accredited professional qualifications for instrumental/vocal music teachers.

Objective Three: Partnerships and Resources

To promote the development of partnerships between schools and outside agencies which are now essential to provide the kinds of creative and cultural education that young people need and deserve.

Funding and Resources

Action by Government

38 The DfEE should enable LEAs through the Standards Fund to employ co-ordinators /curriculum advisers for creative and cultural education, accountable to head teacher boards, to work with schools, to ensure access to specialist advice; liaison with community groups; and co-ordination with other services provided by local government through other departments.

39 The DCMS and DfEE should establish a mechanism and formula to:

a. provide all schools with dedicated funds for creative and cultural programmes and activities;

b. to provide local education authorities with dedicated funds to co-ordinate provision for creative and cultural programmes and activities.

40 The DfEE and the DCMS should develop a directory of funding opportunities available to schools, and collate and disseminate examples of successful funding strategies. This information should be printed and made available on the National Grid for Learning.

41 The DfEE and the DCMS should take action to ensure long-term provision of a single national system of music services after the interim arrangements of the Standards Fund. This system should provide:

a. peripatetic music services which are available to all young people on the same payment basis with remission for those on low incomes;

b. local services to create and update stores of instruments for loan.

The Youth Music Trust should be developed to complement this national system.

42 The Government in association with the Youth Music Trust should initiate and part-fund local schemes for choral music involving schools and the wider community.

43 The model framework developed by the Federation of Music Services and the National Association of Music Educators should be taken as the basis for a national strategy to ensure coherence, consistency and progression in instrumental and vocal music tuition.

44 The DCMS should:

a. establish a coherent system for long-term funding for the development of education programmes by cultural organisations;

b. ensure that cultural organisations allocate core funds to the development of partnerships with the formal and informal education sectors;

c. ensure that the use of funding allocated to cultural organisations for education work is monitored.

45 The Government should examine the feasibility of a tax incentive scheme to encourage business to provide expertise and/or direct funds for the development of creative and cultural education.

Action by Local Education Authorities

46 LEAs should specify support for school improvement in creative and cultural education in their Education Development Plans and consider making creative and cultural education one of the priorities.

47 Good practice in after school clubs should be disseminated to encourage all schools to consider the opportunities for creative and cultural development of pupils as part of their extended provision.

48 LEAs should encourage the exchange of knowledge, expertise and facilities between specialist schools and other schools in the area.

Action by OFSTED

49 OFSTED should conduct an audit of LEA provision for creative and cultural development, including advisory support, music services, youth music groups and theatre in education.

Developing Partnerships

Action by Government

50 The DCMS should:

a. undertake an audit of provision for creative and cultural education in publicly funded cultural organisations;

b. co-ordinate the development of a quality assurance system for partnerships between artists, arts organisations and the formal and informal education sectors.

51 The DCMS in collaboration with the Arts Council and the QCA should develop:

a. guidance on the factors that contribute to successful partnerships between schools and outside organisations or individuals;

b. a national arts education award scheme for schools and arts organisations centred on supporting and encouraging schools and cultural organisations to improve and extend their arts education provision.

52 NESTA should undertake research on approaches to mentoring. This work should be disseminated in collaboration with the QCA for adaptation to and widespread implementation in schools.

53 The DCMS should extend the funding programmes for the development of the creative industries to support partnerships and joint projects with education.

Action by Schools

54 Schools should explore practical ways of developing the use of their facilities for creative and cultural education; to enrich the experience of pupils and of the wider community.

55 Where possible, school governing bodies should designate a member to have responsibility for encouraging links between the school and cultural organisations and to have an overview of the school's policies and programmes for creative and cultural education.

Action by Cultural Organisations

56 All cultural organisations should develop policies and programmes which relate their work to formal and informal education. Such policies should not separate education from the main objectives of the organisation, but should recognise the need to engage with the wider community as a core objective.

Professional Teacher Associations and Subject Associations

57 Professional teacher associations and subject associations should:

a. provide opportunities to discuss the full implications of this report with their members and the ways that it will impact on teaching, learning and teacher training;

b. give guidance to their members on how to respond to this report in positive ways by improving creative and cultural education through their teaching and/or particular subject areas.

New Technologies

Action by Government

58 The Government should:

a. explicitly encourage the creative uses of new technology through The National Grid for Learning;

b. support traditional libraries with a virtual library in every school, with access to dedicated databases and general information banks;

c. set as its goal not just the provision of a computer and an internet/intranet connection in every school, but the provision of a PC to every pupil and teacher's desk;

d. provide hardware and software to ensure that every pupil leaving school has had opportunities to explore the creative possibilities of new technologies.

59 Existing national programmes for the development of computer software to support creative and cultural education should be co-ordinated in such a way as to support the wider needs of education in all sectors.

Appendices

Patterns of Provision

a.   The School Curriculum

a.1.   Our research and consultations provide evidence of significant concerns about the provision for creative and cultural education in many areas of the curriculum. The following information has been compiled using three different sources.

   i.   the statutory provision for each subject or area;

   ii.   the OFSTED view based on inspection data;

   iii.   issues that have been raised through our consultation process by subject specialists in each area. This is not a comprehensive list of issues in each area, but it includes some of the subject specific issues that are not dealt with elsewhere in the report.

The Arts

a.2.   *Art*

   i.   Art is a statutory subject to all pupils in Key Stages 1-3, although from September 1998 the details of the Programmes of Study are not statutory and could be locally determined.

   ii.   According to OFSTED, progress in art is good or very good in one third of primary schools. In secondary schools, progress improves through Key Stage 3 and 4, and post-16 pupils make better progress in art than in any other subject. However, assessment is weak in art compared with most other subjects, and only a small proportion of schools use the end of key stage descriptors.

   ii.   There are concerns about the definition of the subject. Visual arts specialists generally argue that the subject should be named art and design, and include craft activities. Currently, art teaching has a strong fine art emphasis, and design and technology a strong manufacturing one. The National Curriculum has imposed a prescriptive model of art education which emphasises technical skill at the expense of creative and conceptual innovation. In art, especially at Key Stages 3 and 4, there is very little craft and design. The curriculum focuses predominantly on drawing and painting. Cutbacks in specialist trained staff, increased student-staff ratios and timetabling constraints are placing a strain on art and design teachers.

a.3.   *Drama*

   i.   Drama is not a separate subject, but subsumed within the English curriculum, which is compulsory for all pupils in Key Stages 1-4.

ii. OFSTED inspections suggest that too few schools teach drama. Drama receives little attention in primary school inspection reports, but such references as there are confirm its importance. In Key Stages 1-3 provision for drama is poor because of its low status and low levels of funding. Objectives are unclear, teachers lack confidence in teaching it, and practice varies between classes in the same school. Many secondary reports make no reference to drama. Where it is seen, progress improves slightly at Key Stage 3, and then considerably at Key Stage 4, primarily through its popularity as a GCSE course. The 1996-97 OFSTED report acknowledges that "good teaching ensures that pupils have a clear understanding of drama as a separate art form", but the 1997-98 report states that "in English, drama is often under-represented and the contribution it makes to speaking and listening skills varies greatly".

iii. Drama is the fastest growing GCSE subject, apart from business studies. The place of drama in the curriculum is an area of much discussion among specialists. Overall, they agree that it belongs in an arts curriculum, rather than in English. Drama is a powerful way of addressing social issues with young people, and of developing powers of communication and of working in groups. In general, the potential of drama in social education is not adequately harnessed by schools. There are concerns that too little drama is done for its own sake, as an art form in its own right.

a.4. Dance

i. Dance is subsumed within physical education. PE is compulsory throughout Key Stages 1-4, but dance is optional after Key Stage 2. The relaxed requirements for Key Stage 1 and 2 make dance optional throughout compulsory education.

ii. According to OFSTED, dance is taught in most primary schools, and although achievement varies, it is generally well taught in Key Stage 1 and 2. Its inclusion in the programme of activities is often highly dependent on the confidence and knowledge of individual teachers. Dance is provided for the majority of girls at Key Stage 3, but is less frequently available for boys. In primary and secondary schools continuity is often broken, with consequent lack of progression in attainment.

iii. The position of dance within PE has provided short-term security for the discipline, but long-term lack of teachers and too little emphasis on the artistic nature of dance. Most dance specialists would prefer to see dance as an entitlement within an arts curriculum. Alternatively, the title of physical education (PE) should be changed to physical education and dance. The QCA has changed the name of the post responsible for this subject accordingly. Dance has an important place within youth culture. Education is not drawing enough on that wider culture.

a.5. Music

i.   Music is compulsory in Key Stages 1-3.

ii. OFSTED inspections show that for several years, music has been one of the best taught subjects in primary schools. The National Curriculum has resulted in a considerable increase in the amount of music being taught in primary schools. The quality of teaching in Key Stage 3 is improving, and is already very high in Key Stage 4. There is often a lack of continuity in pupils' experience of music, which means that they do not consolidate their knowledge, understanding and skills.

iii. There are problems of equality of access: geographically, economically and in relation to gender and ethnic minorities. Music provision now depends more and more on the enthusiasms of individual teachers than on any principle of entitlement. The United Kingdom offers an unparalleled range of musical activities, both amateur and professional. This range is the envy of our European colleagues, despite a continual diminution of resources and a historical lack of attention by successive governments to music education. Certain trends need to be reversed and some services need to be reinstated if a crisis in music education is to be prevented. Early identification of gifted children or specific talents should be encouraged and supported. There is often a mismatch between the predominantly classical music culture of schools and young people's own musical preferences. There are concerns that the standard of singing is poor in relation to performance and composition.

a.6. Media Education

i.   Media education is subsumed in English, not a discrete area in the National Curriculum.

ii. Not inspected by OFSTED.

iii. Current provision for media education is based on the minimal National Curriculum requirement. It is under-resourced and there is a lack of formal training for teachers of media education, especially in the practical aspect of media work. Only 3.3 per cent of time in GCSE English is devoted to this area. This compares poorly with international models, for example, Australia, where the arts is one of eight areas of learning, and within the arts, media education is clearly identified as one of five subject strands. According to the British Film Institute, there is a wide split between analytical study (critical work) and the development of creative skills through practical work in media education. This is primarily due to the cost and complexity of media production technology.

Technology

a.7. Design and Technology

   i.   Design and technology is a compulsory subject from Key Stages 1-4.

   ii.   OFSTED data indicates that, although achievement continues to improve slowly — particularly in Key Stage 3 — overall achievement remains lower than for other subjects with the exception of information technology. Pupils' skills in making things are often better than their ability to design. Low attainment and slow progress are often associated with teachers' lack of subject knowledge and expertise and by their low expectations of both the most and the least able pupils. OFSTED recognises the continuing need for in-service training.

   iii.   The Crafts Council emphasises that for many schools, the design and technology National Curriculum requires an unrealistic breadth and depth of teacher knowledge. The current Orders do not specifically mention creativity, nor creative activity. Within the creative activity of designing and making there are many opportunities for cultural activities, but these are only infrequently grasped, particularly with older students, due to pressures of generating assessment evidence. Design and technology is intended to provide young people with the opportunities to respond creatively to the challenge of designing and making products. There are opportunities for a broad creative response in which they decide on the overall nature of their design, and on what it will be used for, who will use it and where it could be sold.

a.8. Information Technology

   i.   Information technology is a statutory subject from Key Stage 1-4. In January 1998 the subject became de facto part of the core curriculum as the only foundation subject with compulsory programmes of study to teach.

   ii.   According to OFSTED, the spread of attainment and differing rates of progress, both within and between schools, are wider in information technology than in any other subject. This relatively new subject continues to present the greatest challenge to primary schools despite the heavy investment nationally. One in three schools in Key Stage 1 and half of all schools in Key Stages 2-4 fail to comply with statutory requirements. Achievement in information technology continues to lag behind that of other subjects. At present, too few teachers are qualified to teach this subject and are expected to teach a wider range of technologies than those in which they are adequately qualified. They are expected to teach to an inappropriately large class for such a 'hands on', practical based topic.

   iii.   Centrally co-ordinated funding is required to ensure that teachers continue to be prepared to teach the subject. It may be that due to the specialised nature of information technology it should be resourced regionally, with highly qualified teachers covering more than one school for a given technology. Assessment methods must be developed which better reflect the creative element of the students' work. Students' work is usually assessed individually. However, the development of team working skills is seen as invaluable by future employees. This approach to problem solving is not given sufficient weight at primary or secondary level. Work at secondary school often duplicates that at primary level. The introduction of project-based work at this stage would ensure that the basic grounding in information technology learnt at primary level is built on. Students are increasingly familiar with the use of the Internet, and this should be exploited with industry contributing to the information available. The opportunities for careers in information technology must be actively promoted from Government through industry, and into colleges and schools.

a.9. Science

i. Science is a statutory subject for Key Stages 1-4 with compulsory testing at the end of Key Stages 1-3.

ii. OFSTED reports show that pupils' achievement in science is better than in most other subjects. Progression between Key Stage 1 and 2 and between Key Stage 3 and 4 is often not well co-ordinated: tasks set for children often fail to build on previous learning and little new knowledge is encountered. Work in experimental and investigative science is often narrow, carried out to a format prescribed by the teacher.

iii. The National Curriculum does not support approaches which see science as a creative and imaginative activity. The curriculum is content based and does not encourage creativity; neither does it provide sufficient opportunities for children to develop an understanding of the history of science and the role of different cultures. It does not sufficiently acknowledge the approaches, or roles of different cultures in science. Primary schools have few problems in linking the arts and science in spite of the National Curriculum. For example, children have an opportunity to watch theatre groups introduce science through drama, often helping to make difficult scientific concepts more accessible to them. Science based theatre is an approach which teachers know about and are willing to use, even with restricted school budgets. Science is sometimes recorded creatively, through painting, poetry and role-play. Where children and young people are offered opportunities to link science with the creative arts the results can be very positive and offer pupils the opportunity to view science from different and often unique perspectives. At secondary level, the divide between science and the arts still remains. In the past students were either arts or science. Students who combine science and arts subjects are still the exception rather than the norm, although there is evidence that these barriers are being broken down.

a.10. Humanities

i. Both history and geography are statutory foundation subjects from Key Stages 1-3.

ii. Pupils' progress in geography does not compare well with other subjects, but in history, in more than one quarter of schools pupils' progress is good or very good and the proportion of schools where pupils underachieve is lower for history than for almost all other subjects. Geographical skills are insufficiently practised and consolidated within investigations in Key Stages 1 and 2.

iii. There are grave concerns about the impact of the relaxation of the National Curriculum on humanities subjects at GCSE and A Level. The contribution of the humanities to creative and cultural development is not sufficiently recognised. Most people can see how the humanities can link with creativity, but too few think of them as creative. Yet, for all the strictness of the disciplines, that essentially is what the humanities are. The humanities offers an understanding and an interpretation of human behaviour. The creative process allows for imaginative activity in making and interpreting connections. These skills can help young people to make sense of their environment and past. There is a deeply-rooted sense in which people identify 'their' culture in terms of the past and/or their surroundings.

a.11. Physical Education

i. Physical Education is a statutory requirement for all children in Key Stages 1-4, although the programmes of study are currently suspended.

ii. OFSTED reports that progress in physical education is generally satisfactory or good in about three in ten primary schools and GCSE courses have a positive effect on levels of attainment at Key Stage 4. Short modular programmes, often found at Key Stage 3, limits pupils' progress.

iii. The contribution of physical education to creative and cultural education needs to be more clearly defined. While concentrating on the physical development of children, PE and sport are inextricably linked to cultural values and traditions. An ability to abide by the rules, co-operate with others, play fairly, and applaud a good performance, are sporting conventions which make for law abiding and committed citizens. PE and sport help to reinforce the concept of self-worth within an individual through improved personal performance linked to an increase in knowledge and understanding of one's own quality of performance. The diversity and range of physical activity and sport provides pupils with many opportunities to experience different forms of physical, emotional and social expression. In dance and gymnastics there is a close association with the notion of creativity and æsthetic appreciation, whilst in games the competitive team approach provides opportunities for individuals to share success or failure in a controlled, safe environment. The varied nature of PE and sport provides challenging opportunities for pupils to develop their problem-solving abilities, creative thinking, social skills, and physical prowess as part of their continued development within society. A minimum entitlement to physical education should be guaranteed for all pupils in all schools, along with appropriate training for teachers. A national strategy for sport is lacking. A more co-ordinated approach to the accreditation of sports coaching in all activities should be sought, together with a strategic overview of how national governing bodies of sport can work more effectively and cohesively, both together and with the PE professions, schools, teachers and parents.

a.12. Religious Education

i.   Schools are required to teach religious education (RE) at Key Stages 1-4, but syllabuses are locally determined.

ii. According to OFSTED reports, achievement in religious education has shown an improvement in recent years. There are now fewer schools where pupils underachieve; however, good standards are less common than in most other subjects. In Key Stage 4 in particular, progress in many schools is limited by the lack of time available for the subject, the lack of expertise of many non-specialist teachers and lack of challenge and imagination.

iii. Religious Education in schools has been gradually changing over the past quarter century or so to accommodate religious and secular pluralism. The subject has increasingly been concerned with issues of multi-culture and has shifted from a single religion and rather textual focus, to a concern to a concern with religious and cultural diversity. The shift from a primarily textual approach has generated a variety of approaches to using the arts as a means to enhance religious education, ranging from performance or other forms of artistic practice as a means to spiritual or religious expression to a study of artistic works within religious traditions as a means to understand religious language and feeling. There are several concerns within the RE community in relation to creative and cultural education: that policies on cultural education and development, should take a wide view of 'culture'; the concentration on literacy and numeracy at Key Stage 1&2 could inhibit creative developments in RE; that the introduction of new fields, including citizenship, should acknowledge the importance of the contribution of RE; and that work on spiritual, moral, social and cultural development should fully involve Religious Education.

b   Teacher Education

b.1.   The information in this section mainly represents the official OFSTED and TTA views on teacher training. Comments from the RSA report on teacher training in the arts is also included, as well as some additional information from the consultation. As indicated in Chapter Ten, current provision in teacher training can have far-reaching effects on creative and cultural education. It is therefore important and helpful to know what this current provision entails in each subject area.

Art

b.2.   There are 30 providers of the Postgraduate Certificate in Education in art in England. There are currently about 1000 trainees, of whom about 70-80 per cent go into full-time employment as teachers. Most courses recruit a high calibre of trainee; many are mature students who have engaged in a range of different, but relevant, experiences of the subject, including a number who have previously worked professionally as designers and in various capacities as community artists. Completion rates are good but statistical monitoring is of variable quality.

b.3.   Training in art is predominantly of good or very low quality. The proportion of courses with serious weaknesses (3.7%) is very low. Strengths in the training are the distinctive quality of many of the subject mentors in schools and the model which they provide of good studio and classroom practice. Subject tutors are very good at drawing on the range of talent and experience which the trainees bring with them and challenge individuals to extend their own range of skills and understanding. They also provide a very good lead for trainees in demonstrating how to plan, monitor, display, discuss and assess the work of pupils in the secondary age-range. A small minority of courses have some weaknesses in co-ordination across the partnership.

b.4.   No significant weaknesses were found in the subject knowledge and understanding of the trainees. A high proportion of art courses have good or very good grades in this area of the standards. In planning, teaching and class management, the majority of the art trainees at one course in four are very good and very few courses have a significant minority of only adequate trainees. Planning for progression is a particular strength, though in a few courses progression from Key Stage 2 could be better understood. Trainees show imagination in recognising the needs of individual pupils. The teaching is very often sensitive, confident and challenging. Time and physical resources are managed well, but trainees have limited access to ICT facilities for art in partner schools. Standards are also unusually high in monitoring, assessment, recording, reporting and accountability. The trainees know how to assess pupils' work against the National Curriculum and how to help pupils build up personal portfolios. They provide comment and feedback to individuals, have a good understanding of reporting procedures, and understand the external standards used to judge pupils' work at GCSE, A-level and in vocational courses.

Dance

b.5.   Physical illiteracy is a problem in both schools and teacher education. Too many pupils, and consequently too many of those entering the teaching profession, find difficulty in achieving control and subtlety, moving with sensitivity, exploring, exploiting and understanding the dynamic quality of the movement itself. They find the control of tension and relaxation, clarity and precision in movement, difficult. Too many prospective teachers have limited ability to observe and report intention and meaning, cause and effect, in the movement of others. The circle of deprived physical literacy is thus reinforced.

b.6.   There is an acute lack of teacher training in dance education and a great need for trained specialist teachers in primary schools. Many students are not allowed to do PGCE courses with dance, so they have to do PE courses with a total of 6 hours dance training. It is often difficult for dance PGCE students to find jobs, because schools prefer PE specialists. PE should not be the only training route to dance education. The short-term focus should be on INSET training for dance and the funding to resource it. The opportunity of providing INSET training through ICT should be pursued, as there is currently funding available for ICT development. The dance education sector should not miss the opportunity to establish a place in the National Grid for Learning. Many PE teachers, especially male, are nervous of teaching of dance. Although the PE link can be positive for boys, some male PE teachers are patronising towards dance. Proper training could remedy this situation.

Drama

b.7.   There are 7 secondary PGCE courses offering specialist training in drama. All are being inspected by OFSTED, but so far only one inspection has been completed. Evidence from inspections conducted 4 or 5 years ago suggests that good provision is being offered in at least some of them. From a training point of view, the picture is quite encouraging. Furthermore, evidence suggests that newly qualified teachers (NQTs) are getting jobs and there are sufficient specialist posts available to absorb the number of NQTs available. The TTA is considering whether it should require PGCE drama courses to cover the ITT NC (Initial Teacher Training National Curriculum) for English as well as drama. While most, if not all, drama courses include some training in the teaching of English (reflecting the statutory place of drama within the National Curriculum Orders for English) there is anxiety amongst providers at the prospect of delivering the full ITT National Curriculum for English as well as providing specialist training in drama. Their concern is that this could lead to the demise of specialist drama courses, and consequently have a major impact on the delivery of the subject in schools

Music

b.8. There are 25 providers of PGCE secondary music training in England. The geographical spread of provision leads to clusters (eg. London and South East), and deserts (eg. East Anglia). There is a number of well-established, good courses with full-time tutors, sometimes teams of tutors who provide ITT, in-service teacher training courses (INSET), and also higher degrees in their institutions. However, there are other courses where music is staffed by a part-time tutor who is only responsible for the secondary PGCE and where staffing seems vulnerable and isolated from the institution's overall provision. There has been under-recruitment on almost all courses, perpetuated this year. Music became a shortage subject in 1998-99. There are relatively few students from conservatoires on PGCE courses. There are eight conservatoires nationally, and only London, Manchester and Birmingham PGCE courses are attracting conservatoire graduates.

b.9. Overall, students are well qualified, committed and strong candidates for teaching. However, undergraduate courses are variable — too variable — in their ability to provide a secure foundation for a career in music education. Graduates show an over-emphasis on solo performance study, with a lack of versatility. In particular, many have had little or no training in music technologies, vocal work, composition or world music repertoire. These latter are essential as we approach the millennium. Where students do have strengths in these, they adapt well and quickly to the demands of the National Curriculum, particularly in Key Stage 3. Most students have done GCSE themselves, but the newer elements have not yet penetrated A level or degree courses.

b.10. Partnership between HEI and school music departments relies often very heavily on very small numbers or even single members of staff in schools, which places a heavy burden on mentors. In some regions, HEIs have difficulty in finding sufficient departments of quality for training placements.

b.11. Training in music is good or very good in over four-fifths of courses, but a few courses have significant or serious weaknesses. Those providers which audit musical knowledge, but also provide opportunities to extend and apply it during the course tend to provide training of good quality. Central training sessions, including those involving visiting tutors and mentors, are almost always better than subject training which takes place in schools. Mentors bring many strengths to courses, but most need to have a clearer understanding of the standards as they relate specifically to planning, teaching and managing the music curriculum. On about two-thirds of courses, trainees' planning and teaching are good or very good. However, in one course in three, a significant minority of trainees need to improve, particularly in their teaching in Key Stage 3 when pupils are organised in groups and participating in complex practical workshops.

Design & Technology

b.12.　There are 42 providers of D&T courses in England. Most courses do not attract high numbers of applicants and are unable to meet their target set by the TTA. Over a third of providers are only adequate in their admissions policy and selection procedures. Many recruit trainees from a broad range of degree backgrounds, often poorly matched to the requirements of the National Curriculum in D&T.

b.13.　The quality of D&T training is improving. Two-thirds of courses provide good or very good quality training. However, the proportion of very good training courses is comparatively low. In a third of the courses, significant improvements are required to bring them up to a good standard. Significant weaknesses include low-quality training in the school-based elements of courses, lack of sufficient subject enhancement, and a lack of training in trainees' specialist D&T fields, particularly in food and textile technology. In a minority of providers, some weaknesses in the training are found where staff have not kept up with current developments in the subject, or lack rigour and challenge in their teaching.

b.14.　Trainees' knowledge and understanding are good in just under three-quarters of providers, and, in one case, the majority of the trainees were very good. However, just over a quarter of courses have a significant minority of trainees with only adequate subject knowledge. Three-quarters of courses equip their trainees to plan, teach and manage the D&T curriculum to a good standard, and in one course, the majority of the trainees were very good in these respects. However, few trainees are outstanding, and a quarter of providers produce trainees a significant minority of whom have only adequate planning and teaching skills.

b.15.　Just under half the providers were graded good on their trainees' monitoring, assessment, recording and reporting of pupils' progress and achievement, but none had sufficient numbers of very good trainees to be graded very good. There are significant weaknesses in the standards achieved in this area in just over half of the D&T courses inspected, a higher proportion than in most subjects.

English

b.16.　There are currently 73 training courses for secondary English teachers across the country. Most courses successfully meet the recruitment targets set for English by the TTA and recruit high calibre trainees. Selection procedures are mostly good or very good. Further improvements are required, in a minority of partnerships, in the rigour of selection tasks, particularly to assess the quality and accuracy of applicants' use of English. The training provided by schools and tutors is good or very good in 80 per cent of courses. Strengths exist in the range of approaches covered and training for classroom management. However, training in planning needs sharpening in a significant number of courses, as do arrangements for meeting the diverse range of training needs of trainees. Insufficient time is given to preparation for teaching basic literacy skills on a significant number of courses.

b.17. Trainees in most partnerships achieve good or very good standards in the subject knowledge required to support effective English teaching. Trainees' planning, teaching and class management are at least good in almost all courses. However, one important area in which a significant minority of trainees have shortcomings is the clarity and precision of their planning for pupils' progress in relevant skills, knowledge and concepts.

b.18. Trainees' standards in monitoring, assessment, recording, reporting and accountability are at least good in most courses. However, more consistency is required in the assessment and recording of pupils' performance in speaking, listening and reading, with assessment better used to inform planning and evaluation.

Geography

b.19. There are 42 geography teacher training courses across the country. Admissions policies and selection procedures for geography courses are generally of very high quality and a good number have several outstanding features. High calibre trainees are recruited and there is a very high level of completion and award of teacher status. However, geography is now a shortage subject and not all courses met their target numbers for 1997-98.

b.20. The quality of training and assessment of trees is good or very good in seven out of ten geography courses. However, in two courses, both training and assessment were poor. A distinctive strength in the training is the outstanding quality of much of the teaching by geography tutors. There are also some tutor partnerships where excellent co-operation between mentors and the geography tutor provides challenge and rigorous training. Weaknesses mainly arise from variations in the quality of school departments, insufficient understanding of the QTS standards, or the lack of resources or opportunities, for example for trainees to use ICT in geography lessons.

b.21. In nine out of ten geography courses, trainees' subject knowledge is good and in more than a quarter it is outstanding. Areas of weakness in a minority of courses are the trainees' understanding of progression from Key Stage 2 to Key Stage 3, and their appreciation of the role that geography plays in vocational courses. In nine out of ten geography courses, trainees' planning, teaching and class management are good. They teach lively lessons, with clear exposition, effective questioning and a wide range of teaching strategies and resources. Weaker trainees are not clear enough in identifying geographical learning outcomes and do not plan sound assessment opportunities as part of their lessons.

b.22. Trainees' standards in assessment are good in about seven courses out of ten. Significant weaknesses were identified in just over a quarter of the providers. Geography trainees often know the principles of assessment, but in practice rely too much on written tests and miss opportunities to assess pupils' progress through observation and intervention. Few use assessment information systematically to adjust their teaching.

History

b.23. There are 28 teacher training courses in history in England. On admissions policy, history has a comparatively high proportion of very good grades and a relatively low proportion of adequate grades. Few providers have any difficulty in meeting the TTA's recruitment targets. Completion rates rarely fall below 90 per cent. Some well-qualified trainees are not able to find a post because the demand for history specialists is declining.

b.24. The quality of training in history is almost always good or very good, with a high proportion which is very good. Centrally-provided training has good content, and is taught effectively; feedback from tutors and mentors on class management and teaching methods is often of high quality. The best courses audit, and where necessary, extend trainees' subject knowledge. History trainees are predominantly good in subject knowledge, and in one course in three the majority of the trainees are very good in their grasp of the concepts and content they are teaching. They understand progression through the Programme of Study. Almost all are familiar with examination syllabuses and broader assessment requirements, but the degree of understanding of post-16 history and of ICT as applied in history classrooms varies a good deal between courses.

b.25. In planning, teaching and class management, history trainees are mainly good, and a very much lower proportion of history courses have only adequate standards in this area. Trainees plan effectively for teaching National Curriculum history, have high expectations, present material clearly and with enthusiasm, and are sensitive to individual abilities and needs. Some trainees in a minority of courses have minor shortcomings in planning for progression; for developing pupils' social, moral and cultural understanding through history; and in linking assessment information to planning.

b.26. In monitoring, assessing, recording, reporting and accountability, history trainees perform better than those in most other subjects, but even so this is the weakest area of the standards in the subject. There are strengths in marking, feedback and record-keeping and in the trainees' sound knowledge of the level descriptions and of GCSE assessment. The weaknesses relate mainly to the links between assessment and planning and to the lack of range and depth in the trainees' experience across the age-range.

Mathematics

b.27.   In England there are currently 75 training courses for mathematics
         teachers. The recruitment of suitably qualified mathematicians to train as
         secondary teachers remains a major problem. Despite strenuous efforts,
         the PGCE courses inspected in 1997-98 only recruited to just of 20 per
         cent of their TTA target. There is also a less well-recognised problem in
         retaining trainees until the end of the course. In 1997-98, 26 per cent of
         the trainees recruited failed to gain qualified teacher status. Around seven
         per cent were encouraged to leave during the course because they were
         failing to meet the required standards.

b.28.   A fifth of the training courses are very good; a quarter are adequate, but
         need significant improvement; the rest are good. Four-fifths of the
         centrally-provided training sessions were good and over a third of these
         were outstanding. Trainees work in schools with good mathematics
         mentors were also of good quality. Common weaknesses are a lack of
         clarity and specificity in feedback to trainees on their teaching and
         insufficient guidance on how to assess and record pupils' progress. In a
         third of the courses, there is also a lack of rigour in assessing and making
         good deficiencies in trainees' own mathematical understanding.

b.29.   There were two courses where standards of mathematical knowledge and
         understanding were poor and a small minority of courses where very few
         of the trainees reached a good standard. However, most trainees in most
         courses had a secure understanding of the concepts and skills necessary
         to teach mathematics across the 11-18 age-range. The main weaknesses
         were a shaky understanding of progression from Key Stage 2 and of the
         level descriptions for mathematics.

b.30.   Few mathematics courses achieve very good or good grades for planning,
         teaching and class management. There is some excellent teaching by
         talented trainees, but a large minority rely excessively for their planning on
         schools' schemes of work, and are not precise or methodical enough in
         defining learning objectives for lessons. The range of materials and
         approaches which trainees are encouraged to try out is unduly narrow in
         some schools. Opportunities to use ICT in mathematics lessons very
         considerably; for some trainees, access to ICT in schools is limited
         because of timetable pressure on computer rooms.

Modern Foreign Languages

b.31.   There are 70 HEIs who offer teacher training courses in modern foreign
         languages in England. Many providers try to widen their recruitment base
         by targeting final-year degree students, local residents and graduate
         foreign nationals. The proportion of foreign nationals recruited is rising
         steadily. However, over the two years 1996-97 and 1997-98 there was a
         national shortfall of 27 per cent against the TTA target. The calibre of
         modern language trainees is predominantly good and on average 85 per

cent gain qualified teacher status. This compares reasonably well with other shortage subjects such as mathematics.

b.32.   There is some training of outstanding quality. Most partnerships are good at training their modern linguists in classroom management and whole-class teaching. However, one course in three needs to make significant improvements in assessing, monitoring and enhancing trainees' own command of the languages they teach. One course in four has significant weaknesses in showing trainees how to plan for progression, in training them to assess and record pupils' progress in the foreign language, and in applying the new standards consistently to the assessment of trainees. These weaker courses are predominantly small ones, and almost half are new providers. The main shortcoming tend to be located in the school-based elements of the training.

b.33.   In nine out of ten courses, the majority of the modern language trainees are good or very good in their subject knowledge. In four out of five courses, the majority of the trainees reach good levels of classroom management and subject teaching skill. However, in the one course in five where trainees are only adequate in this area of the standards, planning for progression constitutes the most common significant weakness. In assessment and recording, very high standards are rare and, in one course in three, trainees are significantly weaker in this aspect than in others. This almost always relates to defects in the timing, content and delivery of the training.

Physical Education

b.34.   There are 32 teacher training courses in PE across the country. The level of applications is buoyant. Trainees are selected who are suitable for teaching, and many are enthusiastic and committed games players. However, most applicants have first degrees whose content is not closely related to the PE National Curriculum. Physical education training sessions in the HEIs are consistently of good or very good quality. However, too many physical education teachers in partner schools have yet to recognise and fully implement the stronger training role assigned to them by current government circulars.

b.35.   Trainees' subject knowledge and understanding are good in four out of ten providers, but in more than half the courses inspected, a substantial minority of the trainees have significant weaknesses. This profile is below all other subjects and is a cause for concern. Trainees' planning is conscientious in many aspects, but lacks precision in defining what is to be learned. Half of the teaching is good and half adequate in quality. Class management, organisation and control of pupils are predominantly good but effective learning is not promoted consistently, as a result of weaknesses in initial planning.

b.36.   The weakest standards are in trainees' ability to assess, record and report on pupils' progress and achievement. Only in a quarter of the courses are standards predominantly good. In the other courses, insecurity in defining what is to be learned and the generally weak quality of assessment, recording and reporting in schools undermine their ability to develop effective judgements of pupils' progress and achievement.

Religious Education

b.37.   There are 42 RE teacher training courses offered by HEIs. Nearly half of providers fall short of the TTA target because of shortages of suitable candidates, or, in some case, insufficient good quality RE school placements. The quality of trainees varies widely. Completion rates are variable but, on average, just under 90 per cent. Take-up of teaching posts is high.

b.38.   The great majority of the training in RE is good or very good but, at 28 per cent, the proportion of only adequate training is comparatively high. One factor which impedes trainees in achieving the standards for QTS is the weakness of statutory RE in some of the placement schools. The majority of training sessions in the HEI providers are of good quality. Good quality provision is characterised by partners having shared aims and school-based tasks being jointly planned and integrated into school-based and HEI-based provision. Weaknesses in subject knowledge are generally addressed well.

b.39.   RE trainees invest much time in developing appropriate subject knowledge for teaching their subject. As a consequence, they are good overall in subject knowledge. In one course out of four, the majority of trainees are very good in their understanding of the key concepts, skills and content to be taught. All trainees understand the statutory requirements for teaching the subject to the 11-18 age-range according to a variety of agreed syllabuses. Their understanding of examination courses and broader assessment requirements is dependent largely upon the provision for RE in their placement schools.

b.40.   In planning, teaching and classroom management, RE trainees are good in two out of three courses. The majority of trainees plan their work effectively to meet the requirements of local agreed syllabuses. The best have marked ability in challenging pupils to think, question and respond, with a clear focus on the understanding of beliefs and values. For a minority of trainees, imprecision with teaching and learning objectives results in the choice of less appropriate learning activities. In two courses out of five, a significant minority of trainees do not understand fully the interrelatedness of planning and assessment. However, many have developed particular strengths in marking, feedback and record-keeping.

Science

b.41.   There are 74 providers of science teacher training courses across the country. Science remains a shortage subject. The main shortfall is in physics and, to a lesser extent, chemistry, which leads to science groups in which biologists predominate. Failure to reach the target number set by the TTA is widespread, though some providers meet or come close to the target through intensive recruitment efforts. Courses do not attract science graduates of the highest calibre.

b.42.   Training is good or very good in just under three-quarters of providers, leaving a quarter with a need for significant improvement. Almost half of the centrally-provided training sessions are outstanding. Mentors make an increasingly systematic contribution to the training and four-fifths of school-based sessions are of good quality. Key areas for improvement are the monitoring and extension of trainees' subject knowledge and the consistency of support from science mentors in schools.

b.43.   In four out of five science courses, standards in subject knowledge and understanding are good, and in a small minority, they are very good. Standards in planning, teaching and class management are markedly less good. The breadth of knowledge and expertise required in teaching both National Curriculum science and a science specialism may contribute to this. In about one course in three, the standards are met adequately and few courses achieve the highest grade. Nevertheless, the majority of courses are good.

b.44.   In monitoring, assessment, recording, reporting and accountability, the science grades are significantly worse than in other areas, with slightly more than two-fifths of courses graded adequate against this set of standards. These findings reflect the higher-order assessment skills needed by science trainees and the lack of well-planned opportunities in school science departments that many trainees experience during the PGCE course.

B Abbreviations, Notes and References

Abbreviations

AOT	Adults other than teachers
BECTA	British Educational Communications and Technology Agency
CPD	Continuing professional development
DCMS	Department for Culture, Media and Sport
DfEE	Department for Education and Employment
HEI	Higher education institutions
HMI	Her Majesty's Inspectorate
ICT	Information and Communication Technology
INSET	In-service training
IT	Information Technology
ITT	Initial teacher training
LEA	Local education authority
LMS	Local management of schools
NESTA	National Endowment for Science, Technology and the Arts
NPQHT	National professional qualification for head teachers
NQT	Newly-qualified teacher
OFSTED	Office for Standards in Education
PE	Physical education
PSHCE	Personal, social, health and cultural education (as defined by Stoke Newington School)
QCA	Qualifications and Curriculum Authority
RSA	Royal Society of the Arts
TTA	Teacher Training Agency

Notes

1 The Challenge for Education

1   Digital media, the industry responsible for designing and creating content for the internet and other digital formats, such as CD-ROMs, could create up to 80,000 jobs over the next eight years. Some 20,750 people in the UK are employed in digital media, a sector that barely existed a decade ago, according to a study commissioned by the Digital Media Alliance, a consortium of companies involved with the industry. There are 2,750 digital media companies in the UK with combined annual revenue of £687.5m. Roughly 2,000 freelances, mustering combined annual income of £50m, work in the digital media sector. The study estimates that 500 specialist digital subsidiaries of traditional media groups produce annual turnover of about £187.5m. The work of these companies and individuals has given the UK an international reputation as having "recognised indigenous talent for creative ideas and cultural innovation". The UK's digital media industry has the potential to grow by at least 20 per cent per

year over the next decade, more than double the rate of traditional creative sectors, such as film and advertising. It could then employ 100,000 people and generate annual revenues of £5bn by 2007. The education system needs to be restructured to train the type of skilled employees that the industry needs and eradicate its present skill shortages.

2 Creative Development

1   Ford & Harris III 1992; Taylor 1988: 118-119. Calvin Taylor and associates have traced "some 50 or 60 definitions" of creativity.

2   A survey of teachers and lectures found that there was "a pervasive view that creativity is only relevant to the arts". Fryer (1996:79).

3   These categories develop a distinction between psychological originality and historical originality made by Boden 1990:32).

4   The description of these stages has a long history but is primarily associated with Wallas (1926:80).

5   Guilford (1975:33-46); Perkins (1994:138). Also Welsh (1975:117).

6   Perkins cited in Kirby & Kuykendall (1991:16).

5 Developing the Curriculum

1   Forthcoming OFSTED report under the provisional title of 'Making a Difference'.

2   Christine Agambar HMI (who looks after the Schools OFSTED database) in a speech at OFSTED's Conference 'Good Teaching in the Arts' when 'Arts Inspected' publication was launched at Woodford Lodge, Winsford in Cheshire, Summer 1998.

3   John Hertrich, HMI, OFSTED's Senior English HMI speaking at the NW Drama 3-18 Conference in January 1999.

6 Teaching and Learning

1   What a person does in terms of creativity "will grow out of his or her conception of personal actualities and potentialities" (Perkins 1981:272). For the role of self-image in adult expectations which facilitate creative acts, see MacKinnon (1962), MacKinnon (1970), Bergum (1973), Bergum (1975) and Kirton (1989) all cited in Ford (1995:24). Also Minkin (1997:117-118).

2   On the beneficial effect of the directive to "be creative" see Datta (1963), Cummings, Hinton & Bobdel (1975) and Fontenot (1993) cited in Ford & Gioia (1995:35). Disposition has been judged to be very important in creative behaviour (Craft et al 1997:79 citing Perkins, Jay & Tishman 1993).

3   Craft (1997:28); Fryer (1996:124); Hubbard (1996:47-64); Torrance (1984); Paul, Torrance & Dorothy (1997).

4   Armbruster (1989: 177-182); Pesut (1990:105-110). For evidence to suggest that metacognitive behaviour is modifiable and metacognitive skills teachable, see Nickerson, Perkins & Smith (1985:294-302).

7 Raising Standards

1   For a full description of Project 1000 see Fryer, Creative Teaching and
Learning, Chapman, London, 1996; p111-118. We are grateful to Marilyn
Fryer for helpful advice on the assessment of creativity.

9 Funding and Resources

1   Further information available from the DCMS.

References

ABBOTT, J. 1997. To Be Intelligent. *Education 2000*, December 1997, pp.-8.

ABBOTT, J. 1998. Why Good Schools Alone Will Never Be Enough in *The
Journal, The 21st Century Learning Initiative. March 1998. pp.-9.*

ANDERSON, D. 1997. *A Common Wealth: Museums and Learning in the United
Kingdom.* London: Department of National Heritage.

ARMBRUSTER, B.B. 1989. Metacognition in Creativity in J. A. Glover, R. R.
Ronning and C. R. Reynolds (eds.), *Handbook of Creativity*, New York:
Plenum Press.

BARBER, M. 1994. *Young People and Their Attitudes to School: an Interim Report
of a Research Project in the Centre for Successful Schools, Keele
University.* Keele: Keele University, Centre for Successful Schools.

BAYLISS, V. 1998. *Redefining Schooling: A challenge to a closed society.* London:
Royal Society for the encouragement of Arts, Manufactures and
Commerce (RSA).

BERGUM, B.O. 1973. Selection of specialized creators, in *Psychological Reports*,
vol. 33, pp. 635-639.

BERGUM, B.O. 1975. Self-perceptions of creativity among academic inventors
and non-inventors, in *Perceptual and Motor Skills,* vol. 40, p. 78.

BLACK, P. & WILLIAM, D. 1998. *Inside the black box: Raising standards through
classroom assessment.* London: Kings College London, School of
Education.

BLAIR, M., BOURNE, J, ET AL. 1998. *Making the Difference: Teaching and Learning
Strategies in Successful Multi-ethnic Schools.* RR59. London: DfEE.

BOSTON, B.O. 1996. The changing workplace is changing our view of education
in *Business Week* October 28, 1996 issue, pp. 2-16.

BOWKETT, S. 1997. *Imagine That... A Handbook for Creative Learning Activities for the Classroom.* Trowbridge: Redwood Books.

BULLOCK. 1990. A Case for the Humanities, in *RSA Journal*, vol. CXXXVIII, no. 5410, pp. 664-676.

CRAFT, A. et al. 1997. *Can You Teach Creativity?* Nottingham: Education Now Publishing Co-operative.

CRAFTS COUNCIL. 1998. *Learning through Making: A national enquiry into the value of creative practical education in Britain.* Edited by John Eggleston. London: Crafts Council.

CUMMINGS, L.L., HINTON, B.L. & GOBDEL, B.C. 1975. Creative behaviour as a function of task environment: Impact of objectives, procedures and controls, in *Academy of Management Journal*, vol. 18, pp. 489-499.

DATTA, L.E. 1963. Test instructions and the identification of creative scientific talent, in *Psychological Reports*, vol. 13, pp. 495-500.

DEPARTMENT FOR CULTURE MEDIA AND SPORT. 1998. *Creative Industries: Mapping Exercise.* London: DCMS.

DEPARTMENT FOR EDUCATION AND SCIENCE. 1985. *Better Schools*. London: HMSO.

DEPARTMENT FOR EDUCATION AND EMPLOYMENT. 1997. *Excellence in Schools.* London: HMSO

DEPARTMENT FOR EDUCATION AND EMPLOYMENT. 1998a. *Extending Opportunity: a national framework for study support.* London: DfEE.

DEPARTMENT FOR EDUCATION AND EMPLOYMENT. 1998b. *Statistics of Education: Schools in England 1997.* London: The Stationary Office.

DEPARTMENT FOR EDUCATION AND EMPLOYMENT. 1998c. *Teachers: meeting the challenge of change.* London: The Stationary Office.

DEPARTMENT FOR EDUCATION AND EMPLOYMENT. 1998d. *The National Literacy Strategy: Framework for Teaching.* London: DfEE

DEPARTMENT FOR EDUCATION AND EMPLOYMENT. 1998e. *Reducing the Bureaucratic Burden on Teachers*, in DfEE circular 2/98.

DEPARTMENT OF NATIONAL HERITAGE. 1996. *Setting the Scene: The Arts and Young People.* London: DNH.

FARMER, A. & KNIGHT, P. 1995. *Active History in Key Stages 3 and 4.* London: David Fulton Publishers.

FEDERATION OF MUSIC SERVICES & NATIONAL ASSOCIATION OF MUSIC TEACHERS. 1998. *A Common Approach: A framework for an instrumental/vocal curriculum.* London: Faber Music Ltd.

FONTENOT, N.A. 1993. Effects of training in creativity and creative problem finding upon business people, in *The Journal of Social Psychology,* vol. 133, pp. 11-22.

FORD, C.M., & GIOIA, D.A. 1995. *Creative Action in Organisations: Ivory Tower Visions and Real World Voices.* London: Sage.

FORD, D.Y. & HARRIS, J.J. III. 1992. The Elusive Definition of Creativity in *The Journal of Creative Behaviour,* Vol. 26, No. 3, Third Quarter.

FOX, A. & GARDINER, M.F. 1997. *The arts and raising achievement.* Paper presented to the Arts in the Curriculum Conference organised by the Department for National Heritage and the School Curriculum and Assessment Authority, Lancaster House, London, 24-25 February.

FRYER, M. 1996. *Creative Teaching and Learning.* London: Chapman.

GARDNER, H. 1993. *Frames of Mind: The Theory of Multiple Intelligences.* Second Edition. London: Fontana Press.

GIPPS, C.V. 1994. *Beyond Testing: Towards a Theory of Educational Assessment.* London: The Falmer Press.

GOLEMAN, D. 1996. *Emotional Intelligence: Why it can matter more than IQ.* London: Bloomsbury.

GUILFORD, J.P. 1975. Creativity: A Quarter Century of Progress in Perspectives in *Creativity* by I.I. Taylor and J.W. Getzels. Chicago: Aldine.

HARRIES, S. 1998. *Investing in the arts: How to carry out a school arts audit and compile an arts statement.* London: RSA.

HENDY, J. 1998. *New LEAs: the Second Wave.* Slough: NFER, Education Management Information Exchange.

HILL, R., in association with the Liverpool Institute of Performing Arts. 1997. *The arts, commercial culture and young people: factors affecting young people's participation in artistic and cultural programmes.* Strasbourg: Council of Europe.

HOGARTH, S., KINDER, K. & HARLAND, J. 1997. *Arts Organisations and their Education Programmes.* London: The Arts Council of England.

HOUSE OF COMMONS. 1982. *Public and Private Funding of the Arts.* Eighth Report from the Education, Science and Arts Committee Session 1981-82. London: House of Commons.

HUBBARD, R.S. 1996. *A Workshop of the Possible: Nurturing Children's Creative Development.* Maine: Stenhouse York.

JEFFREY, B.& WOODS, P. 1997. The Relevance of Creative Teaching: Pupils. Views in A. Pollard, D. Thieson and A. Filer (eds.), *Children and their Curriculum: Perspectives of Primary and Elementary School Children,* London: Falmer Press.

KEYS, W., HARRIS, S. & FERNANDES, C. 1995. *Attitudes to School of Top Primary and First-year Secondary Pupils.* Slough: NFER.

KIRBY, D. & KUYKENDALL, C. 1991. *Mind Matters: Teaching for Thinking.* Portsmouth NH: Boynton/Cook Heinemann.

KIRTON, M.J. 1989. Adaptors and innovators at work, in M.J. Kirton (ed.) *Adaptors and innovators: Styles of creativity and problem-solving.* New York: Routledge.

LONGWORTH, N., & DAVIES, K.D. 1996. *Lifelong learning: new vision, new implications, new roles for people, organizations, nations and communities in the 21st century.* London: Kogan Page.

MACKINNON, D.W. 1962. The nature and nurture of creative talent, in *American Psychologist,* vol. 17, pp. 484-495.

MACKINNON, D.W. 1970. The personality correlates of creativity: A study of American architects, in P.E. Vernon (ed.) *Creativity: Selected readings.* New York: Penguin Books.

MACPHERSON, W. 1999. *The Stephen Lawrence Inquiry: Report of an inquiry by Sir William Macpherson of Cluny.* London: HMSO.

MENTAL HEALTH FOUNDATION. 1999. *The Big Picture.* London: Mental Health Foundation.

MINISTRY OF EDUCATION. 1959. *Report of the Central Advisory Committee for Education.* London: HMSO.

MINKIN, L. 1997. *Exits and Entrances: Political Research as a Creative Art.* Sheffield: SHU Press.

MONTGOMERY, D. 1999. *Positive Teacher Appraisal through Classroom Observation.* London: David Fulton.

NATIONAL CAMPAIGN FOR THE ARTS. 1997. *Theatre in Education: Ten Years of Change.* London: NCA.

NATIONAL FOUNDATION FOR EDUCATIONAL RESEARCH (NFER). 1998. *CAPE UK: Stage One Evaluation Report.*

NICKERSON, R.S., PERKINS, D.N. & SMITH, E.E. 1985. *The Teaching of Thinking,* New Jersey: Lawrence Erlbaum.

O'BRIAN, J. 1996. *Secondary School Pupils and the Arts: Report of a MORI Research Study July 1996.* (ACE Research Report No. 5). London: Arts Council of England.

ODEN, M.A. 1990. *The Creative Mind: Myths and Mechanisms.* London: Weidenfeld and Nicholson.

OFFICE FOR STANDARDS IN EDUCATION. 1996. *Exclusions from Secondary Schools:* 1995/6. London: OFSTED.

OFFICE FOR STANDARDS IN EDUCATION. 1998. *Standards and Quality in Education 1996/97: The Annual Report of Her Majesty's Chief Inspector for Schools.* London: OFSTED.

OFFICE FOR STANDARDS IN EDUCATION. 1999a. *Raising the attainment of minority ethnic pupils: Schools and LEA responses.* London: OFSTED.

OFFICE FOR STANDARDS IN EDUCATION. 1999b. *Standards and Quality in Education 1997/98: The Annual Report of Her Majety's Chief Inspector for Schools.* London: OFSTED.

PARSONS, C. & CASTLE, F. 1998. *Trends in exclusions from school - new Labour, new approaches?* In Forum, vol. 40, no, 1, pp 11-14.

PERKINS, D.N. 1981. *The Mind's Best Work.* Cambridge Massachusetts: Harvard University Press.

PERKINS, D. N. 1994. Creativity: Beyond the Darwinian Paradigm in M. Boden (ed.) *Dimensions of Creativity.* London: MIT Press.

PERKINS, D., JAY, E. & TISHMAN, S. 1993. Beyond Abilities: A Dispositional Theory of Thinking in *Merril-Palmer Quarterly* January 1993, vol. 39 no 1 pp. 1-21.

PESUT, D.J. 1990. Creative Thinking as a Self-Regulatory Metacognitive Process — A Model for Education, Training and Further Research in *The Journal of Creative Behaviour,* vol. 24 no. 2, 1990; pp. 105-110.

POLLARD, A., BROADFOOT, P., CROLL, P., OSBORN, M. & ABBOTT, D. 1994. *Changing English Primary Schools? The Impact of the Education Reform Act at Key Stage One.* London: Cassell.

PUTTNAM, D. 1998. The Arts, Communication and New Technologies, in *Facing the Future: The Arts and Education in Hong Kong* by Ken Robinson. Hong Kong: Hong Kong Arts Development Council.

RESNICK, L.B. & KLOPFER, L.E. 1989. *Towards a Thinking Curriculum: Current Cognitive Research.* Alexandria VA: Association for Supervision and Curriculum Development.

ROBINSON, K. (ed.) 1990. *The Arts 5-16: A Curriculum Framework.* Essex: Oliver & Boyd.

ROGERS, R. 1995. *Guaranteeing an Entitlement to the Arts in Schools.* London: Royal Society for the Encouragement of Arts, Manufactures and Commerce (RSA).

ROGERS, R. 1998. *The disappearing arts? The current state of the arts in initial teacher training and professional development.* London: RSA.

ROWNTREE, D. 1977. *Assessing Students: How shall we know them.* London: Harper & Row.

SCHOOL CURRICULUM AND ASSESSMENT AUTHORITY & NATIONAL FOUNDATION FOR EDUCATIONAL RESEARCH 1998. *International Review of Curriculum and Assessment Frameworks.* INCA website:www.inca.co.uk.

SCOTTISH CONSULTATIVE COUNCIL ON THE CURRICULUM. 1996. *Teaching for Effective Learning.* Dundee: SCCC.

SHARP, C. & CATO, V. 1998. *The Attitudes and Concerns of Pupils and Parents. Review of Research Literature for the National Advisory Committee on Creative and Cultural Education.* Unpublished Report. Slough: NFER.

SHARP, C. & DUST, K. 1998. *The Effects of the Educational Reform Act, 1988 on Provision for Arts and Cultural Activities in Schools. Review of Research Literature for the National Advisory Committee on Creative and Cultural Education.* Unpublished Report. Slough: NFER.

STEINBERG, H., SYKES, E., MOSS, T., LOWERY, S., LEBOUTILLIER, N, & DEWEY, A. 1997. Exercise enhances creativity independently of mood, in *British Journal of Sports Medicine,* vol. 31, pp. 240-245.

STOBART, G. & GIPPS, C.V. 1997. Assessment: *A teacher's guide to the issues.* Third Edition. London: Hodder & Stoughton.

TAYLOR, C. 1988. Various approaches to and definitions of creativity. Appendix in Sternberg R. J. (ed.), *The Nature of Creativity: Contemporary Psychological Perspectives.* Cambridge Massachusetts: CUP.

TORRANCE, E.P. 1984. *Mentor Relationships: How they aid creative development, Endure,* Change and Die. Buffalo NY: Bearly.

TORRANCE, E.P. & SISK, D.A. 1997. *Gifted and Talented Children in the Regular Classroom.* Buffalo NY: Creative Education Foundation Press.

WALLAS, G. 1926. *The Art of Thought.* London: Jonathan Cape.

WELSH, G.S. 1975. *Creativity and Intelligence: A Personality Approach.* Chapel Hill: Institute for Research in Social Science, University of North Carolina.

WHITE, J. 1998. *Do Howard Gardner's Multiple Intelligences add up?* London: Institute of Education, University of London.

WILLIAMS, R. 1961. *The Long Revolution.* London: Penguin Books.

WOODS, P. 1995. *Creative Teachers in Primary Schools.* Buckingham: OUP.

YOUNG, J.Z. 1987. *Philosophy and the Brain.* Oxford: Oxford University Press.

C Acknowledgements

Text

Our work has been informed by a broad range of organisations and individuals, including:

- written submissions from over 200 groups, organisation and individuals;
- consultative meetings with specialists in key areas;
- commissioned research and advice from:
  - the National Foundation for Educational Research;
  - the Teacher Training Agency;
  - the Office for Standards in Education;
  - the Department for Culture, Media and Sport;
  - the Qualifications and Curriculum Authority.

In addition we are grateful to Professor Angela Anning (Department of Education, Leeds University); Professor Peter Ashworth (Learning and Teaching Institute, Sheffield Hallam University); Anna Craft (Senior Lecturer, The Open University); Dr Marilyn Fryer (Leeds Metropolitan University and The Creativity Centre, Dean Clough) and Professor John White (Institute of Education, University of London) for particular assistance in providing research advice and discussions of the concept of creativity and the processes of creative education.

We are also grateful to the following people for commenting on drafts of the text:

- Maud Blair (The Open University)
- Peter Cotgreave (Save British Science)
- Anna Craft (The Open University)
- Penny Egan; (Royal Society for the Encouragement of Arts, Manufactures and Commerce)
- Professor Anthony Everitt (Independent)
- Dr. Marilyn Fryer (Leeds Metropolitan University and The Creativity Centre, Dean Clough)
- Rick Rogers (Independent)
- Peter Stark (Gateshead Council)
- Pauline Tambling (The Arts Council of England)

We are grateful to all the schools and organisations that have supplied examples for this report and to everyone who has contributed to our work.

Photographs

We are grateful for permission to re-produce the work of the following photographers:

- Simon Warner p.34
- Chris James p.45, p.126
- Justine (model, Korrina at Models One) p.73
- Gill Watson p.106
- Keith Pattison p.163
- Justin Slee p.167

Cover Photograph:

Tony Stone Images

D Research and Consultations

Consultative Meetings

Specialist consultative meetings were held on the following topics:

Art, Craft and Design
Artists in Education
Arts Education Managers
Creative Development
Dance Education
Drama Education
Fashion Design
Primary Education
Science Education
Secondary School Curriculum
Standards and Effectiveness
Technology Education
Multicultural Education
Work, Creativity and the Economy

The following delegates attended these meetings:

A

Judith Ackroyd	Nene University College
Carol Adams	Shropshire County Education Office
Dr Philip Adey	King's College London
Diane Anderson	Longdale Community School
David Arbuckle	Rover Group
William Atkinson	Phoenix High School
John Auty	Nottinghamshire County Council

B

Prof Michael Barber	DfEE
Ken Bartlett	The Foundation for Community Dance
Norinne Betjeman	Arts Council of England
Julia Bird	Poetry Book Society
Anne Blaber	Children's Music Workshop
Maude Blair	Open University
Penni Blythe	Hamdon Education and Training
Jane Boistelle	Marks & Spencer Plc
Betina Botcher	Marks & Spencer Plc
Steven Bowkett	Independent
Sonia Boyce	African & Asian Visual Artists Association
Jane Brake	Independent
Sally Brampton	Independent
Mike Buchanan	Marks & Spencer Plc
Kate Burnett	Independent

David Bryan	Independent
Paul Bunyan	NIAS, NATE
Stephen Burroughs	The Crafts Council

C

Russell Chalmers	The Holst Group
Patricia Clark	Avondale Park Primary School
Peter Clark	Confederation of British Industry
Veronica Clark	Pashley Down Infant School
Caroline Coates	Independent
Pat Cochrane	Cape UK
Steve Cockett	University of Exeter
Ian Cole	MOMA
John Connell	Intake High School
Ruth Corman	Designer Crafts Foundation
Sarah Coverdale	Arts Council of England
Anna Craft	The Open University
Cecilia Crichton	CHEAD
Michaela Crimmin	RSA
Sue Crockford	123 Productions Ltd
Chris Crowcroft	Foundation for Young Musicians

D

Stephen Dagg	Centre for Young Musicians
Prof Wendy Dagworthy	Central St. Martin's College
Amanda Dalton	The Arvon Foundation
Paul Dash	Goldsmiths College
Heather Dauphin	Hampstead School
Janet Dawson	DfEE
Steven Derrick	Phoenix Dance Company
Helen Dilly	Theatre Royal Bury
Maura Dooley	Independent
Roger Durston	Music Education Council
Sangeevini Dutta	Independent
Maggie Dwyer	TUC

E

Siân Ede	Calouste Gulbenkian Foundation
Claire Edis	St. Clement Danes School
Penny Egan	RSA
Brian Eno	Independent
Rachel Elliott	Green Candle Dance Company

F

Andrew Fairbairn	British Federations of Young Choirs
Patrick Fallon	DCMS
Rosemary Feasey	The Association for Science Education
Tony Fegan	LIFT
Mike Fleming	University of Durham
Helen Fletcher	Far Town School
Linda Florance	CAPITB Trust
Dr Lynda Foster	Independent
Caryn Franklyn	Independent

Moira Fraser Steele	Design Council
James Friel	Independent
Kerry Furneaux	The Crafts Council

G

Sue Gibbs	Theatre de Complicité
Tina Glover	Junction Arts
Brian Godbold	Marks & Spencer Plc
Jackie Goodman	Arts Plan
Marion Gough	Independent
Ruth Gould	Full Circle
Jacqueline Greaves	Ludus Dance Company
Joy Gregory	Independent
Richard Gregory	Independent
Hilary Gresty	VAGA

H

Jane Hackett	Birmingham Royal Ballet
Prof David Hargreaves	School of Education, Cambridge University
Tony Harrington	Northern Stage
Prof Bill Harrison	Sheffield Hallam University
Kim Hasler	Marks & Spencer Plc
Virginia Haworth	Artswork
Penny Hay	NSEAD
Ann Hewitt	Whiteheath Infant School
Claire Hicks	SAMPAD
Nick Higgins	Seagram Europe & Africa
Michelle Hind	Associated Board
Caro Howell	Tate Gallery of Modern Art
Sue Humphries	The Coombes County Infant and Nursery School

I

Ruth Ingledaw	Association for Business Sponsorship of the Arts
Irma Inniss	Independent

J

Sarah Jackson	Stoke Park School
Darryl Jaffray	Royal Opera House
Prof Edgar Jenkins	University of Leeds
Shobana Jeyasingh	Shobana Jeyasingh Dance Company
Veronica Jobbins	National Dance Teachers' Association
Pamela Johnson	Independent
Peter Jones	DCMS
Len Judge	Synetics Education Initiative

K

Andy Kempe	University of Reading
Bob Kelley	The Campaign for Music in the Curriculum
Colette King	Independent
Tony Knight	Qualifications and Curriculum Authority

L

Bill Lind	Ifield Community College
Janet Lovekin	Marks & Spencer Plc

M	Shân MacLennan	Southbank
	Libby MacNamara	Association of British Orchestras
	Chris McIntyre	CHEAD
	Rohini Malik	INIVA
	Ken Mannion	Sheffield Hallam University
	Gayle Markovitz	RSA
	Michael Marland	North Westminster Community School
	Sally Millard	Hampstead School
	Maggie Morris	Laban Centre London
	Gillian Moore	London Sinfonietta
N	Christopher Naylor	Engage
	Jonothan Neelands	University of Warwick
	Frances Newell	Newell & Sorrell
	Mary Newman	DCMS
	Helen Nicholson	Homerton College, Cambridge
	Richard Nott	Workers for Freedom
O	Ian Oag	Allied Domecq Plc
	Margaret O'Brian	South-East Arts
	Pauline O'Keefe	Allfarthing School, Wandsworth
	David Oliver	Folkworks
P	Glynis Packman	Sackville School
	Bob Paisley	CCEA
	Anice Paterson	National Association of Music Educators
	Keyna Paul	Independent
	Roy Peach	London College of Fashion
	David Perkins	Federation of Music Services
	Campbell Perry	Bishopton Primary School
	Cathy Poole	Watershed Media Centre
	Ian Potter	Ousedale School
	Jane Pountney	Children's Music Workshop
	Marcus Powell	Marks & Spencer Plc
R	John Rainer	National Drama
	Caroline Redmond	Independent
	Helen Reeves	Holly Hall School
	Viv Reiss	Arts Council of England
	Simon Richey	Calouste Gulbenkian Foundation
	Damien Robinson	Independent
	Mark Robinson	Cleveland Arts
S	Huw Salisbury	South Camden Community School
	Pete Sanders	Lauriston Primary School
	Henk Schut	Independent
	Anne Schwegmann-Fielding	Independent
	Jo Shapcott	Independent
	Rebecca Sinker	Independent
	Sally Smith	CV Clothing

	Dr Jacqueline Smith-Autard	National Dance Teachers' Association
	Patrick Spottiswoode	International Shakespeare Globe Centre
	Nick Stanley	Birmingham Institute of Art and Design
	Dr John Steers	NSEAD
	Prof Hannah Steinberg	Middlesex University
	Kathy Stonier	Stoke Newington School
	Graham Storrow	Stadley Primary School
	Michael Stoten	The Voices Foundation
	David Sulkin	Independent
T	Margaret Talboys	Qualifications and Curriculum Authority
	Pauline Tambling	Arts Council of England
	Helen Teague	1647 Ltd
	Ron Tendler	Independent
	Elaine Thomas	CHEAD
	Michael Thompson	Design Connect
	Nicola Thorold	Independent Theatre Council
	Alister Tipple	Marks & Spencer Plc
W	Richard Walton	Sheffield Hallam University
	Mike Watkins	London Association of Art and Design Education
	Clare Webster	Independent
	Judith Webster	Royal Philharmonic Orchestra
	Paul Weiland	Independent
	Prof Dick West	Sheffield Hallam University
	Larry Westland	Music for Youth
	Lindsey Wharmby	Lawnswood School
	Prof John White	Institute of Education, London
	Richard Wigley	Hallé
	Colin Wilkinson	Techniquest
	Deborah Williams	DCMS
	Julia Williams	Cheshire County Council
	Mark Windale	Sheffield Hallam University
	Hilary Wrack	Adzido Pan-African Dance Ensemble
Y	Sheila Young	Proper Job Theatre Projects

Written Consultations

Written consultations were received from the following organisations and individuals:

A Action for Children's Arts
Dr Philip Adey, CAT, King's College London
Advisory & Inspection Services Division, Nottinghamshire County Council
Adzido Pan African Dance Ensemble
African & Asian Visual Artists Archive (AAVAA)
Akademi

Antidote, Campaign for Emotional Literacy
The Anti-Racist Teacher Education Network
Area Museum Council for the South West
ARTS Centre for Studies in Science & Mathematics Education
The Arts Council
Arts in Education Service, Leicestershire County Council
Arts in Sandwell
Arts Plan
Art Shape Ltd
ArtsWork
The Arvon Foundation at Lumb Bank
The Associated Board of the Royal Schools of Music
Association for Media, Cultural and Communication Studies
Association for Science Education
Association of British Orchestras
Association of Graphic Design Educators
Axis

B   Bangor University Music Department
BBC Philharmonic
Jo Belloli
Benslow Music Trust
Big Brum Theatre in Education
Birmingham City Council Education Department
Birmingham Repertory Theatre
Bishopton Primary School
Blackpool Borough Council
Maude Blair, Open University
Naz Bokhari, Ernest Bevin College
Bolton Metro
Boomerang Media
Bournemouth Borough Council
Stephen Bowkett
Bradford Metropolitan District Council
Roger Breakwell, Camberwell College of Arts
Bridgebuilder
British Actors Equity Association
British Association of Advisors & Lecturers in Physical Education
British Educational Communications and Technology Agency
British Federation of Young Choirs
British Film Institute
Kate Burnett
Prof Leone Burton, University of Birmingham

C   Calouste Gulbenkian Foundation
David A Calverley
CandoCo Dance Company
Camden LEA
The Campaign for Music in the Curriculum
CAPE UK

Michael Carden
Prof C R Chaplin, Dept of Engineering, University of Reading
The Central School of Speech & Drama
Centre for Race, Culture & Education, Leeds City Council & Leeds Met University
Cheltenham & Gloucester College of Higher Education
Cheshire County Council Advisory & Inspection Service
Cheshire County Council Education Dept
Chicken Shed Theatre Company
Children 2000
Children's Music Workshop
Chisenhale Gallery
City of Birmingham Symphony Orchestra
City of York LEA
Cleveland Theatre Company
Nick Clough
Cloughwood School
Caroline Coates
Stephen Cockett, Lecturer in Drama, University of Exeter
Coin Street
CBI
Contemporary Art Society
Aiden Cook
Martin Coslett
Peter Cotgreave
Sue Cottam, St Osmund's Middle School Dorchester Youth Dance & NDTA
Coventry City Council Leisure Services
Coventry University Performing Arts
Professor Brian Cox
Anna Craft, The Open University
The Crafts Council
Creative Options
Sue Crockford, 123 Productions Ltd
Croydon LEA
The Creativity Centre, Dean Clough
Cumbria Arts in Education

D   DATA
Barrie Day
Deafsite
Derby City Council
Derbyshire County Council
Derby Playhouse
Design Council
Design Museum
Discovery, London Symphony Orchestra
Mildred Dobbs
Dorman Museum

Dorset County Council, Expressive Arts Team
Dorset County Council Music Service
Dudley LEA
Dudley MBC Leisure Services
Dudley Music Services
Karen Dust
The Dyslexia Institute

E   Eastern Arts Board
East Sussex County Music Service
Eco Distribution
Education Extra
Educational Publishers Council, The Publishers Association
Penny Egan, RSA
Engage
The English Association
English National Ballet
Enigma
Brian Eno
Anthony Everitt
The Extension Trust, Tandem

F   Federation of Music Services
Lynda Foster PhD
The Foundation for Community Dance
Mary Fowler, Adviser for English, London Borough of Havering
Prof Peter Fowler, Head of Learning Methods Unit, Liverpool John Moores
University
Dr. Marilyn Fryer, Leeds Metropolitan University and The Creativity Centre,
Dean Clough)

G   Mr Oliver Gill
Prof Caroline Gipps, Kingston University
Global Innovation Network
Glyndebourne Opera
Gavin Graveson, Choral Animation Projects
Judith M Graydon, Headteacher, Parish C of E Primary School
Green Candle Dance Company

H   The Hamblin Foundation
Ms Gerda Hanko
Harris Museum & Art Gallery
Prof Bill Harrison, Centre for Science Education, Sheffield Hallam
University
Mr Olaf Hindmarsh, Teacher Adviser for Art & Design & Co-ordinator for
Artists in Education
The Historical Association, Mr Sean Lang
The Holst Group
Dr Eileen Hooper-Greenhill, Dept of Museum Studies, University of
Leicester

Hounslow Borough Council, Education Dept
Richard Howlett, Hampshire Music Service
Huddersfield Creative Town Initiative
Pat Hughes, Liverpool Hope University

I   IATS, Norfolk County Council
Ifield Community College, West Sussex
Inclusive Theatre, Interplay Theatre Co
Incorporated Association of Preparatory Schools
Incorporated Society of Musicians
Independent Schools' Association
Independent Theatre Council
The Industrial Society
Inspection & Advisory Service, London Borough of Newham Council
Institute of International Visual Arts
Institute of Welsh Affairs
ISA
ISAI Executive, Academic Policy Committee

J   Jabadao
Prof Robert Jackson, Director of Religions & Educational Research Unit,
Institute of Education, University of Warwick
Sarah Jackson, Stoke Park School, Coventry
Prof Edgar Jenkins, Science & Education Policy Unit, University of Leeds,
Gay Jessop, Head of Art & Design, Harrytown RC High School
Jiving Lindy Hoppers
Bev Joicey HMI
Junction Arts, Arts Development Agency for District of Bolsover

K   Keele University, Department of Psychology
Bruce Kent
Barbara Kentish
Ruth Kenward, Music Specialist, Bourne County Primary School
Steven Keogh
Kidbrooke School, Trisha Jaffe
Marilyn Kinnon, Educational Analyst & Teacher
Kneehigh Theatre Trust Ltd
Kokuma
Saville Kushner, Centre for Applied Research in Education, University of
East Anglia

L   LEAP Project, Business Partnership, Tower Hamlets Education
University of Leeds Conference: Creativity in Schools
Leicester City Council, Arts & Leisure Dept, Museums Education
Leicester City Council, Education Dept
Library & Information Commission
Linguistics, Carleton University, Ottowa
Liverpool Dockers & Stevedores Co-Operative & Initiative Factory
Local Government Association
London Arts Board

London International Festival of Theatre (LIFT)
LUTCHI Research Centre
Lyric Theatre, Hammersmith

M   M6 Theatre Company
mac, Birmingham
Maharishi School
Malbank School & Sixth Form Centre
MEC
Prof Peter Medway, School of Linguistics, Carleton University, Canada
Medway Council, Medway Children's University
METIER
Middlesborough Borough Council, Education & Leisure Dept & Dorman Museum
The Midi Music Company, Music House Too
Millennium Appeal
Millennium Challenge
Prof Arthur Miller, Dept of Sciency & Technology Studies, University College of London
Margaret Mills
Mind the Gap Performing Arts
Prof Diane Montgomery, Learning Difficulties Research Project
The Museum of Modern Art, Oxford
Museums Association
Museums & Galleries Commission
Music for Youth
Musicians Union

N   National Association for Education of Sick Children
National Association for Gifted Children
National Association for the Teaching of English
National Association of Advisors in English
National Association of Advisory Officers for Special Education
National Association of Head Teachers
National Association of Music Educators
National Association of Teachers in Further and Higher Education
National Association of Writers in Education
National Association of Youth Orchestras
National Campaign for the Arts
National Centre of Children with High Abilities & Talents
National Dance Teachers' Association
National Drama
National Endowment for Science, Technology and Arts
National Federation of Music Societies
National Foundation for Educational Research
The National Gallery
National Museum of Photography, Film & Television
National Society for Education in Art & Design
National Theatre Education
National Youth Agency

The New Art Gallery
Newham Council, East London
North Cornwall Arts
North Warwickshire Borough Council Leisure Services
North West Arts Board
North Westminster Community School
Northern Arts
Northern Ballet Theatre
Northern Theatre Educational Trust
Nottinghamshire County Council, Education Department
Nuffield Design & Technology

O   Oldbury Wells School
Dr Susan O'Neill, Keele University, Department of Psychology
Opera North
Opt for Art Steering Group
Orchard Theatre Company
Oxfam Education

P   John Palmer, Inclusive Theatre
The Paul Hamlyn Foundation, Patricia Lenkester
Tony Penny
Melanie Peter
Joan M Pick
Pilot Theatre Company
Playtrain
Poetry Book Society
Pop-Up Theatre Ltd.
Ian Potter
Christopher Price
Professional Association of Teachers
Professional Council for Religious Education
Proper Job Theatre Company Ltd.

Q   Queen Elizabeth High School, Kathy White-Webster
Quicksilver Theatre

R   Craig Randolph
Reading Borough Council Museum Service
Caroline Redmond
Religious Education Council of England & Wales
Remembering Education
Dr Malcolm Rigler
Rick Rogers
Royal College of Art, Centre for Drawing Research
Royal College of Music
Royal Institution of Great Britain
Royal National Institute for Deaf People
Royal National Institute for the Blind
Royal National Theatre

Royal Opera House
Royal School of Church Music
Royal Shakespeare Company
Royal Society of the Arts
Royal West of England Academy

S   Sackville School, Glynis Packman
Sainsbury Centre for Visual Arts, University of East Anglia
St Osmund's Middle School
Salongo African & Caribbean Dance & Music Resource Project
Sandwell MBC, Education & Commercial Services Dept
Sassoon Gallery
Saxon Court
School of Drama & Music, University of Exeter
School of Education, University of Wales Institute, Cardiff
Scottish Opera
Seagram Europe & Africa
SEI
Sheffield Galleries & Museums Trust
Shrewsbury Borough Council Museums Service
Shropshire County Council & Telford & Wrekin Council LEA
Rebecca Sinker, School of Lifelong Learning & Education, Middlesex
University
Skillset
Snap People's Theatre Trust Ltd
Society for Storytelling
Somerset County Council, Education Development Service
South Bank Centre
Southend Youth Arts Partnership
Southern Arts Board
SPE
Special Educational Needs National Advisory Council
Staffordshire Education Quality Learning Services
Standing Conference of Young People's Theatre
Peter Stark
Prof Hannah Steinberg
Stoke Newington School, Kathy Stonier
Stoke Park School, Sarah Jackson
Stratford-upon-Avon High School
Surrey County Council, Youth Music & Performing Arts

T   Pauline Tambling, Arts Council of England
Tameside LEA
Jane Tarr
The Tate Gallery
Techniquest
Technology Colleges Trust
Ron Tendler
Thomas Tallis School, Nick Williams

Colin Touchin, University of Warwick
Tower Hamlets Education
TTA
21st Century Learning

U   Unicorn Theatre
United Biscuits (UK) Ltd

V   Values Education Council (VECTOR)
Victoria & Albert Museum
Visual Arts & Galleries Association
The Voices Foundation

W   Walker Art Gallery
Walsall MBC, The New Art Gallery
Warwickshire Artists' Team
Donald Watts
Weekend Arts College
Welfare State International
Dr R N Wells, Analytic Psychotherapist
West Midlands Arts
West Midlands Regional Arts Education Partnership, Dudley
Whitechapel Art Gallery
Whiteheath Infant & Nursery School
Nuala Willis
Colin Wilkinson
Wilnecote High School
Audrey S Wisbey
Women's Playhouse Trust
The Writers' Guild of Great Britain
WWF United Kingdom
Wyke College

Y   Young Writer
City of York Council, Schools Advisory & Support Services
Yorkshire & Humberside Arts Board
Yvonne Arnaud Theatre & Pied Piper Theatre Company